Web API Development for the Absolute Beginner

A Step-by-step Approach
to Learning the Fundamentals
of Web API Development
with .NET 7

Irina Dominte

Apress®

Web API Development for the Absolute Beginner: A Step-by-step Approach to Learning the Fundamentals of Web API Development with .NET 7

Irina Dominte
Iasi, Romania

ISBN-13 (pbk): 978-1-4842-9347-8   ISBN-13 (electronic): 978-1-4842-9348-5
https://doi.org/10.1007/978-1-4842-9348-5

Managing Director, Apress Media LLC: Welmoed Spahr
Acquisitions Editor: Joan Murray
Development Editor: Laura Berendson
Editorial Assistant: Gryffin Winkler
Copy Editor: April Rondeau

Cover image designed by Stefan Schweihofer from Pixabay

Distributed to the book trade worldwide by Springer Science+Business Media New York, 1 New York Plaza, 1 FDR Dr, New York, NY 10004. Phone 1-800-SPRINGER, fax (201) 348-4505, email orders-ny@springer-sbm.com, or visit www.springeronline.com. Apress Media, LLC is a California LLC and the sole member (owner) is Springer Science+Business Media Finance Inc (SSBM Finance Inc). SSBM Finance Inc is a **Delaware** corporation.

For information on translations, please e-mail booktranslations@springernature.com; for reprint, paperback, or audio rights, please e-mail bookpermissions@springernature.com.

Apress titles may be purchased in bulk for academic, corporate, or promotional use. eBook versions and licenses are also available for most titles. For more information, reference our Print and eBook Bulk Sales web page at http://www.apress.com/bulk-sales.

Any source code or other supplementary material referenced by the author in this book is available to readers on GitHub.

Paper in this product is recyclable

I dedicate this book to my daughter and to you, the reader, whether you are trying to learn a totally different domain or just like to keep learning new things.

Table of Contents

About the Author

 **Irina Dominte(Scurtu)** is an independent consultant and trainer, international speaker, software architect, Microsoft MVP for developer technologies, and Microsoft certified trainer (MCT) with a wealth of experience. Having taught classes, workshops, and presentations for over 2,000 hours, Irina is passionate about coding and keeping abreast of the latest trends and best practices in software architecture and .NET.

Twice a year, for five months each time, Irina teaches .NET and C# to aspiring software developers or people interested in software development or seeking to expand their knowledge. She is an active member of the community and has founded the DotNet Iasi User Group and the dotnetdays.ro conference, where she connects with like-minded developers who are eager to share their expertise and insights.

Irina is also a prolific blogger, and her website, `https://irina.codes`, features a wealth of articles on various coding topics. She decided to write this book after learning firsthand how much people struggle to grasp new concepts without proper guidance.

About the Technical Reviewer

Layla Porter is an experienced software engineer and developer advocate specializing in .NET technologies. She's a Microsoft MVP, GitHub Star, and Progress Ninja, and in 2021 she founded the #WomenOfDotNet Initiative. Layla has spoken at developer conferences all over Europe and North America and is a YouTube content creator and streamer. She spends her time hiking, reading urban fantasy, playing video games with her husband, and doting on her two miniature pinschers, Cookie and Lily.

Acknowledgments

The completion of this book wouldn't have been possible without the help and support of many people.

First, I want to thank my husband, who supported me every step and encouraged me. Second, my daughter, Ilinca, who luckily enjoyed going to daycare so I could write this book, and my in-laws, who were there to babysit when I needed them.

Furthermore, I would like to express my appreciation to all those who took the time to review my manuscript and provide constructive feedback that helped refine the content. Special recognition goes to my tech reviewer, Layla Porter, and my friends, Maria Rusu, Andrei Diaconu, and Alexandra Nechita.

Last, but not least, thanks to my former students Tatiana Ciurescu and Cosmin Dumitru, who were brave enough to shift their careers into tech and never stopped learning.

Introduction

This book aims to provide you, the reader, with a step-by-step approach to learning Web API development. We start by introducing basic concepts related to the Web in general and end with more advanced topics like testing an API.

Across the chapters, you will notice a lot of things that might be subject to debate—like splitting the code into different libraries, using different coding standards, or even writing code that requires more lines than I would use in real life.

Everything I choose to use in this book in terms of coding conventions, API architecture, libraries, and topics covered was tested and proved successful over the last eight years. In my spare time, twice a month, I teach .NET to people that come from totally different domains than programming. The vast majority now work in IT, and I dare to think that I made a small contribution to that by using this approach.

PART I

The Basics

CHAPTER 1

Introducing Web API

This chapter introduces you to the world of APIs, including what kinds of APIs are out there, what their purposes are, and how you can categorize them. By the end of the chapter, you will have the correct vocabulary to use when dealing with different types of APIs.

What Is an API?

The term *API* is very widely used in the information technology (IT) industry, and sometimes its usage can be confusing. The term is an acronym for "application programmable interface."

This is in fact the interface that gives a person or a system the ability to interact with a piece of hardware or software through the operations that are exposed.

Think about an API as a remote control, controlling your TV. You press buttons to change the channels back and forth. Something similar happens with APIs. You call methods and endpoints, or set values to properties that are exposed to control aspects of that system.

While regular web applications are intended for humans to interact with, APIs are like web applications but don't have buttons or cute layouts to interact with. Their intent is to be consumed by different "users." In this case, the "user" of an API might be a system or a developer.

There are many types of APIs with different scopes and addressability, and they can be found in different parts of the web, or offline on devices.

© Irina Dominte 2023
I. Dominte, *Web API Development for the Absolute Beginner*,
https://doi.org/10.1007/978-1-4842-9348-5_1

APIs are everywhere. A mobile app, a weather app, your laptop's operating system, a fridge, your smart doorbell, and even your car all expose or use APIs.

In this book, we will focus more on APIs that run on the web over the HTTP protocol, serving data for web applications in JSON format. However, you do need to know about the many types of APIs available. Your browser has an API, your operating system has an API, and you can interact with all of these. We will talk briefly about some of them in the next section.

Categorizing APIs

Now, if we ask ourselves, "What other kinds of APIs exist?" we may not have a simple answer. Categorizing an API is a difficult job because we need to add context to it. Imagine we have a set of LEGO blocks we need to categorize. We might split them by color, or maybe by size. The same happens with APIs—we can find more than one way to categorize them. In the next section, we will talk about a few types of APIs that I have found to be the most common and important.

Types of APIs
Push/Stream APIs

Push/stream APIs are event driven and send real-time notifications to clients. In most cases, a web server will "push" messages or notifications to a web browser. The business domain where you find APIs of this category involves messaging, chats, video, streaming, or payments. There is a significant chance of finding such APIs where time and real-time processing are paramount.

Underneath, these APIs sometimes use protocols like WebSockets or technologies like SignalR.

Native APIs

APIs that are native usually are the interface of a device or a tool, allowing us to interact with the device or tool. For example, web browsers have a JavaScript API embedded that allows them to interpret and execute the JavaScript code used in web applications. The same JavaScript API will allow us to write and execute code directly in the Console tab of developer tools.

In a similar manner, we can access our smartphone's camera or accelerometer through the exposed native API.

SDKs

An SDK, or software development kit, is a package of tools written in different languages that helps developers build applications on top of that package. For example, the .NET SDK provides a set of libraries and tools that can be used by developers to build their own APIs or web applications. SDKs get delivered as installers or as part of an Integrated Development Environment workload and sometimes give you scaffolding capabilities through those IDEs.

Scaffolding is the code generation capability given by some tools or frameworks. It aids the development process by autogenerating code based on predefined options or by taking in some input.

REST

REST, or representational state transfer, is an architectural style in the API world that comes with a set of principles and guidelines about how to design your API and leverage the underlying protocol in the correct way.

REST was first mentioned by Roy Fielding in his dissertation thesis in 2000[1]. Since then, it has gained a lot of traction in the IT industry, but some concepts were misunderstood.

Most of the APIs you will encounter in the web world are written in this way. Not all respect the REST guidelines as they should, and are in fact JSON over HTTP, but this is another subject that we will tackle at the right moment.

We will talk more about REST in a dedicated chapter.

RPC APIs

RPC is a term that means "remote procedure call," and it has been around for a while now in various forms. This model will look like you are calling methods from the same application and using classes from within the same scope or solution, but in fact the methods are hosted on a different machine over the network. One of its main purposes is to make a distributed system look and behave like a monolith.

If we look at Listing 1-1, the method calls seem to be part of the same system, due to how an RPC API looks like. The calls to CreateOrder() and ProcessPaymentFor() are actually calls over the network boundaries, even if the look and feel for developers are local.

Listing 1-1. Code snippet to exemplify RPC

```
var order = salesBoundedContext.CreateOrder(orderRequest);
var paymentStatus = billingBoundedContext.
ProcessPaymentFor(order);
if (paymentStatus.IsSuccessful)
{
    shippingBoundedContext.ArrangeShippingFor(order);
}
```

---

[1] https://resources.sei.cmu.edu/asset_files/WhitePaper/2017_019_001_505040.pdf

With an RPC (and when I say RPC, I am referring to the general concept not necessarily gRPC or other implementation types), the developer will call methods with arguments and get results, but that call will involve a network call over HTTP protocol (in most of the cases). There are plenty of benefits and drawbacks to using such an API, but all deserve a separate section, which is not in the scope of this book.

The Look and Feel of Web Apps

Looking at any web application from the outside—if we are talking about websites or web apps, as those have a layout, buttons, colors, and images that we browse on—we see they have two parts:

- **Frontend** – This runs on the browser and is usually written in HTML, CSS, and JavaScript (or a JavaScript framework like Angular, React, Vue.js). In some cases, people refer to this part of the application as the *presentation layer*. As the name states, the scope of it is to display information to the user, and it should be as dumb as it can be.

- **Backend** – This is written in a server-side language like C#, Python, or Java, and it runs on a web server.

From the developer's perspective, depending on the framework we pick, the separation is not that clear. Most of them have frontend and backend code intertwined or have structures or components that generate HTML code from the server. Such an example can be seen with the ASP.NET MVC framework, where structures like Tag Helpers and HTML Helpers do exactly this: generate HTML from the server.

7

In the example that follows, you can see an HTML Tag Helper that when executed generates an HTML input tag:

```
@Html.TextBoxFor(x=>x.AddedDate)
```

We can say that these application models are like self-contained boxes, as shown in Figure 1-1.

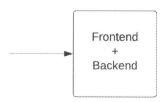

Figure 1-1. *Frontend and backend overview in ASP Razor Pages*

The ASP Razor Pages application model comes with a nice structure, as shown in Figure 1-2, and is very easy to understand and work with.

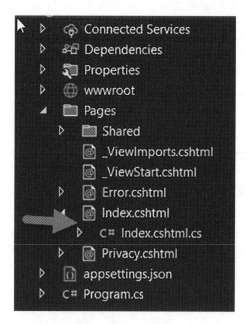

Figure 1-2. *ASP Razor Pages project structure*

Listing 1-2 and Listing 1-3 explore how a page would look in this application model. We should have such source code file pairs for each page we add to our application.

Listing 1-2. Index.cshtml Razor Page client page

```
@page
@model IndexModel
@{
    ViewData["Title"] = "Home page";
}

<div class="text-center">
    <h1 class="display-4">Welcome</h1>
    <p>Learn about
<a href="https://docs.microsoft.com/aspnet/core">building Web
apps with ASP.NET Core</a>.</p>
</div>
```

Listing 1-3. Index.cs—How the code looks likew

```
using Microsoft.AspNetCore.Mvc;
using Microsoft.AspNetCore.Mvc.RazorPages;

namespace WebApplication1.Pages
{
    public class IndexModel : PageModel
    {
        private readonly ILogger<IndexModel> _logger;

        public IndexModel(ILogger<IndexModel> logger)
        {
            _logger = logger;
        }
```

```
public void OnGet()
{

}
```

}

From an architectural point of view, this programming model can be included in the "Onion Architecture" category. As you can see in Figure 1-3, everything is contained in the same app, and all the layers are built around the business domain.

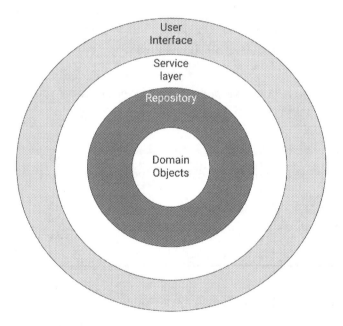

Figure 1-3. *Onion architecture*

Starting from the outermost layer, into to the middle, everything is contained in the same application. It doesn't matter if internally you split the code into multiple libraries for better maintainability and code separation—those libraries will still be strongly coupled. When it comes to deployment and packaging, the code is delivered and treated as a whole.

To be honest, I enjoy writing such apps from time to time, and I rely on them every time I have the opportunity. To me, it is faster and easier to use something that is utterly familiar than to, let's say, set up a React or Angular frontend app and back it up with a standalone API. Nowadays, ASP.NET MVC and ASP.NET Razor Pages or Blazor, are modern, easy to learn, and have a wide addressability—meaning that they will do what they are supposed to do in most cases.

These frameworks have a very well-defined place in the software ecosystem, and they will be used in the future too. Now, most of the enterprise world is more focused on non-functional requirements like scalability, fault-tolerance, maintainability, and extensibility. These requirements go beyond features and functionality to implement. These applications tend to follow different architectures. They have a clear, strict separation of frontend and backend, as shown in Figure 1-4, due to different business needs.

Figure 1-4. *Frontend versus backend separation*

This separation is not only an adaptation to modern times, where developers want to work with the latest tools and tech, but a clear necessity. Sometimes we need to give more computing power to those areas of the business that require it, while others can function well with less computing power.

For example, let's look at an online shop with interesting products. When the products are accessed by a lot of customers at the same time we would need to scale that app section. This way we ensure that pages are loading properly and users don't get errors.

However, the same online shop could have a reporting section that an admin might use once per month; it would be a waste of money to scale it.

Scaling an API typically refers to the process of adjusting the infrastructure and resources supporting the API to handle increasing levels of traffic and usage without degrading performance or reliability. This involves adding more computing resources, such as servers, load balancers, and databases, as well as implementing caching mechanisms, optimizing code, and configuring auto-scaling systems to ensure that the API can handle spikes in traffic and usage.

Splitting the frontend code and the backend code into separate apps is common practice. This way you will have a frontend app, and an API or maybe several APIs that will send data to the frontend, as shown in Figure 1-5. With this separation, we have the luxury of treating different parts of a system independently in a way that might bring benefits to the business.

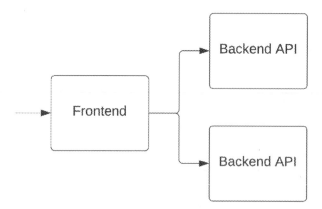

Figure 1-5. *Frontend and 2 backend APIs*

Starting to use a frontend versus backend separation leads to a more granular split of the system. Now we can have a frontend and very specialized APIs that are easy to maintain and deploy. Having a system that is split into several pieces, instead of having just one big block, has a lot of benefits, and we could discuss this in depth. However, I will choose just a few that I find to be notable at this level:

- You can scale only the part of your app that needs scaling.

- You can have different technologies, such as modern frameworks like React or Angular on the frontend, and use powerful languages for the backend.

- You can have separate, specialized, and dedicated teams.

- You can minimize merge conflicts.

- You can have several backends serving one UI.

- You can reuse the backends to serve different types of frontends (mobile apps, web, mobile).

- You can decrease costs and keep them under control.

Enterprise applications will strongly benefit from the granularity offered by modern architectures, as these are the ones that respond to change very well.

What Is a WEB API?

The ASP.NET Web API is a set of libraries that allows us to develop RESTful HTTP APIs (backends) using .NET, C#, or the language we prefer to work with, in .NET.

We need to make a small clarification. You will often hear developers saying "Web API" while referring to generic APIs that serve data to clients. In this book, and in this context, I will refer to the ASP.NET Web API as simply Web API. The expression is shorter like this, and it becomes a known and self-explanatory vocabulary.

Web API gets delivered with the Visual Studio installer, and is available under *Workload* ➤ *Web & Cloud,* as illustrated in Figure 1-6.

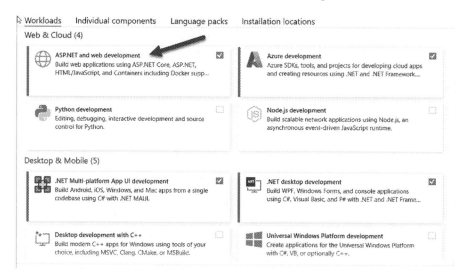

Figure 1-6. *Visual Studio Workload—ASP.NET and Web development*

Having this workload installed will allow us to start our code from a predefined structure, as shown in Figure 1-7.

Figure 1-7. *Web API project structure*

If we run this project, we will see the web browser opening, and the API will just work with dummy data, without us doing any configuration at all. It will load the documentation page that comes by default in the project template, and you'll see something like Figure 1-8, with the small exception that for you, the port might be different than 7038.

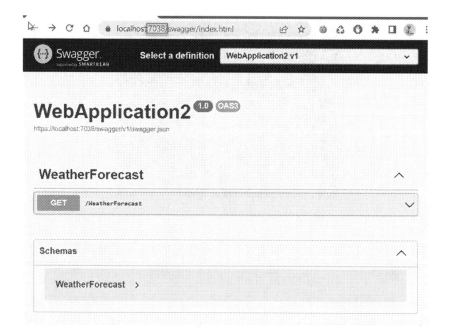

Figure 1-8. *Web API project start screen*

Inside the project structure, everything has a well-defined role in the ecosystem. This is an approach called *Convention Over Configuration* that you'll encounter in all major .NET programming models. In short, this means that as long as you follow the well-established conventions, you won't need to configure anything, and the application will just work. This way you can focus more on developing actual functionality and not lose time doing tedious work. We will talk more about this in Chapter 4.

When to Use WEB API

Web API can be used anytime you want to develop RESTful services over HTTP protocol. Due to its ease of use, it should be the go-to technology option if you have such a scenario. These services might have different response formats: JSON (the default one), XML, or something custom.

These APIs can serve as backends for native mobile applications or as web frontends. They can even be consumed by other backends in point-to-point communication patterns.

There are cases where you will need to make server-to-server requests to implement functionality, and WEB API has classes that allow you to do that.

For example, to process a payment using a payment provider, or to log in a user using Facebook or Google, you might need to interact with their APIs and make an API request from your API.

There are plenty of scenarios where someone might use a third-party API to bring value to a product or a business, or to simply avoid reinventing the wheel.

The World of Web Applications

In the world of speed, we all want to be connected. We start to automate our homes, control things remotely, or integrate with major industry players like Facebook or Twitter.

As developers, these things translate to a different approach when it comes to developing web apps. We now need to manage more than one single application from a single solution, and we don't develop monoliths anymore. We develop multiple APIs that are the building blocks of the same system. We have microservice architectures where we need to manage smaller moving parts and make sure these are running as expected.

Life as developers is not getting any simpler, but one thing is for sure: APIs are here to stay, and we need to learn how to write and manage them.

According to ProgrammableWeb.com, the world's leading source of news and information about web-based application programming interfaces, or APIs, since 2008, the API world had a major growth trend, and that trend continues today (Figure 1-9).

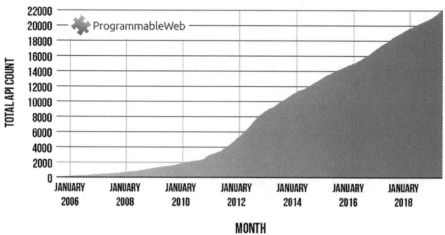

Figure 1-9. *The growth over time of APIs in ProgrammableWeb directory*

This chart is made of 22,000 APIs submitted to the ProgrammableWeb directory, but we know for sure that not all APIs in the world are submitted there, and so we need to take this information with a grain of salt.

Summary

In this chapter, we learned that an API is like a web app that doesn't have a presentation layer and responds only with data in the response body. This data can have different formats, like JSON, XML, or anything custom, specific to the business. We learned about different categories of APIs and had a first look at the ASP.NET Web API. After that, we put everything into context and saw how the web world has evolved and affected the way we write code.

In the next chapters, we will set up our environments, learn must-know WEB concepts that we will use throughout the book, and then start building our API.

CHAPTER 2

Introduction to the Web

In this chapter, we will explore how the internet works and how information travels over the internet. We will learn what happens every time we navigate to a website. All the small blocks in this chapter are very important for any web developer, even if they only write APIs or plan to use other application models, such as .NET MVC or Razor Pages.

We will learn what a *request* and a *response* are, how we can add meaning to them, and how to leverage the underlying protocol. We will use these concepts extensively once we start creating our APIs.

How the Internet Works

It is necessary to start with the basics because it will give us a complete picture of what happens every time we browse on a web page.

Protocols

A *protocol* is a set of rules that defines how data is exchanged within or between computers (machines). Or, in other words, a protocol is a convention between parties regarding the information exchange or communication between them.

© Irina Dominte 2023
I. Dominte, *Web API Development for the Absolute Beginner*,
https://doi.org/10.1007/978-1-4842-9348-5_2

Examples of such protocols include Internet Protocol (IP), User Datagram Protocol (UDP), Transmission Control Protocol, and so on.

Even you and I can establish a protocol. Let's say that you and I decide that we will send messages with words that begin with the letter A—then we could say we have established a protocol between us.

HTTP Protocol

HTTP is the acronym for HyperText Transfer Protocol. It was first coined in RFC1945 in 1996. It started with version 1.0, and since then it has evolved, reaching version 3.0.

HTTP is an application-level protocol with the lightness and speed necessary for distributed, collaborative, hypermedia information systems. It is a generic, stateless, object-oriented protocol that can be used for many tasks, such as name servers and distributed object management systems, through the extension of its request methods (commands). A feature of HTTP is the typing of data representation, allowing systems to be built independent of the data being transferred. (rfc1945, 1996)

With HTTP, the information traveling over the network is in clear text, meaning that with the proper tools a potential attacker might see and use what data travels between the client and the server and back. You can see a schematic flow in Figure 2-1.

Figure 2-1. *Clear text information over HTTP*

HTTPS Protocol

HTTPS (HTTP Secured) is a version of HTTP where the information traveling between the client and the server is encrypted using a certificate that lives on the web server. That certificate is generated by a *certificate authority* for a specific domain and or its subdomain. It has an expiration date, which means that from time to time it needs to be renewed.

HTTPS provides a reasonable security level in unsecured networks, and this means that transmitting sensitive data like passwords or credit card numbers is safe. In this case, a potential attacker cannot see, in clear text (Figure 2-2), what the details transmitted are (as was the case for HTTP).

Figure 2-2. *Encrypted data over HTTPS*

Client–Server Architecture

The client–server architecture is the simplest type of architecture you could ever find in the development world. It involves two entities, shown in Figure 2-3, that are able to communicate and understand what each other wants by decoding the bits and pieces that reach them.[1]

Figure 2-3. *Client-server architecture*

Client

In most cases, the client is the one that initiates the communication by sending a request. We talk more in-depth about requests in a dedicated section.

---

[1] https://datatracker.ietf.org/doc/html/rfc1945

Server

The server is the entity that receives requests from clients, processes them, and generates responses back to them. Of course, the response generation happens if the initial request can be interpreted by the server.

What Is a URL: The Building Blocks

The web is a set of interconnected resources, and those resources need to be addressable. If you want to be reachable by phone, then you'd better have a phone with a phone number and tell people your number. The same happens with resources on the internet by means of a URL.

URL is an acronym for Uniform Resource Locator—a specialized form of a URI (Uniform Resource Identifier), first coined as a term when the web was invented.

The URL is made of a few parts that have meaning for the server, and that help it distinguish what the client wants. No part of it is random, even if some of it might look so. Every single part has a well-defined role. Let's have a look at Figure 2-4 and talk about each individual part.

Figure 2-4. *A URL structure example*

Schema

The schema or protocol shows what is used in terms of transport. Usually, you will find HTTP, HTTPS, or, in some cases, FTP.

The protocol will always be followed by the protocol separator, `://`, and even if we don't often type it ourselves, the browsers add it in for us. In the API world, we will make a clear distinction between HTTP and HTTPS, and we will need to type the correct protocols in the tools we will use for testing our APIs.

```
http://
https://
ftp://
```

Domain

The domain is the part that we type in browsers every time we want to navigate to a specific website, and whether we want it or not, it must be present.

```
https://microsoft.com
https://amazon.com
```

This is sometimes accompanied by a subdomain or a port:

```
https://docs.microsoft.com
http://localhost:4100
```

A *subdomain* is the part that prefixes the domain. Businesses use this to split their website based on a criterion or to make a snapshot of it.

Using subdomains is like arranging a drawer using several small boxes. Each box will hold items that are meaningful to you. A box might hold paper clips or keys, and it might be easier to maintain. The same happens with subdomains.

For example, a URL like `http://2019.myconference.com` may hold a snapshot of the 2019 conference edition, with speakers, talks, partners, and agenda, while `myconference.com` is always the current edition, and current might be 2023 or 2025, depending on the year.

Path

The path in the given example is similar to file paths that we find in operating systems. We often navigate to paths like `C:/Program Files/` or `D:/holidayphotos/2023` to find documents or files that we want. A similar thing happens with the `shoes/sandals` part in our example. Putting everything into context, we found ourselves on `myshop.com`, and more specifically in the `shoes` category, `sandals` subcategory.

As we will see when we start building our API, this path will map to a specific route in our API, and with that it is like finding yourself at a crossroads and deciding which way to go. One path might lead you to one place, another path to another place, and so on.

Query String

The *query* or the *query string* is the part in the URL that should have a filtering effect on the results that come from the server as part of the response.

This is made of *key=value* pair structures, separated by the ampersand (&) symbol. Each such pair has a meaning for the server or the business. Looking at our part example, the string *color=pink&size=35* is made of two such pairs:

- *color=pink* – a parameter named "color" with a value of "pink"

- *&* – separator

- *size=35* – a parameter named "size" with a value of "35"

Now, if we look back at Figure 2-4, with the URL example, we know what we are in: shoes category, sandals subcategory, and from these, we want to filter out only those that meet our criteria: pink color, and a 35 EU size. If this is properly implemented on the server, accessing the

URL in the browser or testing tool, the result we get back should contain exactly what we expect: sandals that are pink and 35 EU size. Nothing less, nothing more.

In a random web page, usually the query strings are changed once the user clicks an option that is supposed to filter the returned results. In Figure 2-5, if we were to click the highlighted option, the results we would see after page reload should match exactly the criteria.

Figure 2-5. *A filter section on an Amazon page*

Fragment

The fragment is the ID of an HTML element in the page, added via the URL. By clicking a URL that has a fragment, usually you will be taken to the same page, but the view will be focused on that HTML element. In this way the browser points you to a specific section of the page. Your action won't cause the current page to reload, so the only movement in the page that you'll see will be the browser positioning over that HTML element.

In the context of APIs, it is unusual to find fragments in the URL, but if you find them, they won't have any effect on the current request. The #JPEG in the following URL is the ID of an HTML element, but in APIs we work only with URLs and data. It won't cause an error, but there will be no actual visual representation of it.

```
https://en.wikipedia.org/wiki/Portable_Network_Graphics#JPEG
```

Request and Response

The request and the response are two building blocks with whom we will be more than familiar by the end of this book. These two parts are the core of any interaction that happens over the internet. We 'ask' something and we get something in response, but we need to know the meaning of each.

Request

A request is like an envelope that travels over the network from the client to the server, carrying information to be decoded (Figure 2-6). It includes a content body (the content of the envelope—the actual letter), some header properties (the recipient), and an HTTP method (indicates how to send the request).

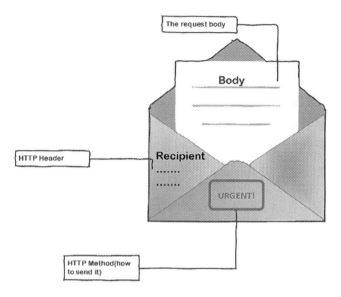

Figure 2-6. *A request is like an envelope*

The request is then processed by the server, and then the server generates a response. There are cases where the request doesn't reach the server, but even so, after a while, a response with a *408 Request Timeout* status code is sent back.

This "envelope" carries information that the server looks at to understand what type of "answer" it needs to send back to the client. This answer will be another type of envelope named *Response*.

The request is made of three parts, as shown in Figure 2-7. We will talk about each of them in more detail in dedicated sections in this chapter.

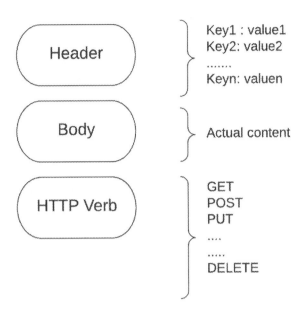

Figure 2-7. *Request anatomy*

- Header – a list of header properties that are sent with the request

- Body – the actual data that is sent in the request, or it might be empty

- HTTP method – showing how to send the request, using one of the categories in the HTTP methods section

Response

Very much like a request, the response is still like an envelope, but this is sent back to the client as a result of request processing. You can see a comparison in Figure 2-8.

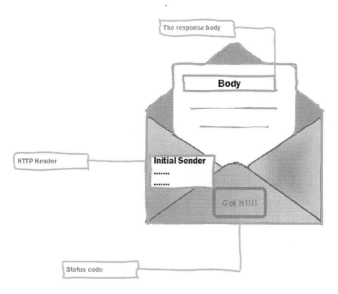

Figure 2-8. *Response like an envelope*

This, too, is made of three parts, but these parts are specific to the response, as shown in Figure 2-9.

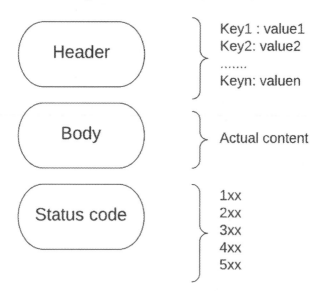

Figure 2-9. *Building blocks of a response*

- Header – properties that are sent with the response

- Body – the actual data that is sent in the response in the format asked for by the client. It may be empty in specific cases

- Status Code – fits in one of the categories in the status codes section

We will go into more depth on these status codes in a separate section.

Request versus Response

If we were to compare the response and the request, they are very similar (with a few nuances), but one has an HTTP method/HTTP verb, and the latter has a status code. We can see the comparison in Figure 2-10.

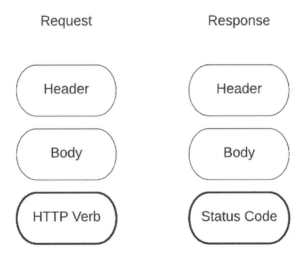

Figure 2-10. *Request versus Response*

Response Formats: MIME Types

A *MIME type,* also known as *multipurpose internet mail extension* type, is a standardized way of identifying the nature and format of a document, file, or group of bytes. RFC6838 describes in more detail the original intent and all the specifications.

When we navigate our computer file system, the extension of each file determines its type. Based on the extension the operating system knows what program to use to open the file. Depending on if the file is a .jpeg or a .png, or a .mp3, it will use different programs.

Browsers, however, can't use extensions to determine the content that needs to be rendered and must instead rely on these MIME types. These are passed as values for different header fields, and help determine the content type.

The structure is very simple. It tries to fit everything formed by bytes into a type and a subtype.

```
type/subtype
```

The type represents the general categorization. For example, video, application, and text are valid types. For a MIME type of *text* a subtype can be *plain*, *html*, or *css*.

There are two classes of the type component: discrete and multipart.

- Discrete – represents a single file or resource, such as a file, a video, or an HTML file to be rendered in browser

- Multipart – represents resources or files comprising multiple chunks that need to be considered as part of a whole

We could talk a lot about MIME types, but for now it is enough to understand where these fit into the ecosystem.

Headers

Headers are also called header properties or fields and are a collection of names and values as described in (rfc2616, n.d.).[2]

Each header field consists of a name followed by a colon (":") and a field value, similar to the following example:

```
Accept:application/json;
User-Agent:TBA;
```

Some of the names for the header fields are defined in RFC standards, and their well-established meanings can't be changed. The same thing happens with some of these header field values.

Some header fields can have a specific meaning if they are present in

- the request;

- the response; or

- the request *and* the response.

For example, if the header field were called Accept, we couldn't change it to "Accepted" because it wouldn't be in the standard anymore.

A header field is just another means of transporting information to the server or back from the server, depending on the case.

Some of these header fields have more meanings, and you'll find them more often as part of a request. Other header fields will have more meanings as part of the response.

For example, as a developer, you can use a header field to depict the client's culture or language, or you can use a header field to send back custom information like API version or a currency value that may be important.

---

[2] https://www.ietf.org/rfc/rfc2616.txt

Header fields should be used in APIs every time you have information to send back and forth that doesn't necessarily belong in a body or a URL query string. In fact, in APIs that are RESTful, leveraging headers as a means to obtain different representations of the same resource is a good practice.

We will now talk more about various header fields that you will likely encounter when working with APIs.

Accept

The Accept header field has a value belonging to a list of standard MIME types, but it can also be custom made.

```
Accept: application/json;
Accept: text/html;
Accept: application/vnd.github.param[+json]
```

This header field tells the server what format of response is preferred by the client. In some cases, a client might need an HTML representation of the resource, and in some other cases a JSON representation of the same resource.

To make a comparison, at a restaurant it is nice to be able to tell the waiter your preference for a certain dish, right? Maybe you want pizza with extra cheese or you want it without onion. The same happens with the client and the Accept header. The Accept header allows the client to specify preferences with regards to the format of the response.

The flow shown in Figure 2-11 happens every time a request is made and reaches the server (if the server is configured to look at the Accept header field). As you'll see later in the book, some servers can be configured to always respond in JSON format and to ignore the Accept header field.

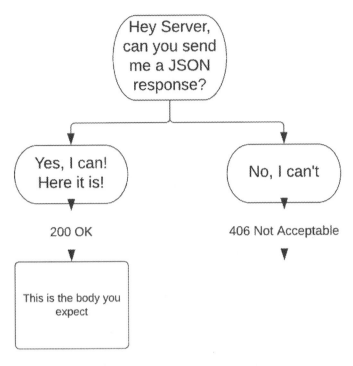

Figure 2-11. *Response generation flow*

Now, if the server looks at the Accept header field, it can determine
whether it can generate a response in the requested format. In the happy
case, the server will return a status code that is in the *2xx Success category,*
along with a response body. In the second case, when the server can't
generate a response body that the client prefers and understands, it will
return a status code in the *4xx Client error category* (406 Not Acceptable)
and an empty response body.

Content-Type

The Content-Type header field also has a standard MIME type as a value.
It can play a double role depending on if it is present in a request or a
response.

```
Content-Type: application/json;
```

First, if it is part of a request, it tells the server what format the body of the request has.

So, by looking at this, the server determines if it can interpret what the format is and continue the processing and then generate a response back.

If the server can't interpret the body, it will respond with a *415 Unsupported Media Type* status code. You can see the flow in Figure 2-12.

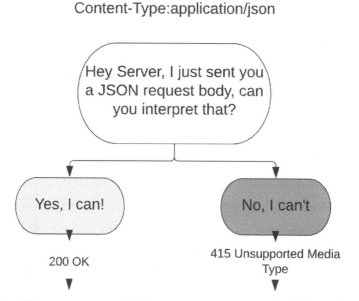

Figure 2-12. *Content-Type header field flow*

In the second case, if this header field is part of the response, it tells the client the format of the body that was sent. By looking at it, the client will be able to see if it can interpret the body.

As we will see later in the book, these two header fields, Accept and Content-Type, play a major role in a process called *content negotiation* that happens under the hood with every single request. This is very important in the API world.

Cache-Control

The Cache-Control header field is one of the most important header fields out there. Some people say that caching is one of the most important specifications of HTTP because it helps increase the perceived performance of web apps. This header field allows us to leverage client-side caching.

Cache-Control is one of the header fields that has predefined values.

- no-cache;

  Cache-Control:no-cache;

- max-age=[value];

  Cache-Control: max-age=604800;

By looking at this header field, if present, a client can store a copy of the response for a later use, or it can see if a previously stored resource is still fresh using the Expires header field.

The Cache-Control header field often works in conjunction with other header fields, such as ETag (ETag, n.d.)[3], If-Match (IfMatch, n.d.),[4] and If-None-Match (IfNoneMatch, n.d.).[5]

HTTP Methods

There are several HTTP methods, but only a few are used in the day-to-day life of a web developer, or at least you will encounter them more often than others. Many years ago, when SOAP services were the standard, some projects were using only the POST method to update something or to get

---

[3] https://www.rfc-editor.org/rfc/rfc9110.html#name-etag
[4] https://www.rfc-editor.org/rfc/rfc9110.html#name-if-match
[5] https://www.rfc-editor.org/rfc/rfc9110.html#name-if-none-match

something, and this practice was sometimes confusing. You had to rely heavily on your business logic to see if a request body had a fresh item (that needed to be inserted into the database) or if it was an update. This was the precursor of the UPSERT command that some developers use today.

In modern times, we should be mindful and use the right method for the right type of operation. Even though there might be two or more ways of implementing a feature, we should strive to use the "best" solution. This means keeping an eye on API design, best practices, lessons learned, and code decoupling, and adding meaning to your endpoints.

GET

The HTTP GET method is described in RFC2616 section 9.3, and as the name suggests, it has the role of requiring something from the server. When it comes to the status codes that you might expect after a GET request, it depends on what features you enable on the server or how strictly you implement your API.

The response to a GET request is cacheable if it has one of the correct caching headers.

POST

The HTTP POST method is described in RFC2616, section 9.5, and is the go-to method every time a new resource should be created or a form is submitted. A POST request usually implies sending data to the server, packed in a request body, with the goal of creating a new record of a specific type or simply sending data.

As a result, the response body should have the newly created entity (with the allocated identifier) and be accompanied by the right status code. In this case, a *201 Created*. To add more meaning to what happened, you should also have a Location header property pointing to the resource URI.

In Figure 2-13, you can see such an example in PostMan (a tool that we will use later in the book):

```
http://localhost:4100/api/speakers/1/talks

{
    "title": "Building APIs like there is no tomorrow",
    "description": "Builing APis is an important and hard
    job. you need discipline and you need to care about your
    consumers"
}
```

Issuing such a POST request to create a new talk for a specific speaker will get a similar response body but with an extra field named ID. This means that our item was successfully created, and the database assigned the ID *316* to it.

```
{
    "id": 316,
    "title": "Building APIs like there is no tomorrow",
    "description": "Builing APis is an important and hard
    job. you need discipline and you need to care about your
    consumers"
}
```

Body Cookies Headers (5) Test Results		Status: 201 Created Time: 6.30 s Size: 392 B
KEY		VALUE
Date	ⓘ	Wed, 13 Jul 2022 08:28:21 GMT
Content-Type	ⓘ	application/json; charset=utf-8
Server	ⓘ	Kestrel
Transfer-Encoding	ⓘ	chunked
Location	ⓘ	http://localhost:4100/api/speakers/1/talks/316

Figure 2-13. *The header fields and status code of a POST response*

PUT

The HTTP PUT method is described in RFC2616, section 9.6, and is the go-to method for updating existing entities. This method replaces the current existing entity, identified by the current URI.

DELETE

The HTTP DELETE method is described in RFC2616, section 9.7, and it should be used in all cases where you want to delete the resource identified by the URI specified. As a successful result, you should receive something around 2XX Success category:

- 200 OK – if an entity body should be returned

- 202 Accepted – if you don't need to wait for or receive an entity body

- 204 No Content – if you want to indicate success but you have no entity body to return

HTTP DELETE should be used wisely because this operation might have a permanent effect.

HEAD

The HTTP HEAD method is described in RFC2616, section 9, as being identical to GET, but is not required to return a body. It will give you an empty body, a status code, and the same headers as for a GET request. In cases where you don't want to consume bandwidth and transfer data over the network, it proves to be very handy because you can inspect the metadata sent.

For example, let's say you send a file or a form to the server that might take a lot to process, and you don't need a response right away. In this case, you can use HEAD to poll the server periodically to see if the operation has been completed.

OPTIONS

The HTTP OPTIONS method is described in RFC2616, section 9.2, and represents a request for information about the communication options available on the request/response chain.

You might make an OPTIONS request to an endpoint to see what the available operations are; for example, to see if a DELETE operation is available on a URL that represents a collection. By issuing a request as follows, the response won't contain a body, but will have the Allow header property, or other header properties, involved in CORS, from which you can extract what is needed, as seen in Figure 2-14.

```
OPTIONS http://localhost:4100/api/speakers/
```

Body Cookies Headers (4) Test Results	⊕ Status: 200 OK Time: 52 ms Size: 117 B
KEY	VALUE
Date	⏱ Wed, 13 Jul 2022 12:35:12 GMT
Server	⏱ Kestrel
Content-Length	⏱ 0
Allow	⏱ GET,OPTIONS,POST

Figure 2-14. *The response to an OPTIONS request*

You may have seen an OPTIONS request made by the browsers as a preflight request to further determine if it is safe to actually make the request. It can't change any resources, which means that the operation is safe, but it lets the server decide if it is acceptable to send another request with the real parameters. You can treat this as a request for "permission to send a request."

Now, since we talked about HTTP methods, it is only fair to introduce an acronym: CRUD, or Create-Read-Update-Delete. CRUD covers every operation that you might do to an item. In business or database terms, you might need to visualize, create, update, or delete a record, and this can be mapped over HTTP methods, as in Table 2-1.

Table 2-1. *Mapping CRUD to HTTP Methods*

	Database/Business Operation	HTTP Method
C - Create	INSERT	POST
R - Read	SELECT	GET
U- Update	UPDATE	PUT
D - Delete	DELETE	DELETE

Idempotent versus Safe Methods

Based on the calling effect, Request for Comments categorizes all HTTP methods as either safe or idempotent. Any HTTP method can have both or none of these attributes at the same time. Knowing about idempotency and safety is important when it comes to testing or consuming an API because it makes us aware of the effects.

An HTTP method is considered to be **idempotent** if no matter how many times the request is made, the result will always be the same (if nothing modifies it meanwhile). For example, if we refresh a page ten times, every single time we will see the same results if nothing gets modified at the server level. The GET HTTP method is idempotent.

An HTTP method is considered to be **safe** if it doesn't modify the state of the resource. HTTP GET or HEAD will just retrieve the resource but never modify it.

POST and PUT are meant to modify a resource, and every time we use such a method it will modify the resource. This means that these are unsafe.

Status Codes

A status code is a three-digit construction used to indicate if an HTTP request was successfully received and processed by the server. Status codes fit in one of the following five categories.

1xx – Informational

Status codes that start with a 1xx are informational and are used when the server needs to send an intermediary response for communicating connection status or request progress. The response won't contain a content body or trailers.

2xx – Success

Success status codes that start with 2xx are indicating that the request has been successfully received and processed. Depending on the status code sent by the server, the response body may be empty or not.

Success status codes:

- 200 OK – The request is received and processed correctly, and a response is generated.

- 201 Created – This is sent in response to a POST request to show that a new resource was created.

- 202 Accepted – This is used when a request is received and processed but the response won't have a body. For example, when something might be sent to be enqueued and no content body is expected back. It is like the server telling the client: "Hey, I got this, but I will process it a bit later."

- 204 No Content – This means the request is successfully processed but no content body will be returned. It is usually used in response to a DELETE request.

3xx – Redirects

Redirects are those status codes that indicate that the current URL will redirect or is redirected to another location. This usually happens in the context of web pages when, for example, you click a link or submit a form, and then suddenly the page reloads and takes you somewhere else. In the context of APIs, you won't encounter them very often.

Redirect status codes:

- 301 Moved permanently – This is used to indicate that the resource has been moved to a new location. This should also come accompanied by a Location header field that contains the new URL.

4xx – Client Errors

Client errors are the category that shows that the client issuing the request has made something preventing the server from processing it correctly. It can be that the URL was not found, there are validation errors, or maybe the user is not authenticated or not allowed to do a specific operation.

Client errors status codes are as follows:

- 400 Bad Request – The server indicates that the request it has received is not well formed. This can mean a lot of things, but most of them are related to the URL itself. For example: a parameter value is missing, or a specific value is not present or correct.

- 401 Unauthorized – You can't prove you are who you say you are.

- 403 Forbidden – I know who you are but you are not allowed to perform the action you want to perform (maybe you want to delete a resource but you don't have the right role).

- 404 Not Found – The URL or the resource is not found.

- 405 Method not allowed – This is used when the server can't process the request based on the HTTP method used. For example, when the client tries to use an HTTP DELETE over a URL that exposes a collection of items.

- 406 Not Acceptable – This means the server can't respond in the format stated in the Accept header field in the request.

- 409 Conflict – There is a conflict due to an internal business rule that might not be obvious at first for the client. For example, the uniqueness of a field on edit.

- 410 Gone – This shows that the resource is not there intentionally and maybe for a limited time, let's say, for maintenance reasons.

- 415 Unsupported Media Type – This indicates that the server refuses to process, or can't process, the request because it doesn't know how to decode the body based on the MIME type of the Content-Type header field.

- 422 Unprocessable Entity – This indicates that the server understands the request body but it can't process it, maybe because of a validation error.

- 429 Too many requests – This indicates that the user
  sent too many requests in a given amount of time.
  This is often accompanied by a `Retry-After` header
  field indicating how long to wait before making a new
  request. Developers often refer to this status code as
  rate-limiting.

5xx – Server Errors

Server errors are the category that states that the server won't be able
to process requests. Unlike client errors, these might need manual
intervention on the code, in order to be fixed. They include the following:

- 500 Internal Server Error – This is used when the server
  can't process that specific request due to something
  internal happening. As a side note, usually a certain
  functionality case is not implemented or not tested,
  and something is broken on the server.

- 501 Not Implemented – This shows when the server
  does not support the functionality needed to fulfill the
  request.

- 503 Service Not Available – This indicates that
  the server can't process the request because it is
  overloaded or is down for a reason. Sometimes the
  server may send a `Retry-After` header property to tell
  the client to wait until it should try the request again.

Cookies

A cookie is a small piece of information with some properties that come from the server. They are usually stored in the client's browser with the purpose of retaining information for later use. Cookies travel in HTTP headers, from the server, and back.

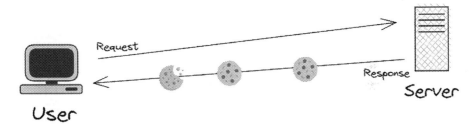

Figure 2-15. *Cookies added in responses*

Because HTTP is stateless, cookies are used as a state management mechanism. You can read more about every component in RFC6265.

These can be written or read from browsers using JavaScript language, which is widely used to develop rich user interfaces. For example, when you log in to a page, you might see a "Remember me" checkbox, which has the purpose of keeping you logged in. This feature is implemented by using cookies, which travel to the server and back as a header field.

A cookie has a few properties, as shown in Figure 2-16.

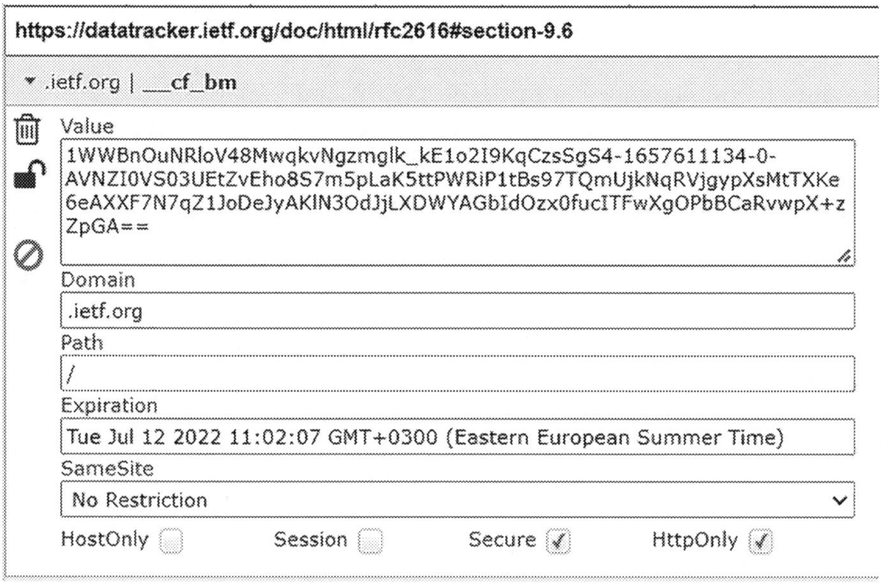

Figure 2-16. *A cookie as shown in EditThisCookie Chrome plugin*

The following are its properties and their purposes:

- *Name*

- *A value* associated with the name

- Assigned to a domain/subdomain or path in the domain

- *Expiration* date

- *HTTPOnly* attribute limits the usage of the cookie to only HTTP, meaning that, for example, the browser APIs omit this cookie.

- *Secure* attribute limits the scope of the cookie to "secure" channels (where "secure" is defined by the user agent).

- *Session* attribute is used to identify the current session.

- *SameSite* attribute limits the scope of the cookie such that it will only be attached to requests if those requests are same-site, preventing information leakage.

If a request is made from an URL like *myapi.com* toward *subdomain. myapi.com* it is a **same-site request** because it's made from a top-level domain to a subdomain.

The opposite of a same-site request is a *cross-site request*. This covers scenarios where a request is made from a URL like subdomain1.myapi.com to subdomain2.myapi.com (a subdomain to another subdomain, or another domain entirely).

A cookie is just another means to transport information from the server and back. Developers shouldn't be afraid to use them if they have the right scenarios. Cookies may play a role in authentication or in keeping data about the current user, and are more front-end facing.

You need to know about their existence in the web context, but you won't deal with them very often when writing APIs. Usually, if there is additional data to be carried back and forth, header properties are used.

Summary

I know that this might be a lot of information to digest, but I tried to present to you, the reader, only those parts that I think are really important.

Using the right HTTP verbs, headers, and status codes is very important when it comes to implementing an API. Not only will you use the specifications correctly, but you will have a clean and well-designed

API, and you will be mindful of your consumers and colleagues. You will help them understand quickly how to operate and consume your API and leverage the existing protocol (HTTP).

In this chapter, we learned about all the small building blocks of the web. The next chapters will be built on these blocks, and you'll get to put everything into practice.

CHAPTER 3

Setting Up the Environment

Before we delve into any theoretical part about APIs, we will get familiar with one of the most used IDEs for .NET development in this section. This is still the go-to option for developing with C#.

Installing Visual Studio

Visual Studio is the go-to IDE for .NET development. If you have never used it before, you can find it on the official website and download it.

```
https://visualstudio.microsoft.com/downloads/
```

Figure 3-1. *Visual Studio available options*

There are three Visual Studio options, but only one of them is free and suitable for learning and non-commercial code—the *Community* edition.

© Irina Dominte 2023
I. Dominte, *Web API Development for the Absolute Beginner*,
https://doi.org/10.1007/978-1-4842-9348-5_3

Click *Free download* and after the download, open the installer. The installer will prompt you to select the "features" you want to be installed. These features are named *workloads*, and the workloads you will need depend on the type of apps you are writing. This is a means of saving disk space on your local machine.

If you ever change your mind and need something extra, you can reopen the installer and select the option you need.

For Web API development, you will need to download the *ASP.NET and web development* workload, as shown in Figure 3-2.

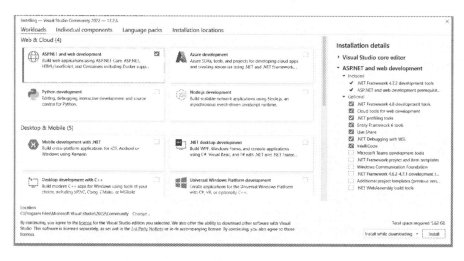

Figure 3-2. *Visual Studio Installer workloads*

When the installation is complete, you can launch Visual Studio by pressing the Launch button shown in Figure 3-3 or simply by searching for it among your computer programs.

Figure 3-3. *Visual Studio after installation*

Postman

To make sure our API works as expected we could as well use one of the existing browsers, but we won't have a complete overview of the entire API ecosystem. To get that, we will need another tool that facilitates testing our APIs.

What Is Postman?

Postman is an API tool for building, consuming, and testing APIs. You will often use it during development for testing your APIs, or any API. It has a lot of features that can streamline API testing. It can let work with different environments, code variables, save URLs with placeholders, organize things according to test cases or scenarios, and automate different things.

You can find Postman on this website: `https://www.postman.com/downloads`. See Figure 3-4.

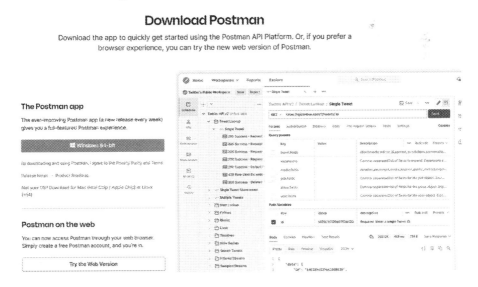

Figure 3-4. *Postman homepage*

You will be prompted to create an account, but it's not mandatory. It helps though because it will allow you to save what you are working on and let you distribute your work across multiple computers. Also, you have the option of using the tool online, which it lets you explore the tool and APIs without installing anything.

To make things even more interesting, as you can see in Figure 3-5, there are a few API collections available that you can use to play around.

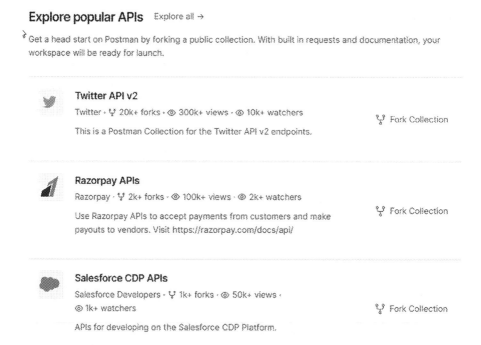

Figure 3-5. Popular API collections from Postman website

For example, if you want to try the Twitter API, you can see how things can be organized in Postman by interacting with an interface similar to what you will get in the installed tool.

In Figure 3-6, the requests are organized in collections and folders, and you get a high-level overview of the request types and a short description of each.

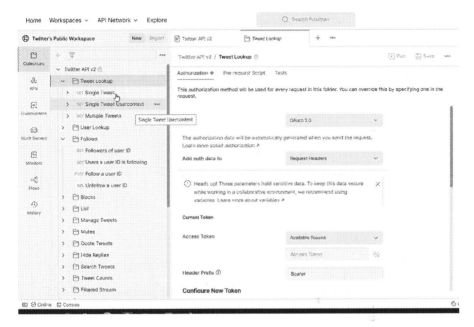

Figure 3-6. *Postman online interface*

Exploring the Postman Interface

When you first open Postman, you will see a lot of toggles and tabs that you will get to use later, but for now, I think is best to focus on the four sections highlighted in Figure 3-7.

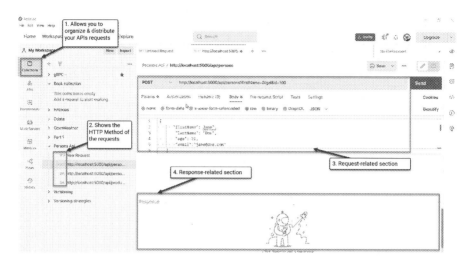

Figure 3-7. *Some Postman sections*

1. *Collections* – This tab allows you to organize
   your API calls. Here, you can give names to your
   collections and create folders and subfolders to
   keep things tidy. Also, to help you deal with tedious
   work, there is a contextual menu for each collection.
   In Figure 3-8, you can see a contextual menu that
   operates on an entire collection.

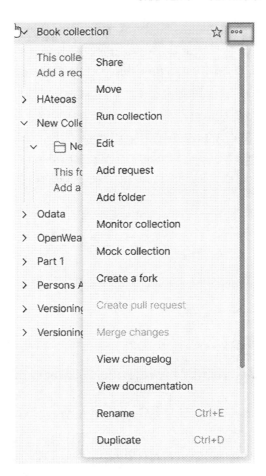

Figure 3-8. *Collections – contextual menu*

You can consider a collection as being a smart folder with files in it. You can share the files, arrange them, and delete them.

2. *Request methods* – Inside the Collections folders and subfolders you can have a high-level overview of what type of requests are available, with a small label where the HTTP method is displayed.

3. *Request section* – This contains everything you can add to a request (headers, query parameters, authentication-related bits, body, scripts that can be run in certain conditions, some settings you can turn on or off at request). Some of these items are just settings that you can tweak in that specific request, and some of them are related to the actual data that gets sent to the server, as you can see in Figure 3-9.

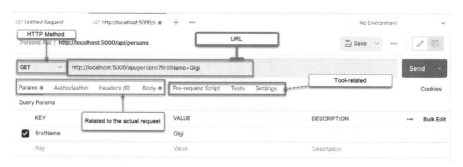

Figure 3-9. *Content related to the request in Postman*

4. *Response section* – This will contain the response body displayed in different forms: prettified, as it comes from the server, and interpreted as HTML as if it were in the browser, as shown in Figure 3-10.

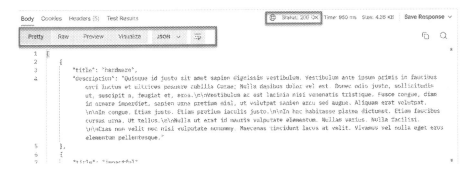

Figure 3-10. *Content related to the response in Postman*

Postman is an easy-to-use yet very complex tool. At first, if you have never used the tool before, it might be a little overwhelming, but don't be afraid to click, test around, and maybe have a look at their learning center: https://learning.postman.com/docs/getting-started/introduction/.

What we have covered here should be enough for you to get started with an API.

Your First Web API Project

Not that we installed the tools that we will use for the development and testing of our API, we will see how to actually create one. We will explore the Visual Studio interface and get familiar with it.

Creating a Project

To create a Web API project, you will need to browse and select the right template from Visual Studio (Figure 3-11). Usually, the templates are either empty—useful when you want to organize things yourself from scratch—or with a basic dummy functionality that is just enough to lead you through that application model.

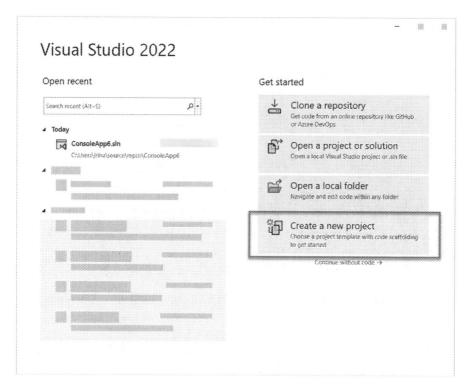

Figure 3-11. *"Create a new project" option*

In Figure 3-12, the ASP.NET Core Web API option is a template for RESTful HTTP services, which can also function as a base for ASP.NET MVC applications. In the following sections, we will focus on creating HTTP services, or APIs that return data.

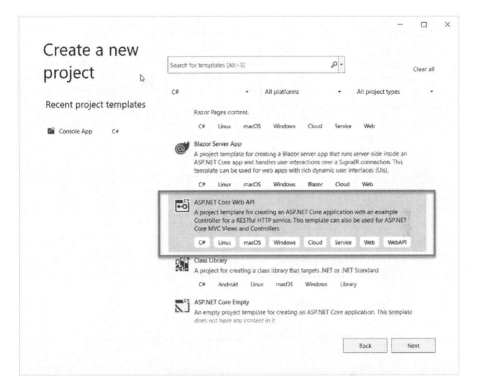

Figure 3-12. *Selecting ASP.NET Core Web API template*

Clicking the Next button will take you to the next step, and you will be required to provide a name for your project and select a location for it, as shown in Figure 3-13.

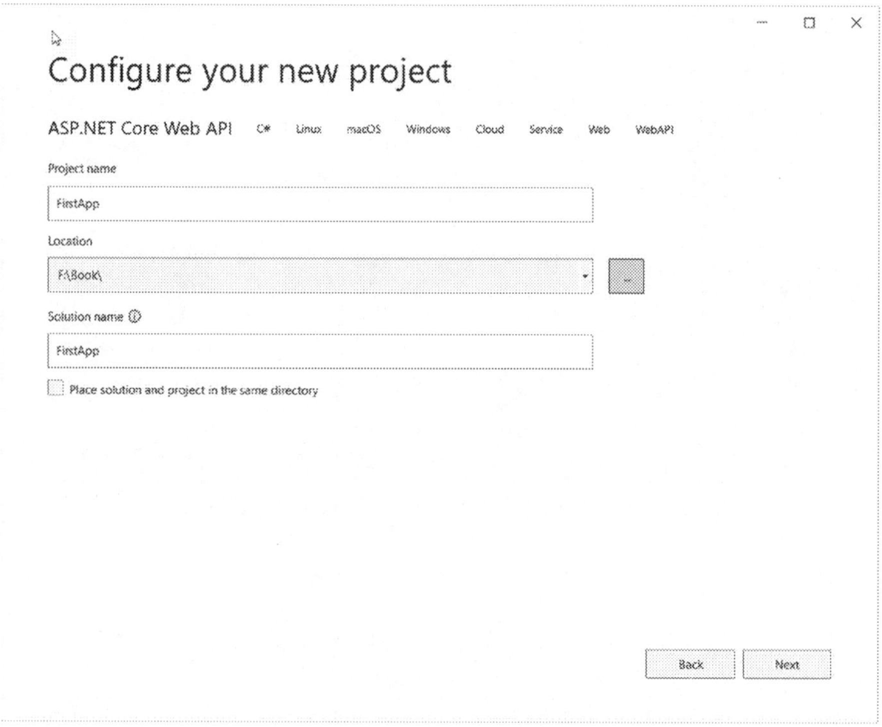

Figure 3-13. *Providing a name and a location for the new project*

After this step, once the name and the location of the project are settled, you can select some additional information regarding the behavior of the current project. Additionally, you can choose if you want to add authentication to your project, use Docker, or choose what is target .NET version is (if you have several versions installed, those will appear here), as shown in Figure 3-14. Unchecking the *Use controllers* option will give you a different programming model—*Minimal API*—but we won't focus on that now. In our case, all other options can be left unchanged.

Figure 3-14. *Creating a new project – Additional information step*

Minimal API is a programming model where the project structure
consists of two files: a JSON file for configuration-related strings, and
a .cs file for the actual code. This model is suited for microservices
architecture and projects where a very focused API is needed.

In the next section, we will explore the generated project structure files
and quickly progress toward issuing our first request.

Exploring the Project Structure

Looking at the Solution Explorer window and the project structure, you will
notice that it is small and made of a series of nodes that can be collapsed
or expanded, folders, and some C# files. We will take a short look at each of
the nodes shown in Figure 3-15, but the highlighted ones will be our focus.

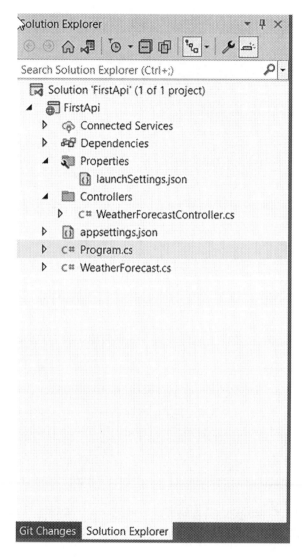

Figure 3-15. *Web API project structure*

- Connected Services – This node will display all the
  services that are used in this project, and those with
  which the project interacts. For example, Azure Key
  Vaults, external services like WCF or gRPC, storage
  accounts, databases, etc.

- Dependencies – References to other projects or libraries in the same solution or library packages installed from public NuGet or other private package managers

- launchsettings.json – Used only locally in the development machine; it doesn't get deployed and it contains info related to each debug profile

- Controllers/WeatherForecastController.cs – The Controllers folder and the files inside contain the logic for your API endpoints. Usually, we will have one Controller file per endpoint (URL), and we will implement HTTP methods inside these controllers. In our example, the WeatherForecastController.cs is auto-generated by the Visual Studio template. It has basic functionality, as shown in Listing 3-1.

Listing 3-1. Content of WeatherForecastController

```
using Microsoft.AspNetCore.Mvc;

namespace FirstApi.Controllers
{
    [ApiController]
    [Route("[controller]")]
    public class WeatherForecastController : ControllerBase
    {
        private static readonly string[] Summaries = new[]
        {
        "Freezing", "Bracing", "Chilly", "Cool", "Mild",
        "Warm", "Balmy", "Hot", "Sweltering", "Scorching"
        };
```

```csharp
private readonly ILogger<WeatherForecastController>
_logger;

public WeatherForecastController(ILogger<WeatherForecast
Controller> logger)
{
    _logger = logger;
}

[HttpGet(Name = "GetWeatherForecast")]
public IEnumerable<WeatherForecast> Get()
{
    return Enumerable.Range(1, 5).Select(index => new
    WeatherForecast
    {
        Date = DateTime.Now.AddDays(index),
        TemperatureC = Random.Shared.Next(-20, 55),
        Summary = Summaries[Random.Shared.Next
        (Summaries.Length)]
    })
    .ToArray();
}
}
}
```

Endpoint is a term that is used often instead of URL in the context of an API.

- appsettings.json – This contains configuration strings or values for different properties that shouldn't be hardcoded in C#. When the app runs, some of them are already interpreted by the platform under the hood and enable or disable something.

In Listing 3-2, which is included in the project, you can see that the default LogLevel is Information, which means the project will log everything for all enabled logging providers, starting with Information and up.

Listing 3-2. appsettings.json Default Content

```
{
  "Logging": {
    "LogLevel": {
      "Default": "Information",
      "Microsoft.AspNetCore": "Warning"
    }
  },
  "AllowedHosts": "*"
}
```

In appsettings.json, we usually add things that can change during the lifetime of a project or are environment dependent. For example, database names and connection strings or some settings (like LogLevel, for example) usually change per environment. You might have (and you should have) a database for development, one for staging, and one for production, and usernames or the actual database names might be different. You can think of this file as being a panel with a lot of buttons that you can turn on or off to make things behave differently.

LogLevel specifies the level from which the app can start outputting data that aid the development process. These properties are classified as either Trace, Debug, Information, Warning, Error, Critical, or None.

Program.cs – This file helps streamline everything. You can write code that reads from appsettings.json properties, or you can define which implementation corresponds to which interface. It can be considered the control room or the core of any application, since everything related to the configuration is done here.

WeatherForecast.cs – A dummy class, containing properties, with the sole purpose of providing the developer with a demo, as shown in Listing 3-3.

Listing 3-3. WeatherForecast.cs Class Content

```
namespace FirstApi
{
    public class WeatherForecast
    {
        public DateTime Date { get; set; }

        public int TemperatureC { get; set; }

        public int TemperatureF => 32 + (int)(TemperatureC /
        0.5556);

        public string? Summary { get; set; }
    }
}
```

Running the Project

Now that we have had a quick look through the project structure and files, we can run the project by pressing Ctrl+F5 or by going into the Debug menu and choosing Start without debugging.

The project will start compiling, output some data, and open a console window similar to that in Figure 3-16.

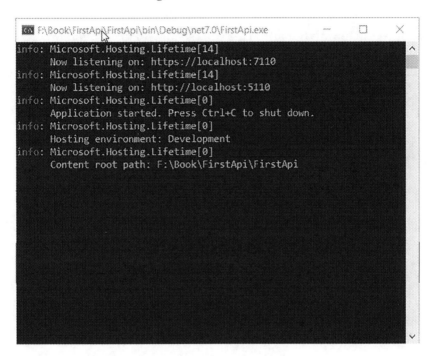

Figure 3-16. *Console API running*

In this window, you can see *info:* messages corresponding to the LogLevel specified in appsettings.json. Based on that setting value— Information—it writes a message in the console every time something significant happens.

Also, in the same window, you can see the URL where the API is running, with one for the HTTP protocol and one for HTTPS. In my case, the application runs on port 5110 for HTTP and 7110 for HTTPS. In your case, it might be different, but this can be customized by adding a setting in appsettings.json.

Along with all these console details, you will notice a browser window opening and displaying a Swagger page, as shown in Figure 3-17. This page shows the request types and additional info about all the requests that could be made toward our app. This will be our API documentation, and we will talk about this in more detail in Chapter 12.

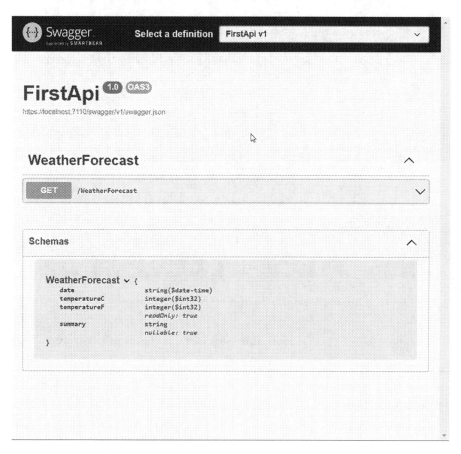

Figure 3-17. A Swagger page

Currently, this Swagger page shows that in our application we have a GET request. We can issue that request by writing the base URLs we've seen in the console and appending /WeatherForecast to it (this is the name of the controller we want to access). In the next section, we will issue our first GET request to https://localhost:7110/WeatherForecast.

Issuing Your First Request

We are finally at the point where we can issue requests (Yay!). With the API running, open Postman. In the URL section, paste the URL of your API and click the Send button.

If at first you do not get a response or receive an error as shown in Figure 3-18, you will need to go to the Settings tab and make sure the SSL verification is turned off, as shown in Figure 3-19.

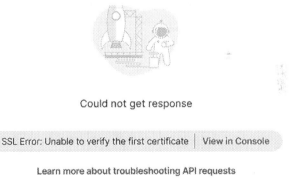

Could not get response

SSL Error: Unable to verify the first certificate | View in Console

Learn more about troubleshooting API requests

Figure 3-18. *Response error in Postman caused by SSL verification*

Figure 3-19. *Turn "Enable SSL certificate verification" on or off*

Once you have done this, you will be able to issue successful requests (Figure 3-20). Don't worry—you won't have to tweak all things every time, as this is something that usually happens with new installs.

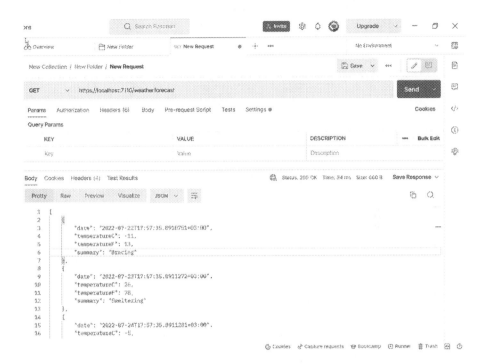

Figure 3-20. *A successful Postman response*

Summary

In this chapter, we installed two tools, set the ground rules for working with Visual Studio and Postman, and saw how to run an API. We will become more familiar with these tools and the project structure in the following chapters.

In the next chapter, we will learn what the main components of Web API are and the role they play in the application ecosystem.

CHAPTER 4

Web API: Building Blocks

In this chapter we will learn a few concepts that help us set the ground for working with ASP.NET Web API. We will learn why some things need to be implementing respecting some rules and how we can leverage what the platform has to offer.

Convention Over Configuration

Convention over configuration is a design philosophy that seeks to apply defaults implied by code structure rather than requiring explicit code.

In other words, as long as we respect the conventions, given there is no need to configure anything else, things will just work. The Web API template is delivered with basic dummy functionality that uses this convention extensively. In Figure 4-1, you can see a project that has two controllers in the Controllers folder, and their names follow the same pattern.

© Irina Dominte 2023
I. Dominte, *Web API Development for the Absolute Beginner,*
https://doi.org/10.1007/978-1-4842-9348-5_4

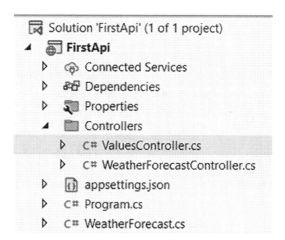

Figure 4-1. *An API with two controllers*

MVC

The model–view–controller (MVC) pattern is an architectural design pattern inspired by the SmallTalk project, dating back to 1978, that aims to decouple and declutter code. The architecture of a project that follows the MVC pattern is rather natural as it is inspired by the actions the user performs on a web page. In a web context, the user will undertake an action, and in response the application will change a data model and generate a view.

In Figure 4-2 you can see the MVC pattern.

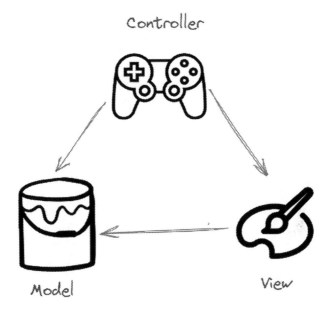

Figure 4-2. *MVC pattern communication*

Model

The *model* is responsible for carrying data to and from the *view*.

View

The *view* is a visualization of the data found in the *model*. It is also responsible for displaying what is graphically transferred in the model.

Controller

The *controller* acts on both the *model* and the *view*. It controls the data flow into the *model* object and will update the *view* whenever data changes.

We can look at the *controller* as being the brain that controls what information is displayed and how.

With MVC, the logic is divided into three chunks that are intertwined but act independently. Of these three chunks, the application logic chunk is changed more frequently than the presentation chunk, and if these two were combined in a single place, our application would be open to unwanted errors, often requiring a lot of retesting.

You will find this architectural pattern in many frameworks because it has a lot of benefits in the long run. An application that doesn't have dependencies scattered everywhere is easier to update, test, debug, and is generally less complex.

We talked about MVC as a design pattern and saw how this applies to the real world. You will encounter, or maybe you already did encounter, ASP MVC projects where the server returns HTML constructs that get to be interpreted by the browser.

In a Web API, the HTML constructs are missing, and the only thing we can get is data in JSON format, XML, or anything custom. We can safely say that a Web API application is similar to an ASP MVC application but doesn't have the presentation layer. We won't see buttons, colors, or any kind of layout in a Web API response.

The API Request Pipeline

Every request that is made to our API has a specific 'road' that it takes inside the platform internals. On that road, the request encounters a few components that have a very well-defined scope. These components, chained one after another form something that we call the "Request Pipeline".

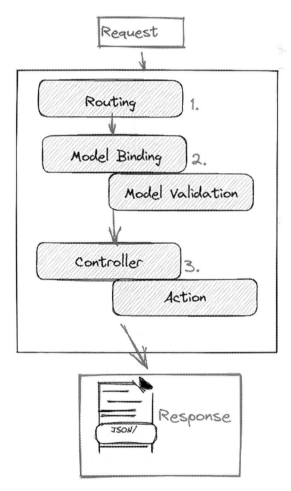

Figure 4-3. *A simplified API request pipeline*

- Routing – tries to match the incoming URL to the route table or conventions. We will see later in this chapter how we can build our endpoints/URLs and hit the right actions by using conventions or templates.

- Model Binding – Helps us obtain, on the fly, values that are sent in different contexts, directly as parameters to our actions. The platform can automatically match different types, values, and names so that we have everything simple at the controller level. The *model binding* mechanism is discussed in more detail in the next sections.

- Controller & Action – At the controller level, inside the action, the `ModelState` can be checked for validity again, or you can look at different properties inside the model and build business logic based on the values.

Controllers & Actions

Controller and actions are the chunks of code we will write most often when we develop APIs. Both have their own particularities and work in conjunction with each other. In the next section, we will explore both, and by the end of the chapter we will have a complete picture about how things work.

Controllers

An API controller is a C# class that has special characteristics and resides in the Controllers folder (if we respect the convention), but it can easily be added at the root level of the project.

Some controllers respect at least one of the conventions, and the first three are more common:

- The name is suffixed with the *Controller* word; e.g., ValuesController, PetsController.cs

- Is decorated with [APIController] attribute

- Inherits ControllerBase class

By respecting these conventions, you will enable the routing mechanism to identify your controllers and the actions inside them. In Listing 4-1 we have an empty controller that is named ValuesController, inherits the ControllerBase class, and is marked as being an API controller by the [ApiController] attribute. On top of this attribute, we have a routing attribute with a routing pattern [Route("api/ [controller]")] that tells the routing mechanism how to match the URL. For example, if a URL has a form like : /api/values it might end up executing an action inside a controller named ValuesController. What action will execute depends on the attribute that decorates the action.

Controllers often group similar action methods together, and these actions handle requests. In practice, a controller is added to take care of a specific entity's operations (CRUD—usually).

Listing 4-1. A GET Action Inside ValuesController.cs

```
[Route("api/[controller]")]
[ApiController]
public class ValuesController : ControllerBase
{

}
```

As we will see later in the book, if we wanted to match an incoming request to this controller, and its content, we would have to issue a request toward https://localhost:port/api/values.

Actions

An action is like a method that can handle requests.

Now, we know that C# classes can contain state and behavior as fields, properties, and methods. These methods are callable and can have parameters and return results.

If we look at Listing 4-2, we will see something similar to a method that has parameters and a return type.

Listing 4-2. An Action Inside Values Controller

```
[Route("api/[controller]")]
[ApiController]
public class ValuesController : ControllerBase
{
  [HttpGet]
  public IEnumerable Get()
  {
     return new string[] { "value1", "value2" };
  }
}
```

If we translate the C# analogy to Web API language, those methods are called actions if they respond to HTTP requests. An action can respond to a specific HTTP method by decorating it with an attribute that corresponds to the HTTP method.

The action in Listing 4-2 responds to an HTTP GET method and returns an array of strings.

When you make an HTTP request to https://localhost:5110/ api/values, the routing mechanism will try to identify an action inside ValuesController that matches in terms of HTTP verbs and parameters.

A few characteristics of actions are as follows:

- Can have simple or complex parameters that get their values from different locations (query string, request body, URL path, service)

- Can be decorated with attributes that correspond to HTTP methods; e.g., [HTTPGet], [HTTPPost]

- Can have return types

You can manually return status codes if you wrap the return type in ActionResult<T> as follows:

```
[HttpGet]
public ActionResult<IEnumerable<string>> Get()
{
    return Ok();
}
```

Action method responsibilities include the following:

- Determine what response type and status code to generate.

- Validate the incoming request.

- Call other underlying services to build the business logic.

Action Return Types

If we talk about HTTP responses, we expect status codes. These status codes are handled and generated by the platform, but very often the business rules dictate what to return from the API.

It might not be a 200 OK in all cases or a 400 Bad Request. It might be a 409 Conflict determined by the uniqueness of a property or a combination of properties. For example, you might require that an `Email` field be unique across your system.

To control everything with fine-grained details we need to understand what types we can return from actions and what the advantages and disadvantages are of each one.

Concrete Type

As in any other C# method, we can return collections of objects, or concrete types, and the framework will take care of generating the status codes for you.

In Listing 4-3, the concrete type returned will be accompanied by a 200 OK status code that is implicit. The platform assumes that if it returns something, that something means that is a successful response.

Listing 4-3. Returning a Concrete Type and a 200 OK Implicit Status Code

```
[HttpGet("{id}")]
public string Get(int id)
{
    return "value";
}
```

Always returning 200 OK is uncommon in real-life scenarios. We usually need to search for something in the database, return the item if we find it, or return a 404 Not Found status code otherwise.

The platform gives us the most common scenarios, but the rest is up to us. To control what status code we return with the actual data, we need to change our return type and use one that will give access to wrapper methods representing status codes. We will see next what options we have for this in the next section, where we talk about `IActionResult` and `ActionResult<T>`.

IActionResult

In Listing 4-4 we see a simple schematic where we implement the case that we talked about earlier. Search for an item, return a 404 Not found status code if you don't find it, or return the item. Right now we don't care about the actual data types, but we will understand what and how we should use them. You will notice that we changed the return type from string to IActionResult.

Listing 4-4. Working with IActionResult Return Type

```
[HttpGet("{id}")]
public IActionResult Get(int id)
{
    var databaseItem = repository.FindById(id);
    if (databaseItem==null)
    {
        //return a Not Found status code
        return NotFound();
    }
    return Ok(databaseItem);
}
```

Using the IActionResult as a return type gives us the flexibility of choosing what status code we should return and when. NotFound() and Ok() are convenience methods inherited from ControllerBase that produce the status for the response.

Methods like Ok() or NotFound() are shorthand for their equivalent new OkResult() or NotFoundResult(), but we should take advantage of every bit of syntactic sugar the platform has to offer, if we fully understand what it does.

"Syntactic sugar" is a term used in computer science to refer to language constructs or features that make the syntax of a programming language more readable or convenient for the programmer without changing the underlying behavior of the language.

ActionResult<T>

Wrapping our concrete return type in ActionResult<T> will give us the same flexibility when returning a mix of status codes, with the addition of the extra casting operation (Listing 4-5). It will infer the type of T and allow us to check what status was returned with the response. This is helpful when writing unit tests.

Listing 4-5. ActionResult<T>

```
[HttpGet("{id}")]
 public ActionResult<string> Get(int id)
 {
     var databaseItem = repository.FindById(id);
     if (databaseItem == null)
     {
         return NotFound();
     }
     return databaseItem;
 }
```

ActionResult<T> versus IActionResult

Using ActionResult<T> will allow the platform to infer what T is, which will be very important when it comes to testing your actions. With testing, you need to check the returned status code and maybe check some field values to make assertions.

Another important distinction between the two is in regards to documenting the API by using the [ProducesResponseType(StatusCodes. Status200K)] attribute. With ActionResult<T> we can use [ProducesResp onseType(StatusCodes.Status200K)], but with IActionResult we need to provide the type of the model by supplying it as the second parameter.

```
[ProducesResponseType(StatusCodes.Status200K, Type =
typeof(ProductModel))]
```

We will talk more in-depth about documenting and testing our API in Chapter 12 and Chapter 13, but we needed to briefly mention this here.

Model

A model is a C# class that has properties and fields used to carry data from the user to the controller, and from the controller to the user.

Conventionally, the model lives in a folder named Models, but it can live in any other folder you like, as long as you can keep the project manageable.

A model is usually a representation of what we have in the database for a certain item, or a real-life representation of something.

If, for example, we have a table named Products, it's not mandatory to expose all the columns through an API. Maybe you have a column that represents the acquisition price, or an acquisition discount, and you don't want that to be publicly accessible. In most cases, you will need some extra properties, a subset of all the columns, or the same columns.

In any scenario, I would advise you to use a Model class because you can decouple representations, and the code will be easier to change. The sole purpose of a Model class is to transport an entity to the outside world (to the API consumers) and back to the server.

The Model class is like a basket that carries back and forth values of the properties. If we look at Listing 4-6 the properties of the class are decorated with special constructs called *validation attributes.*

The System.ComponentModel.DataAnnotations namespace provides the most common validation attributes. We can find things like [Required], [MinLength], [MaxLength], [Email], etc., which cover plenty of real-life scenarios.

With the help of these constructs, we can ensure that the data that is sent to the server is correct, and we can understand what is wrong at the controller level and act accordingly. Depending on how the API is configured, the request might not even reach the controller—if the data sent is not correct—and it might return with a 422 Unprocessable Entity status code.

In general, what "correct" means is up to the business requirements or the development team, but there are a few things that should be obvious enough for us developers. For example, if a field should carry back and forth a property representing an email string, maybe we should make sure that the string provided resembles an email and it has the right format, like something@something.something. Decorating the property with an attribute like [Email] will save us a lot of keystrokes and testing headaches.

Tip   As a best practice, we should always assume that the user will send bad data to the server, and we should try to prevent data corruption downstream. We should try to validate at every possible layer—in the frontend (but in the case of APIs we don't have this layer), in the backend, and at the database level—by having the correct data type for the columns.

Listing 4-6. A Model with Several Validation Attributes

```
public class ShipperModel
{
    [Required]
    [StringLength(24, ErrorMessage = "Phone number cannot
    exceed 24 characters!")]
```

```
    public string Phone { get; set; }
    [EmailAddress]
    public string Email { get; set; }
}
```

DTO

A *DTO* (data transfer object) is a term that you'll often hear when it comes to moving data from one component to another or between different layers of the same app. A DTO is like the cherry filling of the pie—not visible from the outside—whereas a model is like the cherry on top of the pie. Both are cherries, but depending on the location, it is called either a model (visible to the outside) or a DTO (visible only internally to the app).

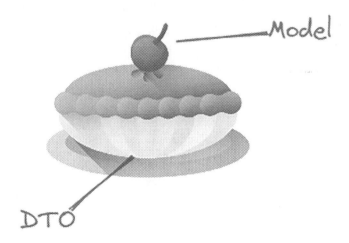

Figure 4-4. *Model versus DTO*

Validating Models

Model validation is the process through which the platform identifies the correctness of the data sent in the request based on the validation attributes we added to the model class.

If you were to have a basket and pick apples in an orchard, I'm sure you would pick the apples that are good-looking and suitable for a pie, and leave the bad ones for a different product (cider maybe). When you pick apples, you validate them, one by one, looking at different characteristics. Maybe you look at the color, size, or how ripe they are. You would want the apples to not be spoiled, or have worms, holes, defects, and so on. You validate each parameter by what is important to you or the intended purpose of those apples. A similar thing happens with each property in the model. These properties are validated in isolation by using the list of validation attributes for each, and then if all of them meet the required list of conditions, the model as a whole is considered to be valid. The validity of the object as a whole is determined by an object named ModelState.

ModelState is a read-only dictionary that contains the state of the model and the model-binding validation.

Using Models

Don't get me wrong, you can work without model classes and you can expose domain entities through the API—nothing is preventing you from doing that. You can and you will work without actual model classes in some scenarios, but from the architectural point of view having two separate entities will give you the most flexibility. You'll say "OK, but I have the same properties in both classes, why should I duplicate code?"

Well, yes, you are right. You have the exact properties, but when it happens that you need to modify what you send through the model, it will be easier to do, and your change won't have cascading effects (Figure 4-5). You won't be forced to touch and change other application areas just to accommodate your changes. That change will remain local if you are using a model and not the domain object.

The intended change

Figure 4-5. *Cascading effects analogy*

Model Binding

Model binding is the mechanism that makes our life easier when using parameters in actions. The values for those parameters get automatically populated from the indicated sources of the incoming request. It can be populated from the query string, form fields, URL path, or request body, using different rules.

The default model-binding mechanism works just fine, by default, because it is part of the convention over configuration philosophy, and we have a way of specifying which is the preferred source to bind from.

We can even write our own *model binder* if we have advanced scenarios. Here are some model-binding sources:

- [FromQuery] – Gets values from the query string

- [FromRoute] – Gets values from route data (URL path)

- [FromForm] – Gets values from posted form fields

- [FromBody] – Gets values from the request body

- [FromHeader] – Gets values from HTTP headers

In Listing 4-7, the ShipperModel parameter is prefixed with a
[FromBody] attribute, which indicates that the values for the properties
should be populated from the body of the incoming request. Further, in
Listing 4-8 you can see an example where a property gets its value from the
querystring, from a parameter named Note.

Listing 4-7. Binding from the Request Body

```
public IActionResult Post([FromBody] ShipperModel model)
{
    if (!ModelState.IsValid)
    {
        return BadRequest();
    }

    var addedShipper = shipperService.Add(model);

    return CreatedAtAction("Get", new { id =
    addedShipper.Shipperid }, addedShipper);
}
```

Listing 4-8. A Property That Should Bind from Request Query String

```
[FromQuery(Name = "Note")]
 public string? NoteFromQueryString { get; set; }
```

We will talk more about model binding in Chapter 10.

Middleware

A middleware is a piece of functionality that gets assembled into an app
pipeline to handle requests and responses, as shown in Figure 4-6. You can
think of middleware as a step in a production line.

Each block can execute some code before or after the next block. You can choose to pass the control to the next middleware or short-circuit the pipeline and be the final middleware.

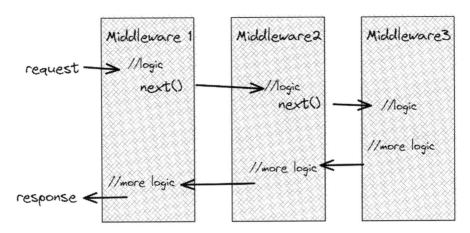

Figure 4-6. *A middleware pipeline*

Using these small constructs, you can "inject" functionality in the request pipeline to extract or add information. For example, you can create a middleware that adds HTTP header fields right before the response is created, or one that catches a specific type of exception and writes a response with a certain message body.

Middleware can be chained one after another to create a rich pipeline. Each middleware component in the pipeline is responsible for calling the next component or short-circuiting it. When a middleware short-circuits the pipeline is called *terminal middleware* because it prevents other middleware components from processing the request.

The order in which each middleware is called matters and can completely make or break functionality. Returning a response instead of passing it to the next middleware can completely modify the response.

In `Program.cs`, you can easily recognize middleware calls by their names. By convention, have .Use*() in their names, and they will call the next middleware:

```
app.UseHttpsRedirection();
app.UseAuthorization();
```

These are extension methods that wrap logic that is written in separate files. As you'll see later, you have several ways of writing middleware: in separate files, wrapping these files in extension methods, or writing the request delegates directly in `Program.cs` as shown in Listing 4-9.

Listing 4-9. Different Middleware Calls

```
app.UseAuthorization();

app.Use(async (context, next) =>
{
    context.Response.Headers.Add("custom-header", "custom-value");
    // Do work that can write to the Response.
    await next.Invoke();
    // Do logging or other work that doesn't write to the
        Response.
});
```

When you write middleware directly in `Program.cs`, there are two types of delegate that you can write: `app.Use()` and `app.Run()`.

The `app.Use()` option gives you access to a parameter called `next`, which represents the next delegate in the pipeline.

The `app.Run()` option doesn't have the `next` parameter, and it terminates the pipeline. Also, `Run()` is a convention, and some middleware can expose this method to imply that the method needs to be run at the end of the pipeline; `app.Run()` is such an example, essentially saying:

"Hey, now that you have run every other middleware, make sure you run me also. I'm the last in the queue."

```
app.Run(async context =>
{
    await context.Response.WriteAsync("Hello from the last
    delegate.");
});
```

If you have several delegates chained, as shown in Listing 4-10, that follow an app.Run() call, the first one executed will finish the request, and everything after it will be ignored.

Listing 4-10. Several Terminating Middleware Components

```
app.Run(async context =>
{
    await context.Response.WriteAsync("Hello from the last delegate.");
});

app.Run(async context =>
{
    await context.Response.WriteAsync("I shouldn't be executed.");
});
app.MapControllers();
app.Run();
```

In this case, a response will be the one in Figure 4-7, irrespective of the endpoint you are calling. Your requests will never reach controllers because the first Run() encountered writes directly in the response stream.

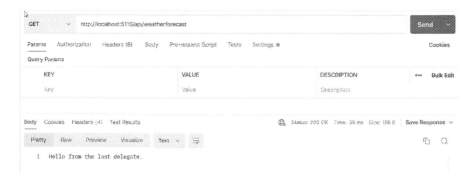

Figure 4-7. *A response from a terminal middleware*

Another thing that needs to be mentioned is that are several middlewares already implemented in the platform, and they have a specific, well-defined order in the execution pipeline. In Figure 4-8, you can see some of the middleware in the platform (some of them are ignored but it doesn't mean they are not important) and the order in which they are executed. Custom middlewares have a defined place, after the Authorization middleware, and that is where, as best practice, we should add them.

There are also different middlewares not shown in Figure 4-8, like `app.UseForwardedHeaders()`, that need to be added first in the pipeline to make sure that subsequent middleware will have access to these added headers if they rely on them. This is used if the hosting of the app is without Internet Information Services (IIS) and `Out-Of-Process`.

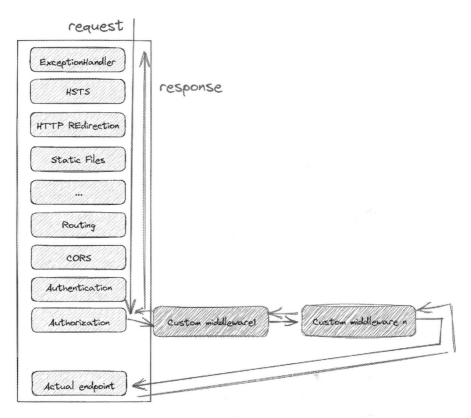

Figure 4-8. *Overview of the middleware execution order*

Middleware can be seen as a global way of streamlining work chunks.
Each chunk has a very well-established role, and the result can be used
as input for the next chunk. It is like you are cleaning up after dinner with
friends, and you share responsibilities. Someone will wash the dishes,
someone will rinse them, someone will dry them, and the last person in
the chain will stack them where they belong. And in this specific process,
the order matters, or you will end up having unwashed dishes arranged
carefully in the cabinet.

Using Map

In addition to what might look like a very linear journey of the request to the controller, and from the controller back as a response, there are places from which you can branch your pipeline if certain conditions are met. For this, we have another convention by using Map.

Listing 4-11. Using Map

```
app.UseAuthorization();
app.Map("/branch1", HandleFirstBranch);
app.Map("/branch2", HandleSecondBranch);

app.Use(async (context, next) =>
{
    context.Response.Headers.Add("custom-header",
    "custom-value");
    // Do work that can write to the Response.
    await next.Invoke();
    // Do logging or other work that doesn't write to the
        Response.

});


app.MapControllers();

static void HandleFirstBranch(IApplicationBuilder app)
{
    app.Run(async context =>
    {
        await context.Response.WriteAsync("Map - First
        Branch");
    })
}
```

```
static void HandleSecondBranch(IApplicationBuilder app)
{
    app.Run(async context =>
    {
        await context.Response.WriteAsync("Map - Second
        Branch");
    });
}
```

By using Map we can provide a path and a second parameter that will handle the request. Usually, the request handler will write directly to the response stream and short-circuit the request and return directly the response. It is advisable to add Map calls before other custom middleware because this way you can speed up the response's return.

In Table 4-1 you can see what should be returned for our example based on the requested URL.

Table 4-1. *Different Responses Based on the Request Used*

Request	Response
http://localhost:5110/ weatherforecast	Hello from the last delegate.
http://localhost:5110/branch1	Map - First Branch
http://localhost:5110/branch2	Map - Second Branch
http://localhost:5110/api/branch2	Hello from the last delegate.

Using MapWhen

If Map allowed us to specify directly a hardcoded path from which to branch, MapWhen will branch the request pipeline based on the result of the given predicate. For this, we can use any predicate of Func<HttpContext, bool> to obtain the value we are interested in.

In the following example (Listing 4-12), the predicate is used to look at a query string variable and extract its value. Make sure you add the MapWhen before a terminal middleware to allow it to run. In Table 4-2 you can see two examples of URLs and the expected response.

Listing 4-12. Using MapWhen to Conditionally Branch

```
app.MapWhen(context => context.Request.Query.
ContainsKey("branch"), HandleThirdBranch);
static void HandleThirdBranch(IApplicationBuilder app)
{
    app.Run(async context =>
    {
        var branchNumber = context.Request.Query["branch"];
        await context.Response.WriteAsync($"Map - branch no:
        {branchVer}");
    });
}
```

Table 4-2. *Different Responses Based on the Request Used*

Request example	Expected Response
http://localhost:5110/weatherforecast	Hello from the last delegate.
http://localhost:5110/ weatherforecast?branch=3	Map – branch no:3

Using UseWhen

UseWhen allows you to do a "detour" in the pipeline, execute some work, and then rejoin the main pipeline. It is like allowing you to leave the party and return afterward once you have finished some chores.

In Listing 4-13, we will still get the results as usual, shown in Table 4-3, but you will also get the logged information in the console, as shown in Figure 4-9.

Listing 4-13. UseWhen

```
app.UseWhen(context => context.Request.Query.
ContainsKey("otherBranch"),
    appBuilder => HandleBranchAndRejoin(appBuilder));

void HandleBranchAndRejoin(IApplicationBuilder app)
{
    var logger = app.ApplicationServices.GetRequiredService
    <ILogger<Program>>();

    app.Use(async (context, next) =>
    {
        var branchNumber = context.Request.Query["otherBranch"];
        logger.LogInformation($"Map - otherBranch no:
        {branchNumber}");

        // Do work that doesn't write to the Response.
        await next();
        // Do some other work that doesn't write to the
            Response.
    });
}
```

Table 4-3. *UseWhen Responses Based on the Request Used*

Request	Response
`http://localhost:5110/weatherforecast`	Hello from the last delegate.
`http://localhost:5110/ weatherforecast? otherbBranch=2`	Hello from the last delegate.

```
info: Microsoft.Hosting.Lifetime[14]
      Now listening on: https://localhost:7110
info: Microsoft.Hosting.Lifetime[14]
      Now listening on: http://localhost:5110
info: Microsoft.Hosting.Lifetime[0]
      Application started. Press Ctrl+C to shut down.
info: Microsoft.Hosting.Lifetime[0]
      Hosting environment: Development
info: Microsoft.Hosting.Lifetime[0]
      Content root path: F:\Book\FirstApi\FirstApi
info: Program[0]
      Map - otherBranch no: 1
```

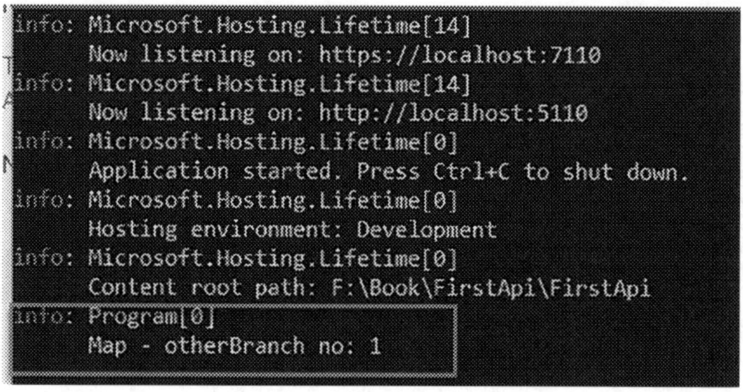

Figure 4-9. *UseWhen – information logged*

Source code: /ch04/FirstApi solution

We will talk more in-depth about middleware in Chapter 9, but for now, this has given you a high-level overview of what can happen internally every time you interact with an API.

Routing

We know that our request travels a specific path inside the platform before we get a response, in the request pipeline. Now we will explore more about the Routing mechanism.

What Is the Routing Mechanism?

The routing mechanism is one of the main parts of the Web API platform. It helps map the request URL to the right controller and controller actions.

To do the matching, it uses the patterns defined in the app and the request verbs and tries to find them in the segments and parameters of the URL.

In Figure 4-10, you can see how a request URL would map to controllers, actions, and parameters. In this example, we have a `PetsController.cs` file with an action named `Edit`, and the action has a parameter named `id` (usually).

Figure 4-10. *Mapping URLs to controllers and actions in an MVC context*

Just by looking at the URL, respecting this convention, we know what action will process the request.

In ASP.NET MVC, the action name can be easily determined from the URL.

If we analyze the same URL in an API context, as in Figure 4-11, the part corresponding to the action name is missing, being determined by the HTTP method used with the request instead. If it's a POST request, it will hit the action in the controller that responds to these kinds of requests.

The HTTP verb that the action responds to is more important, as we will see in the next part.

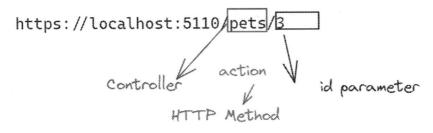

Figure 4-11. *Routing in a Web API context*

Routing can be of two types, as follows:

1. Conventional routing

2. Attribute routing

Of these two, attribute routing is often preferred with Web API.

Either way, you need to be aware of both approaches since you might encounter them in real-life production scenarios.

Even though the approach is global and generic, the patterns applied in order to find the right controllers and actions can be changed by using these two techniques. We will see how we can change these to build complicated endpoints similar to /api/employees/{id}/rewards/ {id}?year=2020. After all, an API is a collection of endpoints that expose data, addressable from the outside world by using URLs.

The purpose of the routing mechanism is to make sure the requests are matched to the right controller and actions based on the pattern that can be inferred from the URL and the verb used with the request. If you want, the routing does pattern matching, and we're the ones that define the actual patterns.

Convention-based Routing

In conventional routing, or convention-based routing, the patterns for each route are defined globally and in one place, using placeholders for every part that is involved in URL generation. This is called *conventional routing* because it establishes a convention for URL paths at a global level. This technique was used long before attribute routing was a thing in .NET, and is more common in ASP.NET MVC applications. Even so, it is used under the hood by default in Web API.

Listing 4-14 shows a default route template with two defined parameters: name and pattern. In addition to these two parameters, you can also specify default values for each, as well as a route constraint. We will talk more about route constraints in Chapter 8, when we will implement our own.

Listing 4-14. The Default Route Template

```
app.MapControllerRoute(
    name: "default",
    pattern: "{controller=Home}/{action=Index}/{id?}",
    defaults: null,
    constraints: null,
    dataTokens: null);
```

- name – a unique name that identifies the route. In case of route failures, the runtime will notify you of issues with the route

- pattern – defines the URL structure and the segments and tokens used for mapping

- defaults – defines default values for tokens in case some are missing from the URL

- constraints – individual constraints for tokens or parameter values

- dataTokens - additional values associated with the route. These don't affect the matching process, but when the route is determined, the values will be added to the RouteData.DataTokens collection property of the controller and can be used in the logic.

Even though we have all these parameters that we can define for a route, the main things considered are controller and action names. Things like namespaces, folder locations, etc. won't matter, but at least we know how things are built.

When we catch exceptions, we are careful to catch them from the most specific to the most general, to make sure at least one catch block will cover the exceptional case we have. The same happens with routes. We should write the most specific one, then move toward the most generic and default for our app. This way, we make sure that no matter how many controllers and actions we create, we can issue requests to them without any hassle. Otherwise, we will always get 404 Not Found status codes, and the requests will never reach a controller.

Note   The terms *endpoint* and *route* are often used interchangeably. Use what you prefer. I use the word *endpoint* when talking about APIs, and *route* if I'm referring to an ASP.NET MVC URL.

In Web API Program.cs, you will see a call to app.MapControllers();. This (among other things) will set a default route template without explicitly showing it. In ControllerBase, the MapDefaultControllerRoute method returns what is shown in Listing 4-15. This way, the platform encourages the usage of attribute routing and makes sure your actions will respond to requests.

Listing 4-15. MapDefaultControllerRoute Return Call

```
return dataSource.AddRoute(
          "default",
          "{controller=Home}/{action=Index}/{id?}",
          defaults: null,
          constraints: null,
          dataTokens: null);
```

A **route template** is a pattern that is used by the routing mechanism to match segments from endpoints.

Attribute Routing

Attribute routing provides a granular way to define your route patterns directly on controllers and actions by decorating them with the [Route] attribute and specifying a string that plays the pattern role. It requires more input from the developer but allows and requires precise control over which route templates apply to each action.

Attribute Routing with HTTP Verb Attributes

There is a special type of attribute that we can use to annotate our controller actions. The names of these attributes have a special form: [HTTP{Verb}], where {Verb} corresponds to one of the known HTTP verbs: GET, POST, PUT, DELETE, etc.

- [HTTPGet]
- [HTTPPost]
- [HTTPDelete]
- [HTTPPut]

Each of these attributes, when added to an action, will make that action respond to a request if the route and verb match.

Token Replacements in Route Templates

Attribute routing comes with a few predefined tokens to cover the most common scenarios. These get replaced with the corresponding values at runtime. The tokens are [controller], [action], and [area].

The tokens are very convenient when you just want to follow what is already established by convention and not customize things. Even when you add a new controller to a project, it is already annotated with the [controller] token to make sure you will be able to create a route easily, as shown in Listing 4-16.

- [controller] replaces the controller name.
  This means that, in the end, we will be able to
  reach this controller's action by calling the /api/
  products endpoint. Respecting the convention over
  configuration, the actual name is Products, and the
  suffix Controller follows the convention.

  We can easily add the token in the route template,
  and it will add the controller name for us, as shown
  in Listing 4-16.

Listing 4-16. Controller Name in Route

```
[Route("api/[controller]")]
[ApiController]
public class ProductsController : ControllerBase
{
 [HttpGet]
  public ActionResult<string> GetMyResponse()
    {
        return "response from Get";
    }

}
```

- [action] replaces the action name in the URL. In Web
  API, the action names are, by default, ignored. The
  attribute that identifies the verb is the one that decides
  which is the right action to use to respond to a request.
  If we want to use the action names as part of the URL,
  we can leverage this attribute, as shown in Listing 4-17.

Listing 4-17. Action Name in URL Example

```
[Route("api/[controller]")]
    [ApiController]
    public class ProductsController : ControllerBase
    {
        [HttpGet]
        [Route("[action]")]
        public ActionResult<string> GetMyResponse()
        {
            return "response from Get";
        }

    }
```

To reach this action, we need to make an HTTP GET request to /api/products/getmyresponse. In this case, whenever we use the [action] token in a route attribute, the actual name given to the action will show up in a URL segment and become relevant to the routing mechanism.

- [area] replaces the area name if that is defined, as shown in Listing 4-18. To reach the endpoint, we will need to make a request that matches the route template: api/admin/products/getmyresponse.

Listing 4-18. Routing with Area Token

```
[Route("api/[area]/[controller]")]
[Area("admin")]
[ApiController]
public class ProductsController : ControllerBase
{
```

```
    [HttpGet]
    public ActionResult<string> GetMyResponse()
    {
        return "response from Get";
    }
}
```

The concept of **"area"** is inherited from ASP.NET MVC and allowed to create "mini-websites" in the same solution with a different layout, styling, and access.

Note   A route with [Route("myproducts")] will match /api/products/myproducts, but the same action with [Route("/myproducts")] will match /myproducts. Adding a slash at the beginning won't combine it with the route defined in the controller, but it will generate a route on its own.

Route Templates

Route templates define the patterns of the URLs expected in the applications by using placeholders. These are strings with placeholders for variables. They are controlled by splitting the URL into multiple segments that, one by one, match the URL.

Route Constraints

To help with parameter matching, we have a series of predefined route constraints available. These can be used in combination with attribute routing. Let's say we need a specific parameter to have exactly x number of characters or to be an integer; route constraints help us enforce that. Most of the predefined ones are related to the data type of the parameters, length, or, in some cases, the format.

Route constraints are used to disambiguate similar routes, not for input validation.

In Table 4-4, you can see a few examples of route constraints and the expected behavior.

Table 4-4. *Route Constraints Examples*

Constraint	Usage Example	Matches Value	Notes
Int	{id:int}	123456789, -123456789	Matches any integer
Bool	{active:bool}	true, FALSE	Matches true or false. Case-insensitive
Guid	{id:guid}	CD2C1638-1638-72D5-1638-DEADBEEF1638	Matches a valid GUID value
Min(value)	{age:min(18)}	19	The matched value must be at least 18
Max(value)	{age:max(120)}	120	The matched value must be at most 120
range(min,max)	{age:range (18,120)}	18, 119	Integer value must be at least 18 but no more than 120

(*continued*)

Table 4-4. (*continued*)

Constraint	Usage Example	Matches Value	Notes
Alpha	`alpha`	acdx, xhex	The string must consist of one or more alphabetical characters, a–z and case-insensitive.
regex (expression)	`{ssn:regex(^\\ d{{3}}-\\d{{2}}- \\d{{4}}$)}`	123-45-6789	The string must match the regular expression

You can also specify multiple constraints for the same parameter by combining them. For example [Route("users/{id:int:min(1)}")] restricts the value of the ID parameter to an integer value bigger than 1.

Dependency Injection

Dependency injection (DI) is a concept that helps us create loosely coupled code, simplifies unit testing, and in general leads to a more maintainable codebase by keeping complexity in check.

DI has many benefits. It helps with SRP (single responsibility principle from SOLID[1]), separation of concerns, and many more principles that if followed help us have "clean code."

Before we talk about injecting dependencies and using dependency injection containers, we need to understand what a dependency is.

---

[1] https://en.wikipedia.org/wiki/SOLID

SRP (Single Responsibility Principle) is a principle in SOLID that says that a class should do one thing only.

What Is a Dependency?

A dependency in our code is something that we need in order to accomplish a task—a library, a class, or a package for a class. It is usually required in the constructor, and without it we can't instantiate the class. We humans are dependent on food, water, sleep, and social media! Similarly, some of our classes need other classes to function properly or to be instantiated.

To put dependencies in a real-life context, if we were to make some pancakes from scratch, we would need to buy the ingredients. There are no awesome pancakes without the proper ingredients. The same happens with code.

When we first start coding, we use classes and we instantiate those classes using the new keyword.

```
var account = new BankAccount();
var myStringBuilder = new StringBuilder();
```

Generally speaking, every time we use the new keyword, we introduce a dependency in our code, making it harder to test and more resistant to change. However, this doesn't mean we shouldn't use that dependency anymore. We just need to think of whether the concrete implementation we are using will ever need to be replaced.

If we look at the following code, it is unlikely that we will ever give our implementation for the StringBuilder type, right? This applies to most of the classes that are part of the core platform, but not to the rest of them.

Types of Dependencies

There are many types of dependencies: implicit, explicit, visible, hidden, volatile, and so on. We can analyze them by so many aspects that we couldn't cover them in a few pages.

In Listing 4-19, Visible Dependencies, we have the constructor of the class Customer, which requires a BankAccount instance, a concrete implementation.

This is a visible dependency because, looking at the implementation details, we see that to create an instance of the Customer class we would also need to pass a BankAccount instance. So, the Customer class depends on the BankAccount concrete type.

Listing 4-19. Visible Dependencies

```
public class Customer
    {
        public Customer(BankAccount bankAccount)
        {
        }
    }
```

Usually, in any given context, the constructor dictates what the class needs (read: "depends on"), and we use it to make sure our classes are structurally healthy.

Let's look at Listing 4-20, Hidden Dependency, in the same manner. The constructor doesn't seem to have any dependency, and it needs nothing to be instantiated. This is only apparent because inside the constructor the class obtains by itself the needed dependency by calling the new BankAccount() and keeping it as a state in a private field.

Listing 4-20. Hidden Dependency

```
public class ModerateCustomer
    {
        private BankAccount savingsAccount;

        public ModerateCustomer() //hidden dependency
        {
            this.savingsAccount = new BankAccount();

        }
    }
```

This type of code is not only closed to changes and extensions, but also violates the Single Responsibility Principle by doing more than it should. The ModerateCustomer class does what it is intended to do (it is not important here, and the code is omitted so that we can focus on the problem at hand), plus obtains the dependencies it needs.

It is as if you are in charge of cooking dinner, which should be your only responsibility, but for you to cook dinner you also need to do groceries or clean up and do the dishes as a prerequisite. Not fun, is it?

Let's look at some different code. In Listing 4-21, Tight Coupling Dependencies, the instantiation of the dependencies is not even done in the constructor, but in private fields, which won't guarantee any structural completeness of the class. The dependency is—if we could quantify it—even bigger. What would happen if the concrete implementation of the SavingsAccount changes, or instead of that we need a BagPurchaseAccount? We would break our code in all the places where this exact class is used. More than that, if we ever want to change it with some other implementation we will need to make changes everywhere the type is used.

Listing 4-21. Tight Coupling Dependencies

```
public class VIPCustomer
    {
        private SavingsAccount savingsAccount = new
        SavingsAccount();
        private CurrentAccount currentAccount = new
        CurrentAccount();//coupling dependency
        public VIPCustomer()
        {

        }

    }
```

If we analyze Listing 4-22, the preferred way of using dependencies, we can observe a few things:

- There are two dependencies in the constructor, so we know we can't create a PerfectCustomer instance without passing these.

- The state is maintained at the class level in private fields (we don't care how it is retrieved for the current example).

- The dependencies ISavingsAccount and ICurrentAccount are abstractions and not concrete implementations.

Listing 4-22. The Preferred Way of Using Dependencies

```
public class PerfectCustomer
    {
        private ISavingsAccount savingsAccount;
        private ICurrentAccount currentAccount;
```

```
public PerfectCustomer(ISavingsAccount savingsAccount,
ICurrentAccount current)//loose coupling dependency
{
    this.savingsAccount = savingsAccount;
    this.currentAccount = current;

}
}
```

The best way to make your code more maintainable is to code against abstractions and to use dependency injection to resolve those dependencies. But, before we can do that, we need to talk more about the mechanism that allows us to write code in such a way that we could swap implementations altogether if we needed to.

Dependency Injection Container

Dependency injection is a specialization of the dependency inversion principle. This is where you let a system pass the dependencies to where they are needed. You pass the responsibility of creating the dependencies yourself to a system that will take care of creating and maintaining their lifetimes.

With dependency injection, you create mappings between abstractions used (usually interfaces) and their concrete implementation(s).

The place where you do these mappings is called the dependency injection container, or inversion of control (IoC) container. The dependency injection container is built-in in .NET, and you can find it in Program.cs. It is currently not represented by a class or an actual method, but it can be configured by calling the right extension methods.

Dependency Injection in ASP.NET Web API

By using the built-in DI container, you can tell the platform: "Hey, whenever you encounter this particular abstraction, make sure you pass this concrete implementation instead."

Figure 4-12 shows one of the most common registration types.

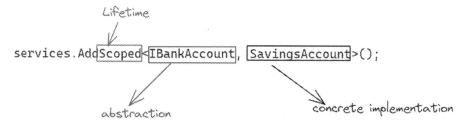

Figure 4-12. *Registration of an implementation*

In this case, for any IBankAccount used in the app, the DI container will resolve it by passing the SavingsAccount concrete implementation. You can specify the service lifetime for every dependency you register by using one of the three lifetime overloads. We will talk in more detail about each of the lifetimes later in this chapter.

By using interfaces instead of concrete types, we can make sure that we can have more than one concrete implementation of the same interface at any given time, and maybe with different lifetimes.

If, let's say, we have a specific code for PostgreSQL and tomorrow we decide to swap it for a SQL database, we won't cause a cascade of changes. We can simply go into the container and make only one change there.

Overall, what is written in the interface is the public contract, and that is the common ground for any two types implementing the same interface, so we won't break anything.

The fact that one class depends on another class, and the second class may depend on another, creates something that is called a *dependency graph*. This dependency graph is resolved by the platform.

> The dependency graph is a set of objects that must be created by the root object (the main object)

.NET uses the DI container to create the dependencies when it activates the controllers. To make sure the controller is fully functional, it will call into the DI container and try to resolve every single dependency that is needed.

So, when we ask for an IBankAccount, it must resolve it and return the concrete implementation that we mapped for it.

Service Lifetimes

The lifetime of a service shows how long an instance of a service lives, or how fresh the instance needs to be. For example, is it new every time it is needed, fresh for every request, or the same instance across the entire app?

The lifetime you use for each service can affect the application's behavior, so it is very important to understand how it works.

> **Service lifetime** shows how long/how a DI container should use a given object to fulfill a dependency.

In the next section, we will talk about each of the lifetimes that a dependency can be registered with.

> You can find the source code for the example in ch04/Lifetime project.

To better understand service lifetimes, in Listing 4-23 I created a class and a set of interfaces implemented by this class. The sole purpose of the MyServiceLifetime class is to return the first four characters in a new GUID every time it is requested. This way we can observe what characters are returned to determine the effect of lifetime types over services.

Listing 4-23. Interfaces Used to Abstract Lifetimes

```
public interface IOperation
    {
        public string LifetimeId { get; }
    }

    public interface ITransientOperation : IOperation
    {

    }

    public interface IScopedOperation : IOperation
    {
    }

    public interface ISingletonOperation : IOperation
    {
    }

  public class MyServiceLifetime : ITransientOperation,
  IScopedOperation, ISingletonOperation
    {
        public MyServiceLifetime()
        {
            LifetimeId = Guid.NewGuid().ToString()[^4..];
        }

        public string LifetimeId { get; }
    }
```

Next, in Listing 4-24, we register our class with different lifetimes so we can see the output from the LifetimeId property.

Listing 4-24. Registering Services

```
builder.Services.AddTransient<ITransientOperation,
MyServiceLifetime>();
builder.Services.AddSingleton<IsingletonOperation,
MyServiceLifetime>();
builder.Services.AddScoped<IscopedOperation,
MyServiceLifetime>();
```

And finally, in Listing 4-25, we add a new controller, named LifetimesController, and we make six mandatory parameters of type ITransientOperation, IsingletonOperation, and IScopedOperation and keep their state on private fields at the controller level.

Listing 4-25. Constructor with Parameters

```
[Route("api/[controller]")]
[ApiController]
public class LifetimesController : ControllerBase
{
    private readonly ITransientOperation transient;
    private readonly ITransientOperation transient2;
    private readonly ISingletonOperation singleton;
    private readonly ISingletonOperation singleton2;
    private readonly IScopedOperation scoped;
    private readonly IScopedOperation scoped2;

    public LifetimesController(
        ITransientOperation transient,
        ITransientOperation transient2,
        ISingletonOperation singleton,
```

```
        ISingletonOperation singleton2,
        IScopedOperation scoped,
        IScopedOperation scoped2
        )
    {
        this.transient = transient;
        this.transient2 = transient2;

        this.singleton = singleton;
        this.singleton2 = singleton2;

        this.scoped = scoped;
        this.scoped2 = scoped2;
    }
}
```

We need two of each type to illustrate the scope within the same or subsequent requests. Next, we will create three endpoints to respond to each of the lifetimes and return the LifetimeId in pairs.

Listing 4-26. Actions

```
[HttpGet("transient")]
public string Get()
{
    return $"LifetimeId-1:{transient.LifetimeId} \
    nLifetimeId-2:{transient2.LifetimeId}";
}

[HttpGet("singleton")]
public string Singleton()
{
    return $"LifetimeId-1:{singleton.LifetimeId} \
    nLifetimeId-2:{singleton2.LifetimeId}";
```

```
    }

    [HttpGet("scoped")]
    public string Scoped()
    {
        return $"LifetimeId-1:{ scoped.LifetimeId} \
        nLifetimeId-2:{scoped2.LifetimeId}";

    }
```

Singleton

The Singleton lifetime gives you the same instance every time it is
requested. The name comes from the *Singleton design pattern,*[2] and it
will serve the same service instance every time it is requested. It doesn't
consider the scope of the request.

```
services.AddSingleton<StripeConfiguration>();
```

This is best suited for things that don't need to take up memory since
those won't change too often. This is suitable for configuration-related
settings used application-wide or read from the appsettings.json.

In our example, if we open the browser and navigate to https://
localhost:7041/api/Lifetimes/singleton or use the Swagger tool or
Postman to issue a request to the endpoint. No matter how many requests
we make, we get the same values back. The highlighted characters in
Figure 4-13 are the same for every request we make to the endpoint.

---

[2] https://en.wikipedia.org/wiki/Singleton_pattern

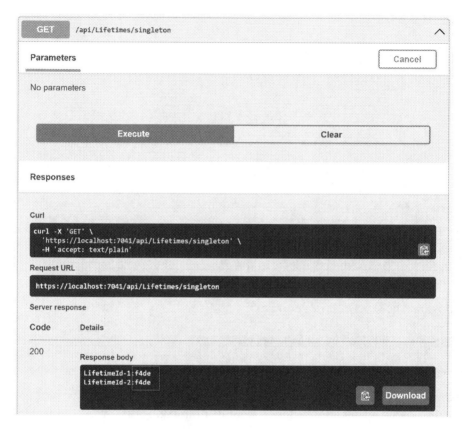

Figure 4-13. *Singleton lifetime*

Scoped

The scoped dependencies are created once per application request (Figure 4-14). In this case, within the same request, our LifetimeIds remain the same, but change for subsequent requests (Figure 4-15).

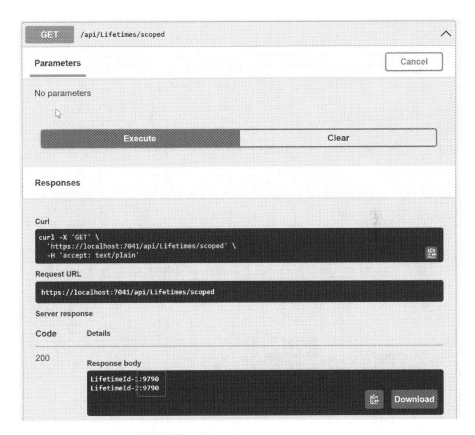

Figure 4-14. *Scoped lifetime*

Figure 4-15. *Second request to the scoped endpoint*

Transient

The transient lifetime will create a new instance whenever that service is requested, no matter the context. It doesn't matter if it is used twice in the same context, it will return a new instance every single time it is needed.

With transient registered services, everything is fresh and newly created, even if it is between subsequent requests or within the same request, as shown in Figure 4-16.

As a result, in the same dependency graph, we might have two or more instances of a given service.

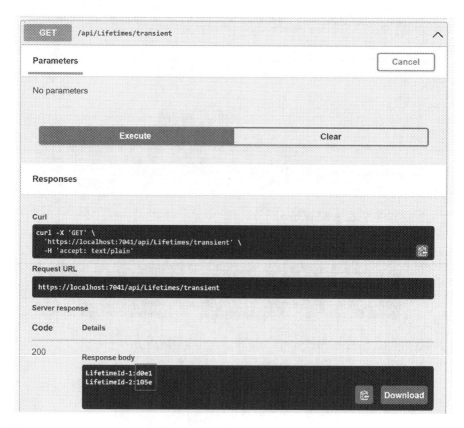

Figure 4-16. *Transient lifetime*

126

As a best practice, we should choose our service lifetimes wisely based on the state of the services that need to be injected. Does the service have a state that should be shared globally? Have no state at all? Or is it a configuration object that needs to be populated and shared across the app?

Table 4-5 summarizes the available state scenarios and the right lifetime for each.

Table 4-5. *Service Lifetimes and Correct Scenarios*

Service state	Lifetime to choose
Global/app level	Singleton
Per request/action	Scoped
Shouldn't share/has no state	Transient

Cleaning Up DI Registrations

When you start adding your registrations, you'll soon notice that the number of lines is increasing exponentially, and it becomes harder to read and find something. This small issue can easily be solved by creating extension methods to logically group some of the lines. What "logically" means is up to you. For example, the code in Listing 4-27 becomes simpler by grouping registrations related to repositories in an extension method (Listing 4-28).

Listing 4-27. Startup.cs with Registrations

```
services.AddScoped(
            provider => new EmailService(
                provider.GetService<IOrganisation
                Adapter>(),
```

```
                  new EmailDispatcherService<AccessEmailQueueOp
                  tion>(provider.GetService<IOptionsSnapshot<Ac
                  cessEmailQueueOption>>(), provider.GetService
                  <IOptionsSnapshot<RabbitConfiguration>>())));

services.Configure<AlertQueueOption>(Configuration.
GetSection("AlertQueueOption"));
services.AddScoped<IExchangeRatesAdapter,
ExchangeRatesAdapter>();
services.AddScoped<ICurrencyAdapter,
CurrencyAdapter>();
services.AddScoped<ICountryAdapter,
CountryAdapter>();
services.AddScoped<ILegalEntityAdapter,
LegalEntityAdapter>();
services.AddScoped<IOrganisationAdapter,
OrganisationAdapter>();
services.AddScoped<IBankAccountAdapter,
BankAccountAdapter>();
services.AddScoped<IUserAdapter, UserAdapter>();
services.AddSingleton<IUserPreferenceAdapter,
UserPreferenceAdapter>();
services.AddScoped<IAlertsService, AlertsService>();
services.AddScoped<IHistoricIntradayRepository,
HistoricIntradayRepository>();
services.AddScoped<IIntradayRepository,
IntradayRepository>();
services.AddScoped<ITransferRepository,
TransferRepository>();
services.AddScoped<IStatementRepository,
StatementRepository>();
```

```
services.AddScoped<ITransactionRepository,
TransactionRepository>();
services.AddScoped<IAlertProcessingRepository,
AlertProcessingRepository>();
services.AddScoped<ICreditStatementRepository,
CreditStatementRepository>();
services.AddScoped<IForwardBalanceRepository,
ForwardBalanceRepository>();
services.AddSingleton<TypeHandler<JObject>,
JObjectHandler>();
AddTypeHandler(new JObjectHandler());
```

Listing 4-28. Creating an Extension Method to Register Services

```
public static void AddRepositories(this IServiceCollection
services)
    {
        services.AddScoped<IHistoricIntradayRepository,
        HistoricIntradayRepository>();
        services.AddScoped<IIntradayRepository,
        IntradayRepository>();
        services.AddScoped<ITransferRepository,
        TransferRepository>();
        services.AddScoped<IStatementRepository,
        StatementRepository>();
        services.AddScoped<ITransactionRepository,
        TransactionRepository>();
        services.AddScoped<IAlertProcessingRepository,
        AlertProcessingRepository>();
        services.AddScoped<ICreditStatementRepository,
        CreditStatementRepository>();
```

```
        services.AddScoped<IForwardBalanceRepository,
        ForwardBalanceRepository>();
        services.AddSingleton<TypeHandler<JObject>,
        JObjectHandler>();
    }
```

You can simply call the extension method, and the code magically becomes easier to read and more manageable, and you know where to find repository-related registrations.

```
services.AddRepositories();
```

Summary

In this chapter, I explained what the building blocks for Web API are and gave a short introduction to each of the mechanisms that make it so powerful, yet so easy to use.

PART II

Implementing an API

CHAPTER 5

Getting Started with Web API

In this chapter, we will implement our first controller actions and understand what a RESTful API is. We will only cover responding to the most common types of requests and scenarios using the right status codes.

A Short Introduction to REST

REST is an acronym for Representational State Transfer, coined in 2000 in Roy Fielding's dissertation thesis.

REST takes a resource-based approach to web interactions. First, you locate a resource, and then you choose to update, delete, or see more details about it.

If your API domain is financial and you have transactions to manage, or if you manage pets, books, movies, and so on — all of these should be treated as resources. These entities are resources that need to be addressable in a unique way and have a URI .

Representational State Transfer (REST) is a collection of six so-called REST constraints. I like to call them guidelines because if these were constraints, more people would respect them. We will talk about each one individually and try to emphasize their importance in an API context.

© Irina Dominte 2023
I. Dominte, *Web API Development for the Absolute Beginner*,
https://doi.org/10.1007/978-1-4842-9348-5_5

Client–Server

The client–server constraint assumes the existence of two entities—a client and a server—that can communicate with each other. The client makes requests, and the server responds to these requests. In this relationship the server is the one that should control what happens and drive the application state (Figure 5-1).

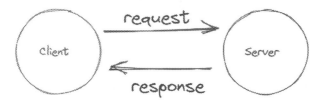

Figure 5-1. *Client-server architecture*

This might be familiar since it is very similar to the client–server architecture we talked about at the beginning of this book, only this goes one step further. It puts the server and the client in a context where they are two completely separate entities, able to evolve independently and be replaced at any given time.

In an ideal RESTful architecture, the server should be the one that drives the application state and be unaware of who the actual clients are. If the client is a mobile app or one written in vue.js, for example, it should make no difference in how the server behaves or its ability to generate correct responses and status codes.

Stateless

The stateless constraint tells us that if the HTTP protocol—which is stateless—is respected, there shouldn't be any state maintained between requests. In other words, the server shouldn't save or memorize information about previous requests.

This means that, by looking at a request in isolation, the server should be able to determine what the client wants and needs, and if there is data that needs to be transmitted, that should be included in the request.

For example, things related to authentication should be contained in every request made, and not be kept at the server level to be accessed. We should not rely on a mechanism that is used to keep the state between client and server, such as hidden fields, sessions stored at the server level, or databases, etc. Anything like that should not be used.

Statelessness as a concept tries to force the user to rely as much as it can on the underlying protocol, HTTP, and leverage its true power. If in any circumstance there is a piece of information that needs to be sent, that information should fit in the URL, header property, or request body.

By doing that, we, or the server, should be able to decipher what is needed just by looking at the request/response main parts.

Caching

The ability to cache data is one of the most important specifications of HTTP. By using the *Cache-control* header, the server is able to tell the consumer that the requested resource can be used and treated as fresh for a specific amount of time.

In Figure 5-2, the last part won't be executed if the data is marked as still fresh in the client response.

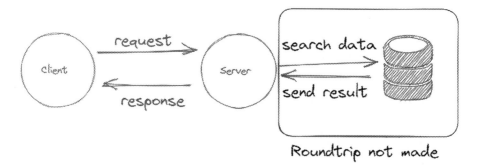

Figure 5-2. *Database not being called when the response is marked as fresh*

We need to keep in mind that to generate a response for a request, the server might make a call, or several calls, to a database, and this might have performance penalties.

Using caching could save the server some database round trips and data transfer. If in our business case a specific resource doesn't change very often, it would be pointless to ask the server to query the database and bring the same data over and over again.

Leveraging caching might increase the perceived performance or can be a major performance gain when combined with in-memory caching mechanisms.

Uniform Interface

The Uniform Interface constraint refers to the addressability, identification and representation of the resources, and it has four sub constraints.

Identification of Resources

States that every resource should be identifiable and addressable by having a uniform resource identifier (URI). Using the URI, a consumer should be able to perform actions over the resource.

Representation of Resources

States that we should work with representations of resources and not directly with domain entities. These representations can be subsets of the domain entities, an aggregation of several entities, or simply copies of these, but not the domain entities directly.

More than that, by leveraging the `Accept` header, we can work with different representations of the same resources. For example, by sending `Accept:application/json`, we get one response, and with `Accept:text/xml` we get a different response—but only if the server knows how to respond with the type asked. These responses might be different not only format-wise but also content-wise.

So, we don't need to create different endpoints every time we need a different representation of a specific resource. A `Speaker` will be the same resource for our application irrespective of whether we represent it as a JSON, XML, or a custom format.

Self-descriptive Messages

In this context, when we talk about messages, we understand we mean requests and responses. Each of them is an entity that should be self-descriptive and have its own meaning. How do we do that? By adding the right headers, status codes, verbs, and media types, as shown in Figure 5-3.

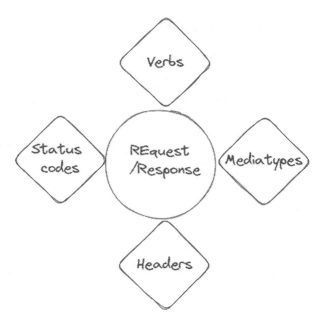

Figure 5-3. *Ways of adding meaning to requests/responses*

HATEOAS

HATEOAS is a tricky and ignored subject when it comes to implementing it. It stands for *Hypermedia as the Engine of Application State* and it means two things in our context:

- Hypermedia
- Content negotiation – allows the server to respond with a different representation of the resource when it receives different values of the Accept header.

Layered System

This architectural style states that between the consumer of the API and the server that generates a response there may be several other servers. If this is the case, the consumer shouldn't be impacted.

The consumer issues a request and gets the response, and that is it. It shouldn't matter that in front of the server there are three, four, or five different layers taking care of aspects like security, forwarding, or anything else required. This enables intermediaries like proxies or gateways to be transparently deployed between the client and the server.

Code on Demand

This constraint is optional. An API can be RESTful without this constraint. This covers situations where we need to send more than static representations of resources as responses. We can send code, usually in the form of a script, that can be executed on the client.

As a side note, this approach was widely used ten years ago to add some dynamic functionality to web pages.

Your First RESTful API

REST is much more than we have talked about here and much more than we will cover in this book. It is an architectural style that not many developers implement to its fullest. Some refer to their APIs as being RESTful even if those APIs don't respect even the most basic of the guidelines of REST.

Introducing CRUD

CRUD is an acronym meaning Create, Read, Update, Delete that comes from the relational database world, representing the four basic operations of persisting storage:

- Create – an item
- Read – a list of resources or an individual resource

139

- Update – an existing resource

- Delete – an existing resource

Let's take an example—we have an online store where we sell socks. We would need to have the ability to create a product, edit an existing one, delete a product, and view the entire list of products or just one.

All these functionalities would give us the option to manage every aspect of a resource (the resource is a product representing a sock, in our case).

When we extend this to our APIs, it means that for any other resource we want to expose through endpoints, for it to be complete we need to allow four operations. Now, we don't manage database operations directly in our code, but through actions that respond to these requests and in turn call other code that takes care of persistence.

In Table 5-1 you can see what type of requests we need to support to allow CRUD for a resource.

Table 5-1. *Mapping Request Types to Database Operations*

	Endpoint operation	Database operation
Create	POST request	INSERT
Read	GET request	SELECT
Update	PUT request	UPDATE
Delete	DELETE request	DELETE

Now that we know all these operations, we should have a look at and put into context the endpoints we need to implement in our API to make sure we cover everything (Table 5-2).

Table 5-2. *All Endpoints to Cover CRUD Operations*

HTTP verb	Endpoint	Description
GET	/api/speakers	Returns a list of all speakers
GET	/api/speakers/{id}	Returns the speaker with the id specified
POST	/api/speakers	Allows the creation of a new speaker entity
PUT	/api/speakers/{id}	Updates the speaker with the given ID with the new properties
DELETE	/api/speakers/{id}	Deletes the speaker with the given ID
HEAD	/api/speakers/{id}	Checks if the speaker with the given ID exists, without returning a body

Getting to Know the Project

You can find the starting point for our app in /ch05/starting_point. In there you will find a new project and a class named `SpeakerModel`.

In our example, we will build an API to manage a conference that takes place every year in several locations. We will have speakers, talks, workshops, and an agenda. We will start from this empty project, and chapter by chapter we will build our API, adding in everything necessary.

Implementing a GET Request

GET requests are one of the easiest to implement because everything is pretty much wired in already in the app.

First, we will create an action that responds to a GET request and returns a list of speakers (Listing 5-1). At this point, we will just focus on how things work and rewrite them later using a more architecturally focused approach, linking them to a real database.

In SpeakersController.cs, we will add a new action named GetAll, which will return an IActionResult. At this moment, it's alright to return an IActionResult and not ActionResult<IEnumberable<SpeakerModel>> from the action because we have only one type returned, and we don't need to write a test for it. We also need to decorate the action with the [HttpGet] attribute to make sure it will respond to the HTTP GET verb.

Listing 5-1. Returning a list of resources

```
[HttpGet]
public IActionResult GetAll()
{
    var speakerList = new List<SpeakerModel>() {
        new SpeakerModel() {
        },
        new SpeakerModel(){ }
    };
    return Ok(speakerList);
}
```

Open Postman and make a GET request to this action.

The URL we need to make the request to is https://localhost:7068/ api/Speakers. Speakers is the controller name, and the action is determined from the verb used when making the request. If everything works as expected, we should get something similar to Figure 5-4, with a 200 OK status code and a list with two empty objects in the body.

Figure 5-4. *Successful response for a GET request*

This type of GET request, which returns a list of items, is often referred to as GetAll to distinguish it from the one returning an individual item.

Now, let's clean up the code. Let's try moving our object creation into the controller's constructor to make sure it's initialized and filled with data when the constructor is created, as shown in Listing 5-2.

Listing 5-2. SpeakersController with SpeakersList

```
private List<SpeakerModel> SpeakersList;
public SpeakersController()
{
    SpeakersList = new List<SpeakerModel>() {
        new SpeakerModel() {
            Email="speaker1@mail.com",
            FirstName="FirstName1",
            LastName="LastName1",
            Id=1
        },
        new SpeakerModel() {
            Email="speaker2@mail.com",
            FirstName="FirstName2",
            LastName="LastName2",
```

```
                Id=2
            },
        };
    }
```

I use `SpeakerList` as the name for a private field here, even though it doesn't respect any conventions, because I want to emphasize somehow that this is dummy data, playing a database role. Later, we will remove it entirely and have a real database instead.

A change such as this forces us to refactor a bit of the `GetAll` action method (Listing 5-3).

Listing 5-3. GetAll Action after Refactoring

```
[HttpGet]
public IActionResult GetAll()
{
 return Ok(SpeakersList);
}
```

Implementing GET and Using an ID

In the previous section, we saw how easy it is to return a list of items with the right status code. In this section, we will return an item only if we can find it in our "database."

To implement the action we will need to do the following things:

- Add an action returning an `IActionResult`, named `GetById`.

- Add an `int` parameter to the action named `id`. This will receive the parameter value from the URL.

- Add a route pattern to match the parameter
  id:[HttpGet("{id}")].

- Search in our list of speakers ("database") for an item
  that matches the incoming id value.

- Return a 404 Not Found status code if there isn't an
  item that matches the id value.

- Return a 200 OK status code and the actual item if we
  found an item that matches the value.

Finally, our method should look like Listing 5-4.

Listing 5-4. GetById Action

```
[HttpGet("{id}")]
public IActionResult GetbyId(int id)
{
    var speakerToReturn = SpeakersList.FirstOrDefault
    (x => x.Id == id);
    if (speakerToReturn == null)
    {
        return NotFound();
    }
    return Ok(speakerToReturn);
}
```

Now that we have this implemented, we can call it from Postman to
test it. But first, one thing to notice is that in our documentation there is
another endpoint that follows the routing pattern that we added. The {id}
pattern will be replaced with the actual value from the request (Figure 5-5).

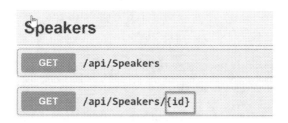

Figure 5-5. *GetById documented by Swagger*

Following the template, we can issue a request to `https://localhost:7068/api/Speakers/1`. We know that we have an item with Id = 1, and in this case, we will get a `200  OK` status code and the actual item in the response body (Figure 5-6).

Figure 5-6. *Success status code for a GetById call*

Now, let's see the second case, where we make a request for an item that has the `Id` value missing, as shown in Figure 5-7.

Figure 5-7. *Not Found status code for GetById call*

We received a 404 Not found status code and a standard
response body having a Content-Type: application/problem+json;
charset=utf-8.

This application/problem+json was first coined in https://
www.rfc-editor.org/rfc/rfc7807 as a first attempt to
standardize the way the APIs treat "problems." This is a means to
try to standardize all the responses for cases that aren't successful.
These response bodies need to have a format that is understandable
and easily identifiable by the consumer. It provides a few default
properties and can be extended with custom members. The idea
behind it is that a Problem can be either business-logic-related
or HTTP-related, and if the consumer can't use the body of the
response, they can easily tell what happened by looking at some
standard fields that are expected to be part of the response.

Implementing a POST Request

If, when we implement GET requests, we only check if the item exists, creating a new item or updating an existing one should always include a data validation step. We should never assume that the consumer of our API will always send good data, and we should prevent data corruption at every layer.

Web API removes most of the tedious work necessary to make sure the data that reaches the server is correct by doing validation for us. Our models are validated by using the datatypes of the properties and the validation attributes added on top of them. If anything is not right, it will return a `400 Bad Request` status code as part of the model validation process.

When the request reaches the server, we will have to perform the following steps:

- Validate the properties sent in the request body, which are already bound to the action's parameters. In this case, as shown in Listing 5-5, `Post(SpeakerModel model)`.

- If everything is valid, then we need to save the item in our database. Usually, the database will automatically assign a value to the property that is a primary key.

- Return the newly saved entity (containing the newly assigned ID) in the response body with a `201 Created` status code.

- Ensure that the response has a `Location` header field pointing to the newly created item URL.

Listing 5-5. Post Action Method

```
[HttpPost]
public IActionResult Post(SpeakerModel model)
{
 //not necessary now
 if (!ModelState.IsValid)
 {
   return BadRequest();
 }

  //assign an Id
  model.Id = SpeakersList.Max(x => x.Id + 1);
  //add  in the 'db'
  SpeakersList.Add(model);
  //return the item with the new assigned id
  return CreatedAtAction(nameof(GetbyId), new { id = model.Id },
  model);
        }
```

In our example in Listing 5-5, the call CreatedAtAction(nameof(Get byId), new { id = model.Id }, model) takes, as a first parameter, the name of an action.

This name could be hardcoded or passed with the help of the nameof operator, and it will help with URL creation. This URL will point to the location where we can return the newly created entity, hence allowing us to "view" it.

In theory, a consumer of our API would be able to access the value sent in the Location header and issue a GET request to it to view all the properties of the newly created item.

In Figure 5-8, if everything is valid when we send the request, then the server will return the response in Figure 5-9. This response has a 201 Created status code, the body contains the entire entity we sent plus the assigned ID, and the Location header points to the URL corresponding to GetById action.

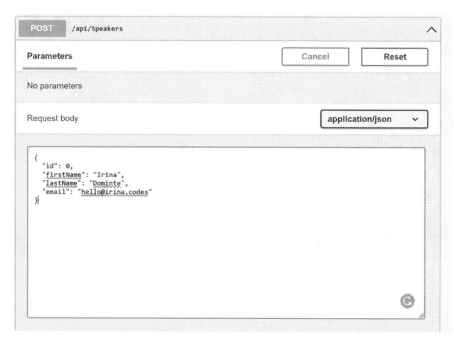

Figure 5-8. *A POST request*

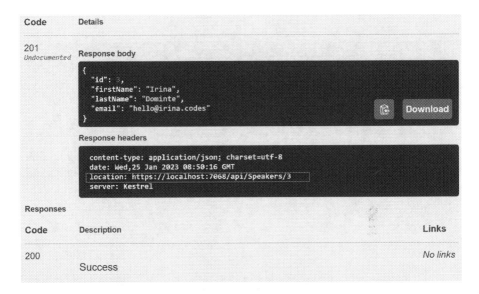

Figure 5-9. *Location header in a response*

We said earlier that a mandatory step in the correct processing of a POST request is model validation. Until now, our SpeakerModel properties have no validation attribute added, but we will want to make sure that for now the Email property has a valid email format.

Open the SpeakerModel class and add the [EmailAddress] attribute on top of our property.

```
[EmailAddress]
public string Email { get; set; }
```

Adding validation attributes and sending requests that don't pass the validation will result in responses that have Content-type:application+problem.

In Figure 5-10, the Email property is not valid. As a result of model validation, the platform will return a response for us that is tied to the encountered error.

151

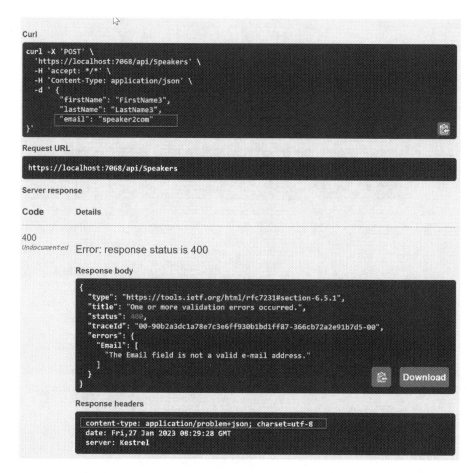

Figure 5-10. *Bad request response*

Once this is implemented, we can take it a step further and say we need to enforce a business rule that will return a `409 Conflict` status code. A good candidate for this business rule would be to make sure the `Email` property of each speaker is unique. For this, we won't implement a special validation attribute now, but rather will manually add an error to the `ModelState`. See Listing 5-6.

Listing 5-6. Manually Adding a Validation Error

```
if (SpeakersList.Any(x => x.Email == model.Email))
        {
                ModelState.AddModelError(nameof(model.Email),
                "Email field should be unique");
                return Conflict(ModelState);
        }
```

The AddModelError method call adds the key Email and the message
"Email field should be unique" to the errors dictionary, and we
can pass it to be returned, or simply return Conflict(), as shown in
Figure 5-11.

Figure 5-11. *409 Conflict status code*

Implementing a HEAD Request

A HEAD request won't have a response body, even if sent from the
controller, as shown in Listing 5-7. A head request can be suitable to check
if an item exists or to access metadata about it, like headers, content type,
or even the size of the response.

Listing 5-7. An Action Responding to a HEAD Verb

```
[HttpHead("{id}")]
        public IActionResult CheckIfExists(int id)
        {
```

```
        var speakerToReturn = SpeakersList.FirstOrDefault
        (x => x.Id == id);
        if (speakerToReturn == null)
        {
            return NotFound();
        }
        return Ok(speakerToReturn);
    }
```

Implementing a PUT Request

Semantically, a PUT request should be used whenever we want to update an existing item based on a unique identifier. As an effect, the whole entity will be replaced, not just the property we want to update.

When we implement a PUT request, we have to send, in the request body, the identifier of the resource and what we want to update. When the request reaches the server, we will have to do the following steps:

- Search in our database for the item that has the identifier sent in the request. We can refer to this as being the "original" item that we need to update.

- If we find it, we need to try to update each property with the new values sent in the request body by calling TryUpdateModelAsync(speakerFromDb);.

- If we don't find the item in our database, we need to return a 404 NotFound status code.

In Listing 5-8 we can see such an implementation. The general rule for implementing an update on an item is to make sure we get the item from the database and then update it property by property with the values we send in our request body. The platform will take care of updating each property for us.

Listing 5-8. A PUT Request Implementation

```
[HttpPut("{id}")]
public IActionResult Update(int id, SpeakerModel model)
{
 var speakerFromDb = SpeakersList.FirstOrDefault(x =>
 x.Id == id);
 if (speakerFromDb == null)
 {
  return NotFound();
 }
  TryUpdateModelAsync(speakerFromDb);
  //update in the database
  return Ok(speakerFromDb);
 }
```

Implementing a DELETE Request

When the request reaches the server, we will have to do the following steps:

- Search in our database for the item that has the identifier sent in the request.

- If we find it, we simply remove it from the database and return a 204 No Content status code.

- If we can't find an item with the specified ID, then we return a 404 Not found status code.

In Listing 5-9 we can see a full implementation of an action deleting an item.

Listing 5-9. A Delete Implementation

```
[HttpDelete("{id}")]
public IActionResult Delete(int id)
{
    var speakerFromDb = SpeakersList.FirstOrDefault
    (x => x.Id == id);
    if (speakerFromDb == null)
    {
        return NotFound();
    }
    SpeakersList.Remove(speakerFromDb);
    return NoContent();
}
```

Best Practices for API Design

There are many considerations when it comes to implementing a well-rounded API, but our purpose here is to learn Web API in a way that will be easy for us to extrapolate later.

I compiled a small list of items that we should bear in mind for RESTful APIs:

- Use nouns instead of verbs, and be specific enough when designing the endpoints; use the right HTTP verbs.

Table 5-3. *Endpoints with Strange Action Names*

Use	Avoid
/api/dogs	/api/getDogs
/api/dogs	/api/createNewDog
	/api/things

- Logical nesting of endpoints – If some resources should be hierarchical, design your endpoints to be nested as shown in Table 5-4.

Table 5-4. *Nested Endpoints Examples*

Examples
/api/dogs/1/owner
/api/employes/{id}/rewards/{rewardId}
/api/speakers/{id}/talks
/api/speakers/{id}/talks/{id}
/api/speakers/{id}/talks/{id}/feedback

- Return standard error codes – Use the standard status codes to add meaning to your endpoints. Not every error is a 400 Bad Request. It could make more sense to return a 409 Conflict or a 433 Unprocessable Entity status code if it helps to differentiate errors.

- Allow filtering, sorting, and pagination of endpoints by using query strings and not different endpoint as shown in Table 5-5.

Table 5-5. *Variations of Endpoints*

Use	Avoid
/api/cats?color=black	/api/cats/blackCats
/api/dogs?sort=age&direction=descending	/api/dogs/OrderByAgeDescending

- Cache data to improve performance.

- Version your APIs if necessary.

- Consider using the Accept header in such a manner that allows you to return different representations of the same resource.

- Have two endpoints for CRUD, not different endpoints for every single operation. Table 5-6 summarizes the list of all operations over a single resource.

Table 5-6. *Endpoints and Possible Operations*

Endpoint	HTTP verb to use
/api/speakers	GET – the entire list of speakers POST – to create a new item
/api/speakers/{id}	GET – a speaker based on ID PUT – update an existing speaker DELETE – delete an existing speaker HEAD – to check if an item exists

Summary

In this chapter, we learned a little about what it means to implement a RESTful API, and we also implemented actions that respond to main HTTP verbs, return static data, and the right status codes to be used. For each of the actions we implemented, we tried to cover the best-case and worst-case scenarios when testing our endpoints either from Postman or the browser, to make sure we understood each step of the process.

In the following chapter, we will take our API to the next level and link it to an actual database instead of returning static data from the controller.

CHAPTER 6

Introducing an ORM

In this chapter, we will learn what an ORM is and how we can easily connect an API to a data store by using such a tool. We will focus on working with Entity Framework Core and SQL Server. Even though there are many relational databases available, in this book we will use SQL Server Express' LocalDB feature. This is installed along with Visual Studio and provides a lightweight SQL Server instance that is ready to use on your machine.

Before we dig into any code we need to understand a few concepts and how they relate to our code.

What Is an ORM?

ORM stands for object-relational mapping and is a tool that helps one to interact with a database in an object-oriented way instead of writing raw SQL queries.

In other words, an ORM allows us to use programming language constructs like classes and objects to perform database operations, such as inserting, updating, and retrieving data, and facilitates database access. An ORM acts like a bridge between our code and the database, making the process of accessing and manipulating data in a database easier, more intuitive, and less error-prone. The goal of using an ORM is to simplify database interactions and make the code more maintainable and readable.

Such a tool will help us map tables with columns to classes with properties and back, as shown in Figure 6-1.

© Irina Dominte 2023
I. Dominte, *Web API Development for the Absolute Beginner*,
https://doi.org/10.1007/978-1-4842-9348-5_6

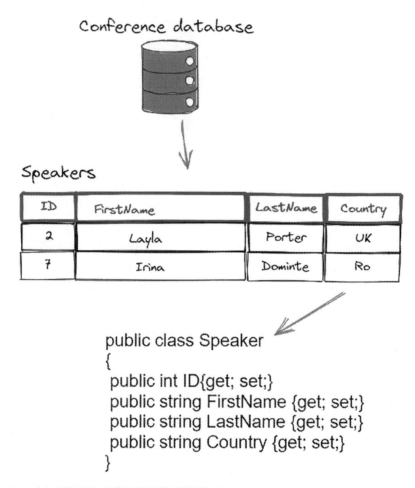

Figure 6-1. *Mapping from a database table to a C# class*

There are many ORMs available, but their goals are the same. Each of them has implementations for many database providers.

A *database provider* is a piece of software that allows the ORM to interact with a specific type of database management system (DBMS), such as Microsoft SQL Server, MySQL, SQLite, or anything else. Usually, this comes as a library and implements the communication between that ORM and DBMS, having specificity for each.

This library knows how to translate the ORM's instructions, which are expressed in a high-level programming language like C#, into low-level database commands specific to the provider in the syntax specific to it.

The fact that an ORM framework typically supports multiple database providers and allows us to use the same ORM to interact with different types of databases can be especially useful for large, complex applications that need to work with several databases.

By using a single ORM for all database types, we can write and maintain a consistent and unified codebase, and we can reuse the know-how we already have.

Introducing Entity Framework

Entity Framework Core (EF Core) is an open-source, lightweight, cross-platform ORM framework for .NET.

EF Core can serve as an object-relational mapper (ORM) that

- enables .NET developers to work with a database using .NET objects;

- eliminates the need for most of the data-access code that typically needs to be written; and

- abstracts and makes database access transparent.

EF Core supports many underlying database engines, like MySQL, Postgres, Oracle, and so forth.

Entity Framework Core Building Blocks

Several components make Entity Framework Core good:

- **Entities** – Each entity is a class that maps to a table in the database.

- **DbSet<T>** – This is a collection of entities that represent the table record.

- **DbContext** – This is the entry point of database access. It manages the entities and the relations between them. We can look at the DbContext as being the database itself, containing tables with relationships.

- **Database Providers** – These are components that allow EF Core to interact with different types of databases, such as Microsoft SQL Server, MySQL, Oracle, SQLite, or anything else. EF Core supports multiple database providers, allowing you to choose the provider that best fits your needs.

- **Connection String** – This is the string of information that defines the parameters needed to connect to a database.

In the following pages, we will dig deeper into EF Core components.

Connection String

A connection string is a string of information that defines the parameters needed to connect to a database in EF Core. The connection string provides information such as the database server name, the database name, authentication details required to access the database, and some additional configuration properties that we can add. It looks like the following:

```
Server= (localdb)\mssqllocaldb.;Database=Conference;Trusted_
Connection=True;
```

In this example, the connection string specifies the server name as (localdb)\mssqllocaldb, which is the local machine, and the database name as Conference. Trusted_Connection=True indicates that a trusted connection should be used, which means that the connection will use the current Windows account for authentication.

A connection string in EF Core for SQL Server typically consists of the following parts:

- **Provider** – The name of the database provider, such as Microsoft.Data.SqlClient

- **Server** – The name or IP address of the server hosting the database

- **Database** – The name of the database to connect to

- **User ID** – The username used to authenticate with the database server (optional)

- **Password** – The password associated with the User ID (optional)

- **Integrated Security** – Specifies whether to use Windows authentication or SQL Server authentication

Examine the following example:

```
Server=(localdb\mssqllocaldb;Database=MyDatabase;User ID=MyUser
name;Password=MyPassword;Integrated Security=False;
```

In Listing 6-1, for example, the ConferenceContext class has two properties, Speakers and Talks, that represent the speaker and talk entities, respectively. The OnConfiguring method is used to configure the database connection for the context. In this example, the connection string is set to use SQL Server with a trusted connection.

Listing 6-1. A Context Class Example

```
public class ConferenceContext : DbContext
{
    public DbSet<Speaker> Speakers { get; set; }
    public DbSet<Talk> Talks { get; set; }

    protected override void OnConfiguring(DbContextOptionsBuilder
    optionsBuilder)
    {
        optionsBuilder.UseSqlServer("Server= (localdb)\
        mssqllocaldb;Database=Conference;Trusted_Connection=
        True;");
    }
}
```

Entity

An entity class is defined as a plain C# class with properties that correspond to columns in the database table. For example, if you have a Speaker table in the database with columns for Id, FirstName, and Bio, you might define a corresponding Speaker entity class as in Listing 6-2.

Listing 6-2. The Speaker class

```
public class Speaker
{
    public int Id { get; set; }
    public string FirstName { get; set; }
    public string Bio { get; set; }
}
```

Afterward, we can use our Speaker entity to perform CRUD (Create, Read, Update, Delete) operations on the Speaker entity, and EF Core will automatically generate the necessary SQL statements.

We could, for example, retrieve all the speakers from the database and store them in a list of Speaker objects, as in Listing 6-3.

Listing 6-3. Using a database context

```
using (var context = new ConferenceContext())
{
    var speakers = context.Speakers.ToList();
}
```

DBSet

A DbSet is a class that represents a collection of entities that can be queried from a database table using LINQ (Language Integrated Query). It is typically defined as a property in a class that inherits from DbContext, which is the main class that represents a database connection and provides a way to access and manipulate the data in that database.

Each DbSet instance represents a collection of entities of a specific type, where each entity corresponds to a row in the database table. You can use DbSet to perform CRUD (Create, Read, Update, Delete) operations on the underlying database table.

Database Context

The DbContext class provides many methods for querying, inserting, updating, and deleting data. It also manages the relationships between entities and provides a way to configure how entities are mapped to the database.

To use DbContext in our application, we typically create a derived class that represents our database context, and then add properties to the class for each entity with which we want to interact. We can then use the context to query and manipulate data in the database. When we make changes to an entity, such as adding, updating, or deleting it, those changes are tracked by the DbContext. Once we have made all of the changes needed, we can call the SaveChanges method on the DbContext to persist those changes to the database as a single transaction.

The DbContext also provides the ability to manage transactions, which is a core functionality of the *Unit of Work pattern*. By using transactions, we can group multiple changes to the database as a single atomic unit, which ensures that all changes are either committed or rolled back (in case of an error or exception).

In addition to tracking changes and coordinating transactions, the DbContext also provides several other features that are common to the Unit of Work pattern. For example, it provides a change tracker that allows us to see what changes have been made to entities, and it provides the ability to attach and detach entities from the DbContext.

When it comes to configuring a DbContext class, we need to use a DbContextOptionsBuilder class. There are three ways to get this builder to pass parameters, as follows:

- With AddDbContext and related methods:

```
services.AddDbContext<ApplicationDbContext>(
        options => options.UseSqlServer
        ("Server=(localdb)\mssqllocaldb;Database=Confe
        renceDemo;Trusted_Connection=True"));
```

- By overriding the OnConfiguring method in the DbContext class:

```
protected override void OnConfiguring(DbContextOptions
Builder optionsBuilder)
        {
                optionsBuilder.UseSqlServer(
```

```
            @"Server=(localdb)\mssqllocaldb;
            Database=ConferenceDemo;Trusted_
            Connection=True");
    }
```

- By being constructed explicitly with the new keyword:

```
using var db = new ConferenceContext();
```

Database Provider

Database providers are components that allow EF Core to interact with different types of databases, such as Microsoft SQL Server, MySQL, SQLite, or numerous others. EF Core supports multiple database providers, allowing you to choose the provider that best fits your business needs.

Configuring Relations Between Entities

There are two ways of configuring relationships between entities in Entity Framework (EF) Core, as follows:

1. *Fluent API* – Fluent API is a way to configure entities and their relationships using a more readable and expressive syntax compared to data annotations. With Fluent API, you can perform configuration tasks, such as defining properties, creating relationships, setting primary keys, and creating indexes, among others.

2. *Data Annotations* – Data annotations are a set of attributes that you can use to decorate your entities to specify certain properties, such as the primary key, required properties, and relationships. Data annotations provide a straightforward way to define the relationships between entities.

Both Fluent API and data annotations have their pros and cons, and the choice between them depends on the complexity of your scenario. For simple scenarios, data annotations might be sufficient, but for more complex scenarios, Fluent API might be a better choice.

Fluent API

Using Fluent API, you can create a model configuration class and use a fluent interface to perform configuration tasks. The fluent interface provides a series of method calls that allow you to express the desired configuration in a readable and concise way. When you need to configure multiple relationships between entities, specify the type of relationships, such as one-to-one, one-to-many, and many-to-many relationships, as follows:

1.   One-to-one:

```
protected override void OnModelCreating(ModelBuilder
modelBuilder)
{
    modelBuilder.Entity<Speaker>()
        .HasMany(s => s.Talks)
        .WithOne(t => t.Speaker)
        .HasForeignKey(t => t.SpeakerId);
}
```

2.   One-to-many:

```
modelBuilder.Entity<Speaker>()
            .HasMany(s => s.Talks)
            .WithOne(t => t.Speaker)
            .HasForeignKey(t => t.SpeakerId);
```

3. Many-to-many:

```
modelBuilder.Entity<Speaker>()
            .HasMany(s => s.Talks)
            .WithMany(t => t.Speakers)
            .UsingEntity<SpeakerTalk>(st => st.HasKey
            (s => new { s.SpeakerId, s.TalkId }));
```

- Setting primary keys:

```
protected override void OnModelCreating(ModelBuilder
modelBuilder)
{
    modelBuilder.Entity<Speaker>()
        .HasKey(s => s.Id);
}
```

- Creating indexes:

```
protected override void OnModelCreating(ModelBuilder
modelBuilder)
{
    modelBuilder.Entity<Speaker>()
        .HasIndex(s => s.Name)
        .IsUnique();
}
```

- Configuring properties:

```
protected override void OnModelCreating(ModelBuilder
modelBuilder)
{
    modelBuilder.Entity<Speaker>()
        .Property(s => s.Name)
```

```
                    .IsRequired()
                    .HasMaxLength(100);
        }
```

Using Fluent API gives developers more flexibility than they have when using data annotations as a result of the granular approach and multitude of methods offered.

Data Annotations

Data annotations in EF Core are attributes that can be applied to entities and their properties to provide additional information and configuration to the EF Core framework. Data annotations can be used to define relationships between entities and configure properties such as primary keys, required fields, and maximum lengths.

Here are some examples of how you can use data annotations to configure relationships between entities in EF Core:

1. One-to-one:

    ```
    public class Speaker
    {
        [Key]
        public int Id { get; set; }
        public string Name { get; set; }
        public int? TalkId { get; set; }
        public Talk Talk { get; set; }
    }

    public class Talk
    {
    ```

```
    [Key]
    public int Id { get; set; }
    public string Description { get; set; }

    [ForeignKey("TalkId")]
    public Speaker Speaker { get; set; }
}
```

2. One-to-many:

```
public class Speaker
{
    [Key]
    public int Id { get; set; }
    public string Name { get; set; }
    public ICollection<Talk> Talks { get; set; }
}

public class Talk
{
    [Key]
    public int Id { get; set; }
    public string Title { get; set; }
    public int SpeakerId { get; set; }
    [ForeignKey("SpeakerId")]
    public Speaker Speaker { get; set; }
}
```

3. Many-to-many:

```
public class Speaker
{
    [Key]
    public int Id { get; set; }
```

```csharp
        public string Name { get; set; }
        public ICollection<SpeakerTalk> SpeakerTalks {
        get; set; }
    }

    public class Talk
    {
        [Key]
        public int Id { get; set; }
        public string Title { get; set; }
        public ICollection<SpeakerTalk> SpeakerTalks {
        get; set; }
    }

    public class SpeakerTalk
    {
        public int SpeakerId { get; set; }
        public Speaker Speaker { get; set; }
        public int TalkId { get; set; }
        public Talk Talk { get; set; }
    }
```

It is easier to understand the structure of your entities and the relationships between them.

Ways of Working with a Database

Depending on the moment when we start to develop our application and the business case we have, there are two options for working with a database. We will discuss specific use cases in the following section and try to show where each type is a good fit.

Database First

The *database-first* approach is used for cases where we already have the database schema defined. Situations where we have a fully created database that won't need changes are rather rare. It may happen when we want to create an application to retire an old one.

The database-first approach is a way of using EF Core to create a model based on an existing database.

The database schema will be used by EF Core (in our case) to generate C# classes. Some of these classes are called *entities* and are generated using the tables and relations in the database. Another class generated is a helper class called `DbContext` that keeps the entities together- and exposes methods for high-level configuration. With these classes, we will have a code-based representation of the database schema.

These entity classes are then used to interact with the database and perform various operations, such as querying data, inserting data, updating data, and deleting data.

We can look at the database-first approach as reverse-engineering a database. It first reads the database schema and pieces of information about tables, columns, constraints, and indexes and uses these to create an EF Core model. Tables are used to create classes (entity types), columns to create class properties, and primary keys to create relationships.

The process of generating C# classes using EF Core is called *scaffolding*.

These generated entities can be customized and extended as needed, but any changes to the database schema will force you to regenerate the model to keep it in sync with the database.

Scaffolding refers to the automatic generation of code based on a predefined model or predefined parameters.

Scaffolding in Entity Framework Core can be performed using the "`dotnet ef dbcontext scaffold`" command in the .NET Core CLI, specifying the database connection string and the output directory for the generated code.

Scaffolding database steps are as follows:

- Install the NuGet package for `Microsoft.EntityFrameworkCore.Design` in the project.

- Install the database provider package[1] for the database schema you want to reverse engineer. (`Microsoft.EntityFrameworkCore.SqlServer` NuGet Package in our case).

- Make sure you have the .NET CLI tools for EF by running `dotnet ef` in a command line. If not, you need to install it by running the following command;

```
dotnet tool install --global dotnet-ef
```

We can also run EF Core commands using PowerShell, but I want you to get familiar with running commands from the .NET CLI family.

To make sure you have it installed, run the `dotnet ef` command again, and you should see something similar to Figure 6-2, as well as a few available commands.

---

[1] https://learn.microsoft.com/en-us/ef/core/providers/?tabs=dotnet-core-cli

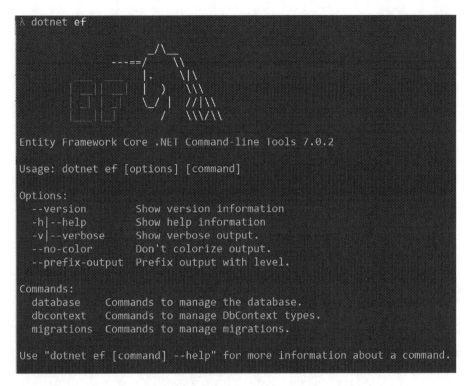

```
λ dotnet ef


            ----==/    \\
                 |.      \|\
                 |  )     \\\
                 \_/ |   //|\\
                   /    \\\/\\

Entity Framework Core .NET Command-line Tools 7.0.2

Usage: dotnet ef [options] [command]

Options:
  --version        Show version information
  -h|--help        Show help information
  -v|--verbose     Show verbose output.
  --no-color       Don't colorize output.
  --prefix-output  Prefix output with level.

Commands:
  database    Commands to manage the database.
  dbcontext   Commands to manage DbContext types.
  migrations  Commands to manage migrations.

Use "dotnet ef [command] --help" for more information about a command.
```

Figure 6-2. *A successful installation of EF Core tool*

Model First

The *model-first* approach in Entity Framework Core is a method of designing your application data model and database schema using C# code to generate a database or to update an existing database.

With this approach, you start by writing code that defines your entities, relationships, and properties, which represent the conceptual model of your data. You can then use EF Core CLI commands or APIs to generate the database schema based on this code and persist your data.

The approach is very convenient for developers and is often used in conjunction with the database-first approach. Changes that happen in code are then applied to the database by using database migrations, as we will see further in this chapter.

Although we have these two ways of working with a database, we will rarely use just one of them. Even if we start from an existing database when our applications evolve, most certainly the database evolves too, and we need to update it to be in sync with our application.

Even if the changes are small, like changing a column data type or the column name, it's still a change that will need to be reflected in both our app and the database.

What Are Migrations?

Migrations help us evolve the database when the model changes and provide a set of tools that allow the following:

- Create an initial database that works with your EF model.

- Generate migrations to keep track of changes you make to your EF model.

- Keep your database up to date with those changes.

- Version control: Migrations allow you to track changes to the database schema and revert to previous versions if necessary. This can be especially useful in a team environment where multiple people may be making changes to the database schema.

- Automated schema management: Migrations can be automated to keep the database schema in sync with the code, reducing the chances of manual errors.

- Increase development speed: Migrations can help improve performance by enabling you to make schema changes without recreating the entire database, which can be a time-consuming operation.

- Support testability: Migrations make it easier to write tests that depend on a specific database schema because you can apply migrations to set up the schema you need before running the tests.

How Do Migrations Work?

EF Core migrations keep track of changes to the database schema by maintaining a history of all the migrations that have been applied to the database. The history of all migrations is stored in a database table called __EFMigrationsHistory_.

Each time you create a new migration using the `Add-Migration` command, EF Core generates a new class that represents the changes you want to make to the database schema. This class is called a _migration_.

The migration class contains two methods: Up and Down. The `Up` method describes how to apply the changes to the database schema, and the `Down` method describes how to revert the changes.

When you run the `dotnet ef database update` command, EF Core compares the current state of the database schema to the target schema defined by your migrations. If there are any differences, EF Core generates the necessary SQL statements to update the database schema to the target state. It then records the migration in the `__EFMigrationsHistory` table so that it knows which migrations have been applied and in what order.

This way, EF Core can keep track of all the changes that have been made to the database schema, and you can easily revert to previous versions of the schema or update the schema to the latest version.

To see a list of all the migrations that have been applied to the database you can use `dotnet ef migrations list` command.

Installing SQL Management Studio

You can connect to a database by using Visual Studio Enterprise, but for the purpose of learning, we want to use SQL Management Studio. This is a widely used tool in the SQL Server database world.

You can find it on Microsoft's website if you search for the name.

Linking Our Project to a Database

We worked so far with dummy data, returning static data every time. Now we will evolve our API and explore how we can link a database to our project, or generate a database from our project.

Generate Tables from Our Project

Start by opening /ch6/start project. You will notice that in the start project, we now have a folder named Domain, with the following classes:

- Speaker
- Talk
- ConferenceContext

We will start to link our project to a database by installing the following NuGet packages:

- Microsoft.EntityFrameworkCore
- Microsoft.EntityFrameworkCore.SqlServer
- Microsoft.EntityFrameworkCore.Design

After installing these, we will need to make sure our ConferenceContext inherits DbContext class and points to the database we would want to connect in our OnConfiguring method.

Now we can add each DbSet for our models to make sure they are a part of what we consider ConferenceDemo database, as shown in Listing 6-4.

Listing 6-4. Creating the Initial DbContext

```
public class ConferenceContext:DbContext
{
  public DbSet<Speaker> Speakers { get; set; }
  public DbSet<Talk> Talks { get; set; }
}
```

Now that we have added this, it's time to open Microsoft SQL
Management Studio and log in using our local credentials, as shown in
Figure 6-3.

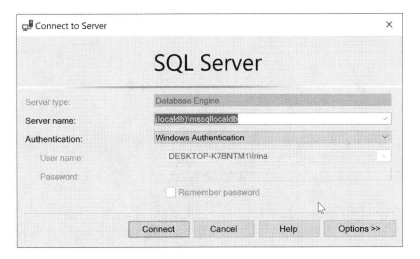

Figure 6-3. *SQL server login screen*

After the login process, if everything is successful, something similar
to Figure 6-4 will be shown. On the left-hand side, we will see the Object
Explorer panel. In this section, you can see numerous nodes, which you
can expand if you want. Under the Databases node, you will see all the
databases on this server.

Right now for us, the node is pretty much empty since it's the first time
we are working with it.

Figure 6-4. *Object explorer in SMSS*

Here, we will manually create a new database named ConferenceDemo, as shown in Figure 6-5.

We can also instruct Entity Framework to create it for us, but for now I prefer this option just to make sure things will work smoothly.

New Database...
Attach...
Restore Database...
Restore Files and Filegroups...
Deploy Data-tier Application...
Import Data-tier Application...
Start PowerShell
Reports ▶
Refresh

Figure 6-5. *New database option*

Now that we have an empty database, we can navigate to our project folder in a command line and are ready to run our first migration. We will create a migration named InitialCreate by using the following command:

```
dotnet ef migrations add InitialCreate --project ConferenceApi
```

After running it, if everything worked, you should see a success message, as shown in Figure 6-6, as a result of running the command.

Our command uses the dotnet CLI to add a migration with the name InitialCreate to a project in our solution named ConferenceApi (Figure 6-6).

I often like to use flags for commands because it makes it clearer and it is easier to tell what is wrong in case something does not go as expected.

Using the --project flag is very useful when we have more than one project in one solution. It allows you to specify directly which one you are targeting with the script without changing directories. In our specific case, we can run the command without the --project flag if we change our directories to make sure we run it from the folder where our .csproj lives.

Figure 6-6. *Adding InitialCreate Migration*

Our command executed with success and created a new folder in our project named Migrations (Figure 6-7).

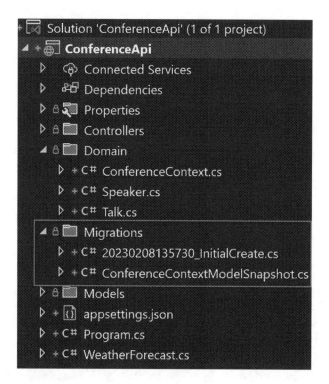

Figure 6-7. *Generated Migrations folder*

Every migration we add will have a file under this folder with a name similar to what we see here. The `{Timestamp_MigrationName}.cs` file format name contains two methods: `Up` and `Down`.

These methods contain code that will help when we apply the migration to the database or when we want to revert a migration (Figure 6-8).

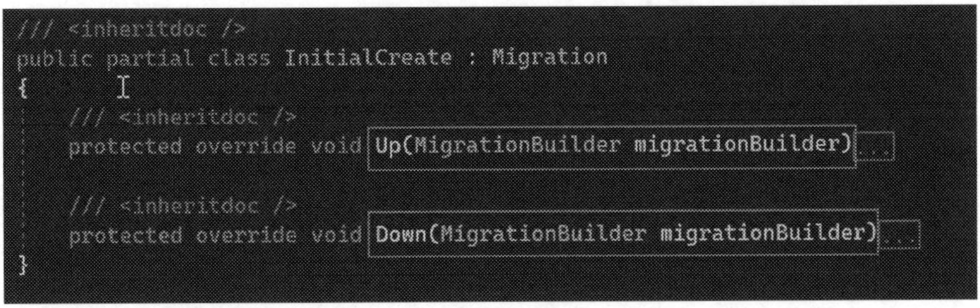

```
/// <inheritdoc />
public partial class InitialCreate : Migration
{
    I
    /// <inheritdoc />
    protected override void Up(MigrationBuilder migrationBuilder) ...

    /// <inheritdoc />
    protected override void Down(MigrationBuilder migrationBuilder) ...
}
```

***Figure 6-8.** InitialCreate generated file*

The next step in our process will be to apply the newly created migration to our empty database. To do that we will need to run the following update command (with or without the --project flag):

```
dotnet ef database update
```

As a result, EF Core will inform us that migrations are applied as shown in Figure 6-9.

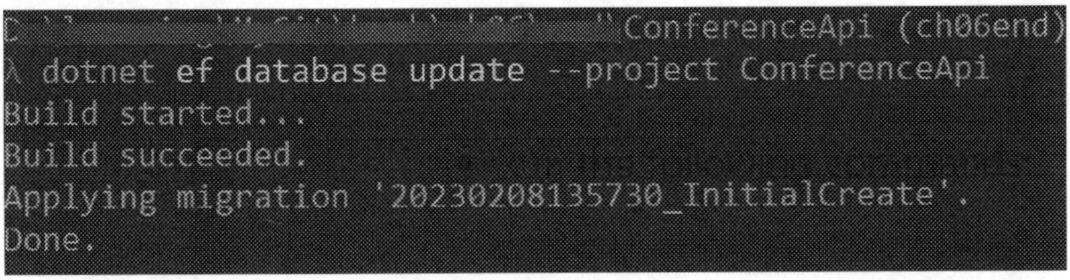

```
                                    ConferenceApi (ch06end)
\ dotnet ef database update --project ConferenceApi
Build started...
Build succeeded.
Applying migration '20230208135730_InitialCreate'.
Done.
```

***Figure 6-9.** Migration applied success message*

Our end goal is to obtain a database with tables and relations between them that are a representation of our code.

In Figure 6-10 we can see the result. We have two tables that correspond to our entities, Speakers and Talks, and a third one, __EFMigrationsHistory, that holds the migrations history.

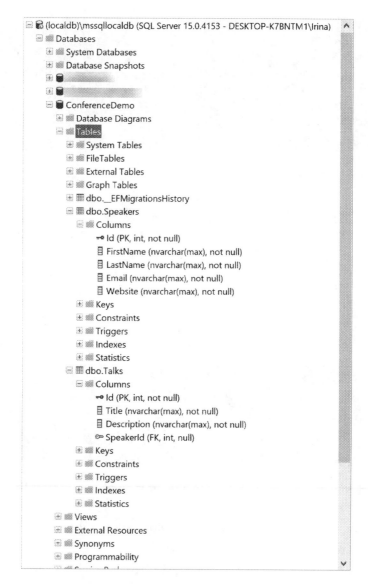

Figure 6-10. *Database updated with tables*

Scaffold Entities from an Existing Database

Because I want you to get familiar with using the CLI and EF Core, we will start from an empty project and reverse-engineer a database. Our database was already created in the previous step, so we only need to run a few commands to see how EF Core scaffolds code for us.

Go ahead and open the ch6/scaffold_project folder and open the ConferenceApi solution from there. Then, navigate to the solution folder in a cmd and run the following long command:

```
dotnet ef dbcontext scaffold "Data Source=(localdb)\
MSSQLLocalDB;Initial Catalog=ConferenceDemo" Microsoft.
EntityFrameworkCore.SqlServer --project ConferenceApi
```

If the command runs with success, in our solution folder we will have the entities and the database context similar to those in Figure 6-11. We notice that while the entity names are what we expect them to be, the class inheriting from DbContext has the same name suffix as our database name: ConferenceDemo.

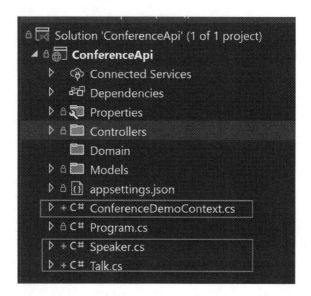

Figure 6-11. *Scaffolded entities*

In Listing 6-5 you can see that, by default, EF Core uses Fluent API to configure the entities. We can change that after we learn what available command flags we have.

Listing 6-5. Database context Content

```
public partial class ConferenceDemoContext : DbContext
{
    public ConferenceDemoContext()
    {
    }

    public ConferenceDemoContext(DbContextOptions<ConferenceDemo
    Context> options)
        : base(options)
    {
    }
```

```
public virtual DbSet<Speaker> Speakers { get; set; }

public virtual DbSet<Talk> Talks { get; set; }

protected override void OnConfiguring(DbContextOptionsBuilder
optionsBuilder)

    => optionsBuilder.UseSqlServer("Data Source=(localdb)\\
    MSSQLLocalDB;Initial Catalog=ConferenceDemo");

protected override void OnModelCreating(ModelBuilder
modelBuilder)
{
    modelBuilder.Entity<Talk>(entity =>
    {
        entity.HasIndex(e => e.SpeakerId, "IX_Talks_
        SpeakerId");

        entity.HasOne(d => d.Speaker).WithMany(p =>
        p.Talks).HasForeignKey(d => d.SpeakerId);
    });

    OnModelCreatingPartial(modelBuilder);
}

partial void OnModelCreatingPartial(ModelBuilder
modelBuilder);
}
```

The OnModelCreating method contains code that configures the generated entities using Fluent API. In there you will also see a partial method stub OnModelCreatingPartial, which allows you to extend the configuration in a separate method and a separate file. Using it will prevent code loss or unwanted overriding in case you ever need to scaffold the database again.

Now that we have the entities and the context generated by EF Core, let's delete them and try to control the output folder and the name of the context. To do that, we have to understand the commands that we run (Table 6-1).

Table 6-1. *EF Core Command Flags*

Flag	Example	Description
--context-dir Data	--context-dir Data	Specifies the folder for the generated context
--output-dir Models	--output-dir Models	Specifies the folder for the generated entities
--context-namespace	--context-namespace DbContext.Namespace	Specifies the namespace for the context
-namespace	-namespace Your.Namespace	Specifies the namespace for the entities
--context	--context ConferenceContext	Specifies the wanted name for the context
--data-annotations		Allows you to use data annotations instead of FluentAPI
--force		Will override existing classes in case of error
--table	--table MyTable	Scaffolds just the specified table

Now, let's open our project and delete the three generated classes: Speaker, Talk, and ConferenceDemoContext. We delete them to recreate them again in a specific location and with specific names.

We will run the following command:

```
dotnet ef dbcontext scaffold "Data Source=(localdb)\
MSSQLLocalDB;Initial Catalog=ConferenceDemo" Microsoft.
EntityFrameworkCore.SqlServer --output-dir Domain --context
ConferenceContext
```

And if everything works as expected, we will have output in our previously empty Domain folder in the project, as in Figure 6-12. We see here that our context now has a different name, ConferenceContext, as we specified with the --context flag in our command, and they reside in the Domain folder, as we specified with --output-dir flag.

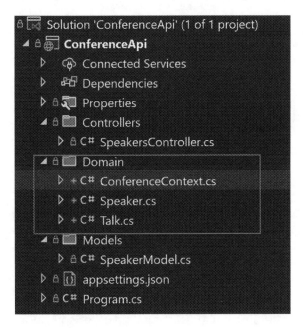

Figure 6-12. *Scaffolding in a specific folder*

Exercise   Delete the content of the folder and scaffold the entities again, this time by adding the `--data-annotations` flag to the command. Observe the generated entities.

Querying Data

Since we now have a database and some tables to play with, the next step is to change our application logic in such a way that responds to our needs in a performant manner.

Interfaces Used for Query Results

When it comes to accessing a query result we have two available options: using what the DbSet is returning, or using one of the interfaces discussed next.

IQueryable

The `IQueryable` interface in Entity Framework Core (EF Core) is a type that represents an enumerable collection of entities that can be queried, filtered, or further processed. EF Core returns `IQueryable` from the `DbSet` property of a `DbContext` by default.

The interface extends the `IEnumerable` interface and adds support for LINQ query expressions. `IQueryable` allows you to build a query incrementally by adding a filter, sorting, and other conditions and then executing the query only when it is enumerated.

This approach enables EF Core to optimize the query and translate it into a single optimized database query rather than executing separate queries for each operation. EF Core returns `IQueryable` from the `DbSet` property of a `DbContext`, which you can use to query and filter entities.

IEnumerable

The IEnumerable interface is a standard .NET interface that represents a collection of elements that can be enumerated (iterated over). The interface defines a single method, GetEnumerator, which returns an IEnumerator that is used to iterate over the elements in a collection.

The IEnumerable interface is implemented by various types in .NET, including arrays, lists, and dictionaries, and it provides a common way to iterate over elements in a uniform manner.

From a DbSet, we can call the ToList method to make sure we load the data in memory. This can have a significant impact on performance for large datasets.

IQueryable versus IEnumerable

IEnumerable and IQueryable both have their advantages and disadvantages in EF Core. The determination of which is better depends on the specific scenario and the needs of your application, but we need to be mindful of what we use. I've seen many projects where performance could have been better if the right interfaces would have been used.

IEnumerable is better for scenarios where you need to retrieve all data from the database into memory and perform in-memory operations, such as filtering and sorting. When using IEnumerable, EF Core executes the query and loads all data into memory immediately, which can have a significant impact on performance for large datasets.

IQueryable is better for scenarios where you need to perform operations on the database server, such as filtering, sorting, and paging, before returning a subset of the data to the application. IQueryable enables you to build a query incrementally and execute it only when it is enumerated, which can significantly improve performance for large datasets by reducing the amount of data that needs to be processed in memory.

Loading Related Data

Sometimes, doing a simple database query is not enough and there are specific scenarios where we also need to return related data from our tables. To do that we have a few strategies available.

Lazy Loading

Lazy loading is a technique in EF Core where related data is loaded on demand instead of being loaded eagerly with the main entity.

It helps to minimize memory usage and improve performance by loading data only when it's needed.

Eager Loading

Eager loading is a technique in EF Core where related data is loaded along with the main entity at the time the main entity is queried. Unlike lazy loading, where the related data is loaded only when it is accessed, eager loading loads the data into memory as soon as the main entity is retrieved.

You can see this in action by using the Include method as shown in Listing 6-6.

Listing 6-6. Loading Talks for Speakers

```
using (var context = new ConferenceContext())
{
    var speaker = context.Speakers.Include(b => b.Talks).
    FirstOrDefault();
}
```

Eager loading can improve performance by saving a database roundtrip, but it can also hurt it if you load too much or unnecessary data.

Executing Raw SQL

Using EF Core doesn't constrain us to using only LINQ to access and filter data. We can also execute functions, stored procedures, and raw SQL code from C# code, as shown in Listing 6-7.

Listing 6-7. Executing Raw SQL from C#

```csharp
using (var dbContext = new MyContext())
{
    // Set up your SQL statement
    string sqlStatement = "SELECT * FROM Speakers WHERE
    Country='USA'";

    // Execute the SQL statement and get the results
    var results = dbContext.Speakers.FromSqlRaw(sqlStatement).
    ToList();

    // Do something with the results
    foreach (var result in results)
    {
        // Do something with each result
    }
}
```

Summary

In this chapter, we learned about what an ORM is and how many benefits it has when we work with databases. After that, we had a look at Entity Framework Core and connected our API to a database using two approaches, code first and database first, and we added our first migration.

CHAPTER 7

Getting Organized

In this chapter, we will take our first step into organizing our project into separate layers. We will add class libraries, move some code around, populate our database, and have a working endpoint at the end.

A **class library** is a collection of reusable code that can be used by multiple applications. It consists of a set of classes, interfaces, and other types that define common functionality that can be used across different projects. Its purpose is to be used by other projects, and it can't function as a standalone application.

Now, you will hear a lot of debate around the split we will make here. Some developers prefer to make folders instead of class libraries because they consider it to be easier, or consider the layers split unnecessary.

The reason I prefer doing it here is that you will often find that real-life applications have more than one project in the solution, and I want you to become familiar with working with other project types too. Another reason I want to do this split is that the difference between what is a *model* and what is a *domain* object becomes clear.

Everything we apply in this book in terms of code has an ulterior didactic reason, and that's why I ask you to follow along.

© Irina Dominte 2023
I. Dominte, *Web API Development for the Absolute Beginner*,
https://doi.org/10.1007/978-1-4842-9348-5_7

Splitting Code into Layers

Splitting code into layers is a common design practice in software development and has several benefits, as follows:

- **Separation of concerns** – Layers allow developers to separate different concerns and responsibilities within an application. This makes the code easier to understand, maintain, and test, as each layer has a specific responsibility and can be modified and tested independently.

- **Reusability** – By breaking down the code into smaller, reusable components, developers can write less code, reduce duplication, and increase the overall maintainability of the application.

- **Testability** – Layers can be tested individually, making it easier to identify and fix bugs and improve the quality of the code.

- **Scalability** – By separating the code into layers, it's easier to add new features and scale the application without affecting existing functionality.

- **Flexibility** – Code that is organized into layers is easier to modify, refactor, or replace without affecting the rest of the application.

Overall, splitting code into layers helps to structure the code, make it more maintainable, and improve the overall quality and stability of the application.

Figure 7-1 shows an outside-in view of our target application. Any request will go through our API endpoints—and all the infrastructure related to our API—and pass through the service layer and data layer, working its way to the database. The domain layer can be considered a "helper" layer because it simply holds the entities.

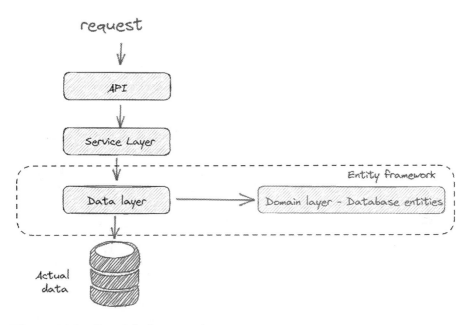

Figure 7-1. *Outside-in overview*

In our code, each of the mentioned layers will be a separate class library.

In the end, code-wise, our application will have separate layers, as shown in Figure 7-2. We will start with the domain and work our way up to the controllers in ConferenceAPI. This will give us a better understanding of how a request will travel from the API level to the database and back.

Figure 7-2. *Target project architecture*

In the source code folder under the ch07/start folder, open our project. Here, right-click on the solution icon, and select "Add new project."

From the options list, select Add ➤ New Project ➤ Class library (Figure 7-3).

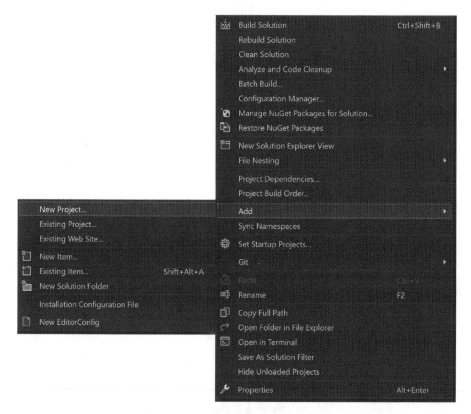

Figure 7-3. *Add New Project*

Use this option to add three new class libraries, named as follows:

- Conference.Data

- Conference.Domain

- Conference.Service

You can give them any names you like, as long as you know what their scope is, but I like to use this common convention. Subjectively, I find it keeps the solution tidy. In the next section, we will re-scaffold the database and, layer by layer, refactor our project.

Domain Layer

Our domain layer (`Conference.Domain` project) will contain domain entities (class entities), our database context, and any extensions that we might need.

A domain entity is a representation of a real-world object or concept in the context of the problem domain of a software application. It is a fundamental building block in the domain layer of the application and represents a distinct, meaningful concept in the business domain.

For example, in an e-commerce application, a domain entity might be a customer, an order, a product, or a shopping cart. These entities have properties that describe their state and behavior and define how they interact with other entities in the system.

A domain entity is used to model the domain and provide a foundation for the implementation of business logic and rules.

In our project, we need to recreate the entities by running one of the commands we learned in the previous project. We do this by installing the three required NuGet packages and then navigating, in a command line, to the `Conference.Domain` folder.

NuGet packages required are as follows:

- Microsoft.EntityFrameworkCore.Design

- Microsoft.EntityFrameworkCore

- Microsoft.EntityFrameworkCore.SqlServer

By running the following command, we will end up with our entities in a separate class library, which is desired:

```
dotnet ef dbcontext scaffold "Data Source=(localdb)\
MSSQLLocalDB;Initial Catalog=ConferenceDemo" Microsoft.
EntityFrameworkCore.SqlServer --output-dir Entities  --context
ConferenceContext
```

Now that we have scaffolded our database, let's add the connection string in our application entry point, ConferenceApi. At this point, we have classes in a library, but these are just isolated files and we can't use them.

Open appsettings.json and add a property name ConnectionStrings, as shown in Listing 7-1. You'll notice that as soon you start typing, the IDE will suggest the correct options.

Listing 7-1. An Empty ConnectionStrings Node in appsettings.json

```
{
  "ConnectionStrings": {},
  "Logging": {
    "LogLevel": {
      "Default": "Information",
      "Microsoft.AspNetCore": "Warning"
    }
  },
  "AllowedHosts": "*"
}
```

The ConnectionStrings node is a standard node, under which we can add all the connection strings to our databases (assuming we have more than one). Adding the connection string under this node will provide us with out-of-the-box methods to access it from our Program.cs, the place where we will wire everything together. The platform already has some implementations like GetConnectionString("ConferenceDatabase"), which relies on this node to access the database.

Let's add the correct connection string (the one we used for scaffolding) and give it a name, as shown in Listing 7-2.

Listing 7-2. Our First Connection String

```
"ConnectionStrings": {
  "ConferenceDatabase": "Data Source=(localdb)
  \\MSSQLLocalDB;Initial Catalog=ConferenceDemo"
}
```

We gave our connection string a name, ConferenceDatabase, and we will use this name to register the dependency in Program.cs.

To register the DbContext in our application, we need to use the AddDbContext extension method, as shown in Listing 7-3.

Listing 7-3. Registering the DBContext

```
builder.Services.AddDbContext<ConferenceContext>(options =>
{
        options.UseSqlServer(
builder.Configuration.GetConnectionString(
"ConferenceDatabase"),
    m => m.MigrationsAssembly("Conference.Domain"));
});
```

At this moment, you will notice that the ConferenceContext class used by the extension method is nowhere to be found. We wrote it, but it exists in a separate class library that has nothing to do with our project.

To fix the error, we have to make sure that ConferenceApi knows about our Conference.Domain project and can find the class that we need.

Right-click ConferenceApi's Dependencies node and select "Add project reference," as shown in Figure 7-4.

Figure 7-4. *Add an existing project as a reference*

From here, the next window that is displayed will show us all the project references that we can add, but for the time being, we need only the Conference.Domain one.

We check the option corresponding to the Conference.Domain project, and when the window closes we will be able to import the namespace that contains our ConferenceContext class (Figure 7-5).

```
using Conference.Domain.Entities;
```

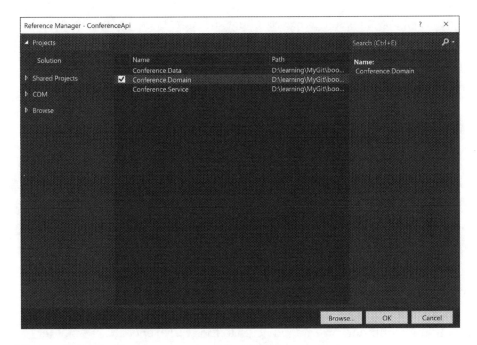

Figure 7-5. *Reference manager for ConferenceApi*

The next step for us is to ensure we have everything in a good state. This means we need to remove the hardcoded connection string we have in the ConferenceContext class and use the ConnectionString we added in appsetting.json.

We can remove the OnConfiguring method in the class, with all the lines shown in Listing 7-4, or use the cli command --no-onconfiguring.

Listing 7-4. ConferenceContext Class

```
protected override void OnConfiguring(DbContextOptions
Builder optionsBuilder)
#warning To protect potentially sensitive information in your
connection string, you should move it out of source code.
You can avoid scaffolding the connection string by using the
```

Name= syntax to read it from the configuration - see https://
go.microsoft.com/fwlink/?linkid=2131148. For more guidance
on storing connection strings, see http://go.microsoft.com/
fwlink/?LinkId=723263.

```
=> optionsBuilder.UseSqlServer("Data Source=(localdb)
\\MSSQLLocalDB;Initial Catalog=ConferenceDemo");
```

The connection string that used to be hardcoded here will be passed through our Dependency Injection container, and the behavior will remain the same. It's not a good practice to hardcode values, especially connection strings, because they are usually different for each environment and get committed to the source control, where are unwittingly exposed.

We have made sure everything is in the right place, and now we need to add an initial migration. We did this before, but we have since added a new project.

In the command prompt, navigate to the Conference.Domain folder, we will have to run dotnet ef migrations add InitialCreate. If we run this as it is, we will be notified that there is no database provider configured for this DbContext, as shown in Figure 7-6.

Figure 7-6. *Migration error*

The error happens because Entity Framework Core doesn't know where to connect to in order to find the database. It can't find the database provider. We are running the command in the Conference.Domain folder, and this project folder has no reference to anything. It has no way of knowing where the database is, or how to connect to it. We passed the connection details in our DI container, in our main application, but in this case, we need to tell the command where to find it.

To fix it and point it in the right direction, we will have to add a --startup-project flag that points to the ConferenceApi folder, like in Listing 7-5.

Listing 7-5. Migrations Pointing to the Project Entry Point

```
dotnet ef migrations add InitialCreate --startup-project
../ConferenceApi
```

Now that we have told the command where to find the connection to the database, it will execute successfully and generate our migrations the same way we have seen in the previous chapter and create a `Migrations` folder in our project (Figure 7-7).

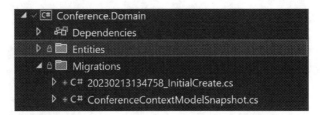

Figure 7-7. *Migrations added*

Data Layer, Implementing a Repository

The data layer in a web application refers to the component responsible for accessing and manipulating data. It is responsible for communicating with the data storage mechanism, such as a database, and providing a consistent and unified interface for accessing and manipulating the data. The data layer often implements data access patterns, such as the repository pattern, which provides a separation between the data storage mechanism and the rest of the application.

This makes it easier to change the data storage mechanism in the future, as only the data layer needs to be modified, rather than the rest of the application. The data layer can also provide caching, filtering, validation, and other data-related services to the rest of the application.

The data layer is a core component of a well-architected web application, as it is responsible for managing the data and providing a unified interface for accessing and manipulating it.

In our case, EF Core `DBSet` classes behave like repositories. We could use them as they are, but our goal is to have a minimum separation of concerns. You will have plenty of time to experiment afterward.

In our `Conference.Data` project we need to add a new file named `SpeakersRepository`; it is where we will implement CRUD methods. Our class needs to access `ConferenceContext` to have access to the database. This means we will need to reference the `Conference.Domain` project.

Right-click the Dependencies node and select the "Add Project reference" option, in the same way we did earlier for `Conference.Domain`. You will endup having something similar to Figure 7-8.

Figure 7-8. *Conference.Data project with Conference.Domain referenced*

In `SpeakersRepository` we will need to inject `ConferenceContext` in the controller and store it as a private field at the class level, as shown in Listing 7-6.

Listing 7-6. SpeakersRepository with ConferenceContext Dependency

```
public class SpeakersRepository
{
    private readonly ConferenceContext context;

    public SpeakersRepository(ConferenceContext context)
    {
        this.context = context;
    }
}
```

The next step in our journey will be to have an interface that SpeakersRepository will implement. These methods will provide CRUD operations for our SpeakersController.

We can start with the definitions in Listing 7-7 and work our way toward implementation.

Listing 7-7. ISpeakersInterface Content

```
public interface ISpeakersRepository
{
    Speaker Add(Speaker newSpeaker);
    IQueryable<Speaker> GetAll();
    Speaker Get(int id);
    Speaker Update(Speaker speaker);
    bool Delete(Speaker speaker);
    bool SpeakerExists(int id);
    bool IsEmailUnique(string email);
}
```

We can use the cursor over the ISpeakersRepository interface and press the "Ctrl+ ." keyboard shortcut.

We can right-click the ISpeakersRepository interface and select "Quick actions and refactorings."

This IDE shortcut will show us a few options, one of which is to implement the interface. Choosing it will save us some precious time, and it will allow the IDE to generate method stubs for us. We can see the options in Figure 7-9.

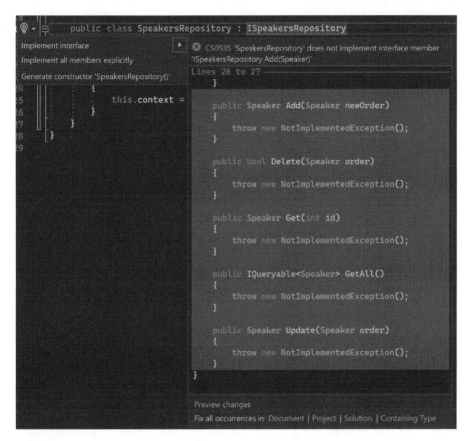

Figure 7-9. *Visual Studio quick action "Implement interface"*

Service Layer

The service layer in a web application refers to the software layer that usually contains business logic and acts as an intermediary between the presentation layer (e.g., the user interface) and the data storage layer (e.g., a database). It is responsible for enforcing business rules, performing data transformations, and providing a consistent interface for data access.

A service layer is used for several reasons, as follows:

- **Separation of Concerns** – The service layer separates the business logic from other parts of the application, allowing for better organization and code maintenance.

- **Reusability** – Services can be reused across different parts of the application, reducing the amount of code duplication and making it easier to make changes in the future.

- **Testability** – The service layer can be tested independent of the rest of the application, making it easier to ensure that the business logic is correct and functioning as intended.

- **Flexibility** – The service layer can be updated or replaced without affecting the rest of the application, making it easier to make changes and improvements to the business logic over time.

Using a service layer is generally considered good practice in web application development, even though at the beginning it acts just as a pass-through layer.

By encapsulating the business logic in a service layer, developers can make changes to the application more easily and with less risk of introducing bugs or breaking existing functionality.

However, it's important to note that like all design patterns and architectural concepts, the use of a service layer is not a one-size-fits-all solution. It depends on the specific requirements and constraints of the application and the team developing it. In some cases, a service layer may be over-engineering or not necessary, and in those cases, alternative approaches should be considered.

Getting back to our code, we need to create a SpeakersService class and a contract for the Conference.Service project (Listing 7-8).

This is similar to what we did for the SpeakersRepository, but the dependency passed in the constructor will not be the ConferenceContext, but the public contract of our repository: ISpeakersRepository.

Listing 7-8. SpeakersService Constructor

```
public class SpeakersService
{
    private readonly ISpeakersRepository
    speakersRepository;

    public SpeakersService(ISpeakersRepository
    speakersRepository)
    {
        this.speakersRepository = speakersRepository;
    }
}
```

We will need to add a reference to our Conference.Data project to have access to anything related to the repositories we implement, as shown in Figure 7-10.

Figure 7-10. *Conference.Service library referencing Conference.Data*

With the reference added we can now focus now on exposing
the same methods through the ISpeakerService as we did for the
ISpeakerRepository, but with a few changes. In Listing 7-9, notice that
the GetAll method now returns an IEnumerable instead of an IQueryable.
These are all the differences for now, but before we end the chapter we will
have more.

Listing 7-9. ISpeakersService Content

```
public interface ISpeakersService
{
    Speaker Add(Speaker newSpeaker);
    IEnumerable<Speaker> GetAll();
    Speaker Get(int id);
    Speaker Update(Speaker speaker);
    bool Delete(Speaker speaker);
    bool CheckIfExists(int id);
    bool IsEmailUnique(string email);

}
```

We will now use the same approach, making sure ISpeakerService is
"implemented" with stubs with the help of Visual Studio. I won't add all
the implementation here because it's redundant, but we should have the
code as shown in Listing 7-10.

Listing 7-10. SpeakerService Signature

```
public class SpeakersService : ISpeakersService
{
...
}
```

We are not done yet, as we need to link everything in our main project, ConferenceApi. At this moment, everything referenced by this project is shown in Figure 7-11.

Figure 7-11. *ConferenceApi and project references*

Now that we have everything prepared, we need to register our dependencies in the Program.cs to make sure the platform will know what concrete implementations to return and for what abstractions, as follows:

```
builder.Services.AddScoped<ISpeakersRepository,
SpeakersRepository>();
builder.Services.AddScoped<ISpeakersService,
SpeakersService>();
```

Introducing AutoMapper

AutoMapper is an object mapping library for .NET. It provides a simple way to convert between objects, such as between a domain model and a view model, without having to write a lot of boilerplate code.

An *object mapping library* is a software library that provides a way to convert between objects, typically in different formats or representations. The term "convert" can be understood as "transform".

Even if two objects have the same properties, one by one, if the name is different, converting from one to another would be tedious work.

In Figure 7-12, converting from a Speaker type as a source to a SpeakerModel type as a destination will require some assignments. Even though our classes have properties with the same name and type, to do a conversion between them we would need to do manual work. This manual work involves taking each property and doing an assignment from the source class to the destination class. Only in this way we can make sure the conversion/transformation is done correctly.

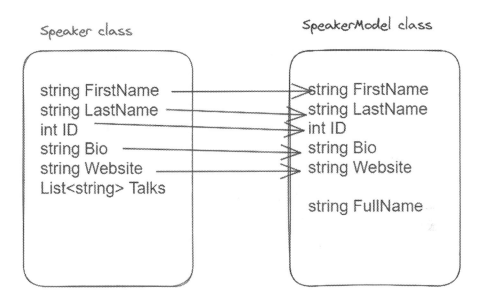

Figure 7-12. *Converting from Speaker to SpeakerModel*

In our example, we have a small number of properties, but imagine having two objects with 40 properties to map from one another.

AutoMapper to the rescue! It will remove this tedious work, and it can even help us map from complex properties or do computations or other things that might come up in the conversion.

AutoMapper uses a configuration-based approach to map between objects. We define the mapping between the source and destination types using a Fluent API or attributes, and then AutoMapper takes care of the rest. It looks at each class member, or we could even configure where to look to find values to map.

AutoMapper uses the conventions we write, called *profiles*, and helps us write cleaner, more maintainable code by simplifying the process of converting between objects.

The main benefits of using AutoMapper are as follows:

- **Simplifies code mapping** – By using AutoMapper, you can avoid writing a lot of manual mapping code, which can be repetitive and error-prone.

- **Increases maintainability** – AutoMapper makes it easy to update your mappings as your application evolves, which makes your code easier to maintain over time.

- **Reduces the risk of introducing bugs** – Having centralized locations for mappings instead of scattering code that transforms objects to other objects all over the place makes the code less error-prone.

- **Improves readability** – By removing manual mapping code, you can make your code more readable and easier to understand.

Installing AutoMapper

To use AutoMapper in our project, we will have to install the following NuGet packages:

- AutoMapper
- AutoMapper.Extensions.Microsoft. DependencyInjection

After we have done that, we need to add the right middleware to our project, as follows:

```
builder.Services.AddAutoMapper(AppDomain.CurrentDomain.
GetAssemblies());
```

The conventions through which we tell AutoMapper how to map an object to another one are simply classes that extend the `Profile` class from the AutoMapper library.

In our project, so far, we will need to map from a `Speaker` object (our domain object) to a `SpeakerModel` object (which we use to return data from the API), and back.

To be able to do that without doing manual assignments, we will create a new folder named `Mappings` in our `ConferenceApi` project, and in there we will add a new class named `SpeakerProfile`. The structure in Figure 7-13 and these names are just suggestions, and you are not required to name them as I do, but it is easier to follow along if you do so.

Figure 7-13. *Adding folders to organize mappings*

The purpose of this folder is to keep all present and future mappings needed for our API.

In Listing 7-11, we extended the AutoMapper's `Profile` class, and in our constructor, we defined a mapping between two types, in one direction, and reverse. These two types won't need additional configuration, as what AutoMapper uses is enough.

Listing 7-11. Mapping from Speaker to SpeakerModel

```
public class SpeakerProfile : Profile
{
    public SpeakerProfile()
    {
        CreateMap<Speaker, SpeakerModel>();
        CreateMap<SpeakerModel, Speaker>();
    }
}
```

With this mapping done, we need to tell the AutoMapper that we created a profile mapping and need it to be considered, which we do by adding `builder.Services.AddAutoMapper(typeof(SpeakerProfile));` in `Program.cs`.

Wire Everything

In the previous sections, we passed through all the steps necessary to build our small project architecture. Now that we have done that, we need to replace our dummy "database" in `SpeakersController` with our actual database.

Revisiting the controller, we need to remove the parameter-less constructor that introduced a hidden dependency and add one that requires an `ISpeakersService` in the constructor, as in Listing 7-12.

Listing 7-12. SpeakersController Constructor

```
private readonly ISpeakersService speakersService;
    public SpeakersController(ISpeakersService
    speakersService)
    {
        this.speakersService = speakersService;
    }
```

Implement SpeakersRepository

To make sure we reach the database, we will need to access the database context, reach into our DBSets, and do operations over them. The DbSet acts like a regular list, and we can use LINQ with it. We can add, remove, update, delete, and filter the results, as we would do with any other List<T>.

For the SpeakersRepository, we already have the interface defined, as it was handled in the previous section, and now we have to implement every single method specified in the interface. In the end, our concrete implementation for this interface will be similar to what is shown in Listing 7-13.

Listing 7-13. SpeakerRepository Full Implementation

```
public class SpeakersRepository : ISpeakersRepository
{
    private readonly ConferenceContext context;

    public SpeakersRepository(ConferenceContext context)
    {
        this.context = context;
    }

    public Speaker Add(Speaker newSpeaker)
    {
        var addedItem = context.Add(newSpeaker).Entity;
        context.SaveChanges();
        return addedItem;
    }

    public bool SpeakerExists(int id)
    {
        return context.Speakers.Find(id) != null;
    }
```

```csharp
public bool Delete(Speaker speaker)
{
  var deleted = context.Speakers.Remove(speaker);
  context.SaveChanges();
  return deleted != null;
}

public Speaker Get(int id)
{
    return context.Speakers.Find(id);
}

public IQueryable<Speaker> GetAll()
{
    return context.Speakers.AsQueryable();
}

public Speaker Update(Speaker speaker)
{
    var updatedEntity = context.Speakers.
    Update(speaker).Entity;
    context.SaveChanges();
    return updatedEntity;

}

public bool IsEmailUnique(string email)
{
    return !context.Speakers.Any(s => s.Email == email);
}
}
```

The methods that modify the database data by removing, adding, or updating records need a call to context.SaveChanges().

The database context also behaves like a Unit of Work pattern by using the ChangeTracker object. As we make changes to instances of our entity classes, these changes are recorded in the ChangeTracker and then written to the database when we call SaveChanges. The database provider is responsible for translating the changes into database-specific operations.

The fact that the context behaves like a unit of work enables us to make several operations and commit them at once, since SaveChanges is transactional.

Let's take an example. For our Add method, although we add a Speaker entity to the Speakers DbSet, the actual database insert is not executed until we call SaveChanges. After this call, the entity is inserted into the database, where it receives a primary key. By accessing the Entity property we can return the item that was just inserted along with its primary key. The Id property of our Speaker object will have a real value now (Listing 7-14).

Listing 7-14. SaveChanges in Add Method

```
public Speaker Add(Speaker newSpeaker)
        {
                var addedItem = context.Add(newSpeaker).Entity;
                context.SaveChanges();
                return addedItem;
        }
```

In our case, the call to commit changes to the database is in the repository method. This means we won't need to call it outside of this method because it happens as part of the Add flow. This works for specific cases when we don't need to commit several operations at once, but in the future, we might consider removing the call from the actual flow by extracting it in a standalone method as shown here:

```
speakerRepository.Add(item);
speakerRepository.SaveChanges();
```

Implement SpeakersService

Since we have the data access all set up, we need to implement the service layer. In this particular case, our SpeakerService class will act as a pass-through, and it won't have additional business logic in the methods. Even so, this layer is the perfect place for any changes that we will need to add in the future. Maybe we will need to add pagination or filters for our results. I know that you might consider it unnecessary, but for learning purposes, we will add and use it. Listing 7-15 shows what a full implementation for our service looks like now.

Listing 7-15. SpeakerService Implementation

```
public class SpeakersService : ISpeakersService
{
    private readonly ISpeakersRepository speakersRepository;

    public SpeakersService(ISpeakersRepository
    speakersRepository)
    {
        this.speakersRepository = speakersRepository;
    }

    public Speaker Add(Speaker newSpeaker)
    {
        return speakersRepository.Add(newSpeaker);
    }

    public bool CheckIfExists(int id)
    {
        return speakersRepository.SpeakerExists(id);
    }
```

```csharp
    public bool Delete(Speaker speaker)
    {
        return speakersRepository.Delete(speaker);
    }

    public Speaker Get(int id)
    {
        return speakersRepository.Get(id);
    }

    public IEnumerable<Speaker> GetAll()
    {
        var speakers = speakersRepository.GetAll();
        return speakers;
    }

    public bool IsEmailUnique(string email)
    {
        return speakersRepository.IsEmailUnique(email);
    }

    public Speaker Update(Speaker speaker)
    {
        return speakersRepository.Update(speaker);
    }
}
```

Make SpeakersController Changes

With two layers implemented, it's time to make changes in our controller
and get rid of our dummy database, SpeakerList, and also put our
mappings to work. We will start by changing the controller and injecting
the right dependencies, IMapper, which is the AutoMapper's interface, and
ISpeakerService, keeping them as private fields at the class level.

Listing 7-16. SpeakersController with IMapper and ISpeakerService
Dependencies

```
private readonly ISpeakersService speakersService;
private readonly IMapper mapper;

public SpeakersController(ISpeakersService speakersService,
IMapper mapper)
{
    this.speakersService = speakersService;
    this.mapper = mapper;
}
```

In the next section, we will see how our actions are changing, and we
will test them in Postman.

Retrieve All Items

The scope of this action is to return the list of all speakers in our system
as a response to HTTP GET requests (Listing 7-17). We will call the GetAll
method of our speaker service for this, and replace the SpeakerList. In the
future, this action can very easily receive an object as a parameter that can
take care of filtering data.

Listing 7-17. GetAll

```
[HttpGet]
public IActionResult GetAll()
{
var speakers = speakersService.GetAll();
return Ok(speakers);
}
```

Now, it's the perfect time to revisit a few of the concepts discussed in a previous chapter about action return types and to clarify a few aspects related to using IActionResult or a concrete type.

Notice that our method returns a list of objects belonging to the domain class. This is of type Speaker, and we mentioned that this is not a good practice. It can be done, but in our case we would want to return a list of SpeakerModel instead of Speaker. This will help us keep things separated and concise, because, as you'll see later, by default, a Speaker object will have a collection of Talks attached, and we don't need that. We want to fine-tune and control everything that is exposed from our endpoints, and we use a model to allow us to do that.

To make the data transformation from Speaker to SpeakerModel, we need to use the mapper. This will help us transform from a source object to a destination object, as shown in Listing 7-18.

Listing 7-18. GetAll with Mappings

```
    [HttpGet]
public IActionResult GetAll()
{
    var speakers = speakersService.GetAll();
    var speakerModels = mapper.Map<IEnumerable<SpeakerModel>>(
    speakers);
    return Ok(speakerModels);
}
```

Another aspect we need to clarify is that of the IActionResult return type.

We know that this is very permissive when it comes to the data returned. It provides a flexible way to return different types of responses, including HTTP status codes, JSON, or XML data. However, it does not provide any information about the data that is being returned from the action method.

In our applications, we should aim to have strongly typed return types because it will help with testing. Also, the code is more clear, since we can tell what the return type is just by looking at the action name. For that, we will replace `IActionResult` with `ActionResult<IEnumerable<Speaker Model>>`.

This is a generic class that implements an `IActionResult`. It allows the action method to return an object of a specific type, T, as well as an HTTP status code. This approach provides a more explicit and type-safe way to return data from an action method that also comes with extra benefits:

- By specifying the type being returned, the compiler can perform additional type checks and ensure that the returned object is of the correct type.

- The client code can directly consume the data returned by the action method without having to perform additional type conversions or deserialization.

- It makes it easier to write unit tests for action methods, as the returned object's type is known beforehand.

Retrieve an Item by an ID

In our `GetById` action, the changed code is highlighted in Listing 7-19. We simply call the `Get` method from `SpeakersService` with the parameter we receive in the URL.

Listing 7-19. GetById Changes

```
[HttpGet("{id}")]
public IActionResult GetbyId(int id)
{
    var speakerToReturn = speakersService.Get(id);
    if (speakerToReturn == null)
```

```
{
    return NotFound();
}
return Ok(speakerToReturn);
}
```

Create a New Item

Our action that accepts POST requests now needs to check if the email sent in the request is unique by checking the actual database data. For that, we implement a method that looks for uniqueness in the database and returns a Boolean value. If we find the email value in the database we will need to notify the caller that we have this internal business rule and stop the execution. On the other hand, if the email check passes, we will insert the new item and return a 201 Created status code, along with a Location header field containing the URL where we can find it. The URL for the Location header field is generated by using the CreatedAtAction method and passing three parameters. The first one is the name of the action taking care of individual item retrieval (GetById), the second is the newly assigned ID of the item, and the third is the actual model or newly added entity (Listing 7-20).

Listing 7-20. Post Action

```
[HttpPost]
public IActionResult Post(SpeakerModel model)
{
    if (!speakersService.IsEmailUnique(model.Email))
    {
        ModelState.AddModelError(nameof(model.Email), "Email
         field should be unique");
        return Conflict(ModelState);
    }
```

```
///transform the entity from model to domain
var speakerToAdd = mapper.Map<Speaker>(model);
speakersService.Add(speakerToAdd);

//return the item with the newly assigned id
return CreatedAtAction(nameof(GetbyId), new { id =
speakerToAdd.Id }, model);
}
```

Update an Existing Item

Our Update action will have the same code structure, with the small change that, this time, we will call the database and retrieve the existing item (Listing 7-21). If the item we are looking for exists, it will update all the properties and send it back to be updated.

Listing 7-21. Update

```
[HttpPut("{id}")]
public IActionResult Update(int id, SpeakerModel model)
{
    var speakerFromDb = speakersService.Get(id);
    if (speakerFromDb == null)
    {
        return NotFound();
    }
    TryUpdateModelAsync(speakerFromDb);
    //update & commit changes in the database
    speakersService.Update(speakerFromDb);

    return Ok(speakerFromDb);
}
```

Delete an Item

To delete an item, we will first need to check if we have such an item. If we don't find it, we need to inform the caller by returning a 404 Not found status code.

Otherwise, we need to retrieve the entire item from the database, remove it, and commit the changes by using our Delete method (Listing 7-22).

Listing 7-22. Delete Action

```
[HttpDelete("{id}")]
public IActionResult Delete(int id)
{
    var speakerFromDb = speakersService.Get(id);
    if (speakerFromDb == null)
    {
        return NotFound();
    }
    speakersService.Delete(speakerFromDb);
    return NoContent();
}
```

Check If an Item Exists

Checking if an item exists using an HTTP Head request means checking if the ID bound from the URL can be found in our database table. If we can't find it, we need to return a 404 Not Found status code, or otherwise a 200 OK.

We could also return an object from the action, but the response sent to the client won't have a body representation, and it would be useless to transfer the entity between the database and the server. One of the powers of HTTP HEAD is that it won't have a response body, thus optimizing a bit the data transfer (Listing 7-23).

Listing 7-23. Head

```
[HttpHead("{id}")]
public IActionResult CheckIfExists(int id)
{
    var speakerToReturn = speakersService.CheckIfExists(id);
    if (speakerToReturn == false)
    {
        return NotFound();
    }
    return Ok();
}
```

Try It Out

Now that you have a complete picture of how things work, you can do a small exercise to test the know-how accumulated so far.

You can implement a Talks controller by yourself, following the same steps we applied for the Speakers controller.

The following is a small list of tasks that you can follow to finish implementing the functionality. Starting from the interface shown in Listing 7-24, provide implementations for everything else.

Listing 7-24. ITalksRepository Interface

```
public interface ITalksRepository
{
    Talk Add(Talk newTalk);
    IQueryable<Talk> GetAll();
    Talk Get(int id);
```

```
Talk Update(Talk talk);
bool Delete(Talk talk);
bool TalkExists(int id);
}
```

Tasks to implement:

- Add a `TalksRepository` class.

- Implement the `ITalksRepository` interface.

- Provide implementation logic for the `ITalksRepository` methods.

- Register the interface and the class in the DI container.

- Add an `ITalksService` interface.

- Add a `TalksService` class that implements the `ITalks` service.

- Register the interface and the class in the DI container.

- Create a controller named `TalksController`.

- Provide a constructor for the controller, injecting the right dependencies.

- Implement a `GetAll` action that returns the list of all talks.

- Implement a `GetById`.

- Implement an `Update`.

- Implement a `Put`.

- Implement a `Delete`.

Summary

In this chapter, we took another step toward developing our full-blown API. We have split our code into separate class libraries and referenced the libraries where we needed them.

We introduced some layers in our small architecture, which is a common practice for organizing the structure of software systems. We delved into the three common layer types in software architecture, namely the domain layer, the data layer, and the service layer. Then, we introduced AutoMapper to help us easily convert between object types. Mapping between different types of objects within the software system plays a critical role when dealing with complex systems that have multiple data sources, and the mapping between the various data models is often necessary.

Then, we made changes to our existing code to use our layers and access the database to retrieve data.

Having a well-organized architecture and the right tools helps teams understand the system's behavior, reduces complexity, and provides a clear separation of concerns, leading to more robust and efficient software systems.

In the next chapter, we will dig deeper into what routing is, implement a route constraint, and see how we can leverage routing to access hierarchical resources.

CHAPTER 8

Routing

We talked briefly about routes in Chapter 4. The routing mechanism determines which action to execute when a request is made to a specific URL, based on templates we define or on conventions already established in the platform.

In this chapter, we will talk more in-depth about routing and review what a route constraint is. I will also focus on defining routes and using them to process incoming requests so that the user can reach the controllers and actions.

By the end of this chapter, you will have a good understanding of routes and the routing mechanism and will be able to define complex routes to fit different business scenarios.

What Is a Route?

A route in a Web API is a pattern that defines how an incoming URL (usually) maps to a specific action in a controller.

For each route template, we can define the following:

- Strings that are expected to always be there

- Strings that are expected to vary

- Default values

- Optional values

- Constraints on segments

© Irina Dominte 2023
I. Dominte, *Web API Development for the Absolute Beginner*,
https://doi.org/10.1007/978-1-4842-9348-5_8

Overall, when it comes to APIs, we create endpoints that expose resources, and these resources need to have a URL that is descriptive or fits the business' needs.

Not only that, but each endpoint also needs to be addressable. We also need to make sure that our API consumers will get the data they expect whenever they call these URLs. This means that we have to make sure that the parameters we have in a URL as part of the path or query strings are valid and allowed.

The routing system has the following functions:

- Examine the incoming URL to figure out, based on all the templates defined, which controller and action will handle the request.

- Generate outgoing URLs.

To make a more childish analogy, the routing mechanism is solving a puzzle every time we make a request and trying to find the right controller and the right action based on the route templates we have defined.

Route Templates

A route template is made of small chunks called segments, and it can contain parameters that get replaced from the URL, have default values, or are fixed strings.

Depending on the type of routing preferred, conventional or attribute-based, the templates are defined globally or individually for each action.

For every action that we want to receive a request, we can define templates that specify the pattern of that URL. For example, we could define a route template to match URLs with a specific format, such as api/{controller}/{action}/{id}.

This way, whenever a consumer issues a request, it will have to have a URL that fits the pattern so that the routing mechanism can identify the right controller and action for it.

The HTTP verb used with the request also helps with the routing matching but only after a pattern is identified.

Table 8-1 shows how a route template can match a URL.

Table 8-1. *Route Pattern Examples*

Route template pattern	Matching URL
`{controller}/{action}/{id?}`	/api/Products/Edit/ /api/Products/Edit/2
`{controller=Products}/{action=Edit}/` `{id}`	/api/products /api/

Route Segments

A segment is a small section separated by the / character. We can have as many fragments as we need. Combined, these fragments make the URL path. ASP.NET is very versatile and allows us to define segments by allowing us to append fixed strings to variable or dynamic ones.

For example, the path /api/{controller}/{action} has three segments (Figure 8-1):

1.   **api** – is a fixed string. This can't be omitted or changed, and it needs to be present in the incoming URL

2. {controller} – will be replaced with the controller
    value in the URL. It can't be omitted, but the value
    for it can change. We can use different controller
    names, and the value will be inferred each time
    from the URL.

3. {action} – will be replaced with the action value
    determined from the URL

Figure 8-1. Segments in an example URL

Static Route Segments

Not all segments in a URL need to be variables. We can have routes that
have static segments that never change no matter what the controller,
action, or verb used. To accomplish this, we don't need to go into every
controller and customize this.

For example, api/speakers can easily be transformed to /api/
internal/speakers or /api/reporting/feedbacks by adding another
segment in the template, like in Listing 8-1.

Listing 8-1. Adding a Static Segment in a Template

```
app.MapControllerRoute(
    name: "internal route",
    pattern: "api/internal/{controller=Values}/{action}");
```

Using the same approach, we can also change the name we require for some segments by appending or prepending strings to the route parameters.

In Listing 8-2, we have an example where we add the prefix My to the name of the controller, which will make our endpoint accessible by using /api/MyValues/getAll.

Listing 8-2. Prepending a String to the Controller Name

```
app.MapControllerRoute(
    name: "internal route prepended",
    pattern: "api/internal/My{controller=Values}/{action}");
```

The text My will be prepended to the ValuesController.

In Listing 8-3, we add the "s" near the parameter, and now we will be able to call /api/valuess/getall to access the endpoint.

Listing 8-3. Appending a Static String to a Controller Name

```
app.MapControllerRoute(
    name: "internal route appended",
    pattern: "api/internal/{controller=Values}S/{action}");
```

Route Parameters

Route parameters are sections of the URL that can vary and help with template matching. These are defined by placing them in braces, such as {id} or {country}. When we declare them like this, the parameters become mandatory segments in a URL, and we need to provide some values for them.

For route parameters, we can define default values, make them optional, or ensure they are valid by using constraints.

- {controller=Values} defines the default controller as being ValuesController. This means that in our URL we could have /api/values, but also /api and we will still end up in ValuesController.

- {id?} makes the parameter named id optional, meaning that the URL can function even without having it present. A matching URL can be /api/Values/2, but also /api/values since the {id?} part can be omitted.

The difference between optional values and default route parameters is as follows:

- A route parameter with a default value always produces a value.

- An optional parameter has a value only when a value is provided by the request URL.

Route Tokens

Route tokens are special constructs made of a series of keywords that have stable meaning that help with template matching. These are reserved keywords, and we will find them often applied to controllers and actions.

These tokens are [action], [area], and [controller]. These get replaced with the values of the action name, area name, and controller name.

Route Values

Route values are the values extracted from a URL based on a given route template. Each parameter defined in the route template will have an actual value extracted from the incoming URL.

Convention-based Routing

Convention-based routing comes from the ASP.NET MVC and was carried over into Web API. The convention-based, or conventional, routing was the first type of routing introduced with the appearance of ASP MVC 2. At that time, it was a major "discovery" and simplified the creation of URLs a lot. I think that was the first moment when developers started to pay attention to what a route should look like.

The conventional default route format handles routes more succinctly, as it has the developer define routes more generically or globally, but it is not the preferred way of working when it comes to Web API.

When we want to use convention-base routing we need to define route patterns in `Program.cs` as shown here. However, these route patterns won't be considered unless we remove the `[ApiController]` attribute from the controllers for which we want to use conventional routing.

```
app.MapControllerRoute(
    name: "default",
    pattern: "{controller=Home}/{action=Index}/{id?}");
```

Attribute Routing

Attribute routing is the preferred routing mode when it comes to APIs. By default, any new controller added will be decorated with the [ApiController] attribute, which makes attribute routing a requirement. This means that actions won't be accessible via conventional routes defined by UseEndpoints, UseMvc, or UseMvcWithDefaultRoute.

To use attribute routing we simply need to decorate controllers and actions with the templates we want, using the [Route] attribute. This type of routing requires more input for each route but allows for precise control of which templates apply to each action.

Each segment defined on an action gets appended to the previous route segments "inherited" from the controller class, if those are defined (Listing 8-4).

Listing 8-4. An Attribute Routing Example

```
[Route("api/[controller]")]
[ApiController]
public class AwesomeController : ControllerBase
{

    [HttpGet]
    public IActionResult MyAction()
    {
        return Ok("Awesome controller-get ");
    }
}
```

In this case, the route token [controller] added to the controller class will be our starting point for URL matching. This means that a URL matching our route template will be /api/awesome because of how things work. The controller name gets replaced in the route token, and our action has no other routing template. At the same time, it is the only action at the controller level that responds to a GET request and is therefore treated as the default.

If we add a few more templates to our action, as shown in Listing 8-5, we will have several URLs that will match.

Listing 8-5. Several Routes Declared on an Action

```
[HttpGet]
[Route("")]
[Route("Home")]
[Route("Home/Index")]
[Route("Home/Index/{id?}")]
public IActionResult MyAction(int? id)
{
    return Ok("Awesome controller-get ");
}
```

First, starting with the pattern defined at the controller level, which in our case is /api/awesome, every segment we define at the action level will be appended to our "root" pattern, for each pattern we define here.

Even our Swagger page will show all the different URLs that will match our controller action, as shown in Figure 8-2.

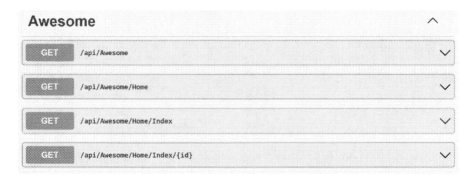

Figure 8-2. *Routes matching our route patterns*

With this being done, we need to look at what happens. Normally, each route pattern defined on top of an action gets constructed by being appended to the route pattern defined on top of the controller. By using defining routes that begin with / or ~/, as shown in Listing 8-6, we are able to prevent them from being constructed this way.

Listing 8-6. Attributes That Exclude the Normal Creation Flow

```
[HttpGet]
[Route("")]
[Route("/Home")]
[Route("/Home/Index")]
[Route("/Home/Index/{id?}")]
public IActionResult MyAction2(int? id)
{
    return Ok("Awesome controller-get ");
}
```

In Figure 8-3 you can see the endpoints Swagger has identified. The first route is the only one that appears to be in the normal generated flow because of the empty string added in the route pattern.

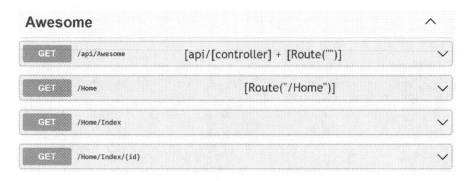

Figure 8-3. *Routes outside of the creation flow*

Furthermore, if we add ~/ to the route pattern on top of an action, we will force the routing mechanism to completely ignore the pattern defined at the controller level.

Looking at Listing 8-7, we have another action named MyAction3 that responds to a GET request. To access it, we will need a URL like this: / instead of /api/MyAction3.

Listing 8-7. Adding a Route as "Root"

```
[HttpGet]
[Route("~/")]
public IActionResult MyAction3(int? id)
{
    return Ok("Awesome controller-get ");
}
```

What we notice now is that the topmost pattern on the controller is completely ignored and the pattern added to our action takes precedence. This way we prevent a route from following the creation convention, and we pull it from the normal flow (Figure 8-4).

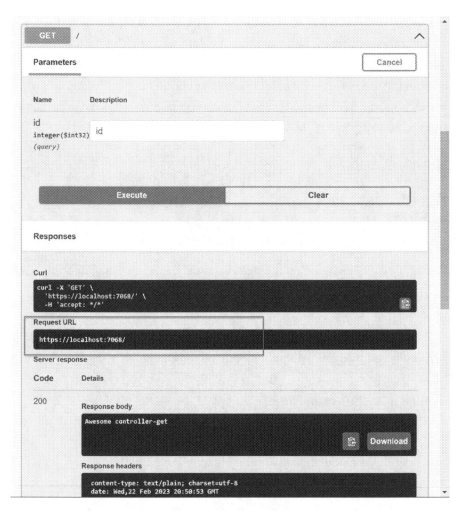

Figure 8-4. Using the browser to test a call

Route Template Precedence

Now that we have covered how we can add different routes to an application and play around with creating complex routes, we need to understand how the route selection works. We might have scenarios where we won't get the result we expect, and here are some possible reasons why:

- Templates with more segments are considered more specific.

- A segment with literal text is considered more specific than a parameter segment.

- A parameter segment with a constraint is considered more specific than one without.

- A complex segment is considered as specific as a parameter segment with a constraint.

- Catch-all parameters are the least specific. See *catch-all* in the "Route Templates" section for important information on catch-all routes.

How to Customize Routing

Customizing routes is part of the development process. Whether we like it or not, whenever we develop functionality, we also need to expose that functionality using a URL. This URL needs to be customized to fit what we want to expose to the outside world. As you will see in the next sections, a controller name might not have anything to do with the URL we are using from the outside.

To summarize, we have a few options when it comes to customizing routes, as follows:

- Route Templates – Used to create routes from a series of input parameters.

- Route Constraints – We can define custom constraints that determine if a URL matches a specific route. For example, you can create a custom constraint to match only integers or to match a specific range of values.

- Route Parameters – We can specify optional or required parameters in our routes. For example, we can specify that a route requires an ID parameter or that it has an optional sort parameter.

- Custom Route Handlers – We can define custom route handlers that handle requests for specific routes. For example, we can create a custom route handler that authenticates a request before processing it.

- Route Ordering – We can control the order of routes by specifying the order in which they are added to the routing configuration. This allows us to specify which routes take precedence over others.

We have all these tools available—we only need the specific scenarios.

Route Constraints

Route constraints in Web API are restrictions applied to a route parameter with the purpose of limiting the range or types of values that can be passed to that parameter. For example, you might want to restrict a route parameter to only allow integer values, be part of an allowed string list, or only accept values that match a specific pattern.

Route constraints are specified as part of the route template and can help to enforce the intended usage of a route, improve the performance of the routing system, and prevent security issues such as URL manipulation attacks. Constraints are separated from the segment variable name with a colon (the : character).

In Listing 8-8, the :int constraint specifies that the id parameter in the route must be an integer. If a request is made with a non-integer value for the id parameter, the routing system will not match this route—it will fall back to the default route (if there is one defined) or will instead return a 404 Not Found status code along with a problem+json message body.

Listing 8-8. Using a Standard Constraint In Table 8-2 we can see a few examples of how a given URL maps to controller and actions

```
[Route("api/products/{id:int}")]
public IActionResult GetProduct(int id)
{
    // Code to retrieve a product with the specified id
}
```

Table 8-2. *URLs Mapped to Controllers*

Example URL	Will map to
/api/speakers/ hello	Controller=Speakers action that responds to a GET Id=null
/api/speakers/1	Controller=Speakers action that responds to a GET Id=1
/api/speakers/1/2	No match, too many segments

Creating a Custom Route Constraint

To create a custom route constraint in Web API, we need to implement the IRouteConstraint interface and register it with the routing system.

The IRouteConstraint interface requires us to implement a single method, Match, which takes two arguments, the HttpContext and the IRouter for the current request, and returns a Boolean indicating whether the constraint is satisfied or not.

Here's an example of a custom route constraint that only matches routes where the value of a parameter is a valid email address (Listing 8-9):

Listing 8-9. Email Constraint

```
public class EmailRouteConstraint : IRouteConstraint
{
    public bool Match(HttpContext httpContext, IRouter
    route, string routeKey, RouteValueDictionary values,
    RouteDirection routeDirection)
    {
        if (!values.TryGetValue(routeKey, out var value) ||
        value == null)
        {
            return false;
        }

        var email = value.ToString();
        return Regex.IsMatch(email, @"^\w+([-+.']\w+)*@\w+([-
        .]\w+)*\.\w+([-.]\w+)*$");
    }
}
```

To use this constraint, we need to register it with the routing system in our Program.cs class (Listing 8-10).

Listing 8-10. Registering the Constraint Map

```
builder.Services.AddRouting(options =>
{
    options.ConstraintMap.Add("email", typeof(EmailRoute
    Constraint));
});

// ...
```

ConstraintMap is a dictionary that allows us to define custom constraints globally and then apply them to specific routes. The name we register here—"email"—is the name of the constraint that we can use globally every time we need to use this constraint, as many times as we need.

To use our custom constraint we simply add it near the route parameter where we want it to be applied (Listing 8-11).

Listing 8-11. Using the Created Constraint

```
[Route("api/users/{email:email}")]
public IActionResult GetUserByEmail(string email)
{
    // Code to retrieve a user with the specified email address
}
```

In this example, the :email constraint specifies that the email parameter in the route must match the custom email constraint. If a request is made with a non-matching value for the email parameter, the routing system will not match this route and will instead return a 404 Not Found error.

Now we can add another endpoint to our SpeakersController that receives an email parameter, as shown in Listing 8-12.

Listing 8-12. Complete Code for Our Action

```
[HttpGet("{email:email}")]
public IActionResult GetByEmail(string email)
{
    Speaker speakerToReturn = null; //speakersService.Get(id);
    if (speakerToReturn == null)
```

```
    {
        return NotFound();
    }
    return Ok(speakerToReturn);
}
```

Available Constraints

In Table 8-3, you can see a small list of already-made constraints that are the most likely to be encountered and also cover a huge number of scenarios.

Table 8-3. *Standard Available Constraints*

Constraint format	Matched format	Description
minlength(value)	{username: minlength(4)}	String must be at least four characters
maxlength(value)	{filename: maxlength(8)}	String must be exactly eight characters long
length(min,max)	{filename: length(8,16)}	String must be at least 8 and no more than 16 characters long
guid	{Id:guid}	Matches a valid Guid value
range(min,max)	{age:range (18,120)}	Integer value must be at least 18 but no more than 120
alpha	{name:alpha}	String must consist of one or more alphabetical characters, a–z, and be case-insensitive.
datetime	{dateOfBirth: datetime}	Matches a valid DateTime value in the invariant culture
bool	{active:bool}	Matches true or false. Case-insensitive

The constraints can even be combined to make sure we cover every scenario we need. You can see some examples here:

- `{id:int:min(1)}`

- `{pubdate:datetime:regex(\\d{4}-\\d{2}-\\d{2})}"` – Will match a date that has this specific form "yyyy-mm-dd". An invalid date such as '2012-56-44 will fail to match because it is not a valid date.

You can see what is available by consulting the following: `https://learn.microsoft.com/en-us/aspnet/core/fundamentals/routing?view=aspnetcore-7.0#route-constraint-reference`.

Creating Hierarchical Routes

In the previous chapter, you had to implement the `Talks` endpoint as an exercise. If you didn't do it, you will find the implementation under the `/ch08/start` folder in the source code. We will leverage the existing implementation and make the needed changes to the route templates so that we will be able to retrieve a talk only if we know the speaker ID.

We will want to access all the speaker's talks, and a specific talk based on the ID, as shown, specific to the two endpoints we learned:

- `/api/speakers/2/talks`

- `/api/speakers/2/talks/10`

We will start by creating a new controller, which we will name `TalksForSpeakersController` since we already have one named `Talks` and we want to leave that as it is. This new controller will have three dependencies, as shown in Listing 8-13.

Listing 8-13. Constructor and State

```
[Route("api/[controller]")]
[ApiController]
public class TalksForSpeakersController : ControllerBase
{
    private readonly ITalksRepository talksRepository;
    private readonly ISpeakersService speakersService;
    private readonly IMapper mapper;

    public TalksForSpeakersController(ITalksRepository
    talksRepository,
        ISpeakersService speakersService, IMapper mapper
    )
    {
        this.talksRepository = talksRepository;
        this.speakersService = speakersService;
        this.mapper = mapper;
    }
}
```

In our controller, we need the following:

- IMapper because we will need to map from a Talk object to a TalkModel class that will be created

- ISpeakersService, allowing us to check if a speaker exists

- ITalksRepository, which contains the code related to talks

In this controller, I wanted to use the ITalksRepository instead of creating a service for it because I wanted to show you that this can also be done.

If you haven't already, we will first add a TalkModel and create an AutoMapper mapping for it as shown in Listing 8-14. This type will be returned from our two actions.

Listing 8-14. TalkModel and Mapping Profile

```
public class TalkModel
{
    public int Id { get; set; }
    public string Title { get; set; } = null!;
    public string Description { get; set; } = null!;
}

  public class TalkProfile : Profile
    {
        public TalkProfile()
        {
            CreateMap<Talk, TalkModel>();
        }
    }

public class TalkProfile : Profile
{
    public TalkProfile()
    {
        CreateMap<Talk, TalkModel>();
    }
}
```

Next on our list would be to add an action responding to a GET request, from which we will return a list of TalkModel for the specified SpeakerId (Listing 8-15).

Listing 8-15. Implementation of GetTalksForSpeaker

```
[HttpGet]
public ActionResult<IEnumerable<TalkModel>>
GetTalksForSpeaker(int speakerId)
{
    if (!speakersService.CheckIfExists(speakerId))
    {
        return NotFound();
    }
var talksForSpeaker = talksRepository.GetTalksForSpeaker(
speakerId);
var talkModels = mapper.Map<IEnumerable<TalkModel>>(talksFor
Speaker).ToList();
return Ok(talkModels);
}
```

The code can be written more concisely, but I prefer to write it as verbosely as I can because it is easier to understand each step.

Returning to the routing part, our controller needs to be accessed only by passing a speakerId parameter, and we will add the route attribute shown in Listing 8-16. Adding this will force every action in our controller to be accessed by using this as the "root" URL.

The {speakerId} route parameter will be populated from the URL and bound by the Model Binding mechanism to the action's parameter.

Listing 8-16. Controller-level Route Template

```
[Route("api/speakers/{speakerId}/talks")]
[ApiController]
public class TalksForSpeakersController : ControllerBase{...}
```

In Figure 8-5 you can see a one-to-one mapping from a URL to a route template. If the URL segments match the template, the parameters in the route will be bound to the parameters.

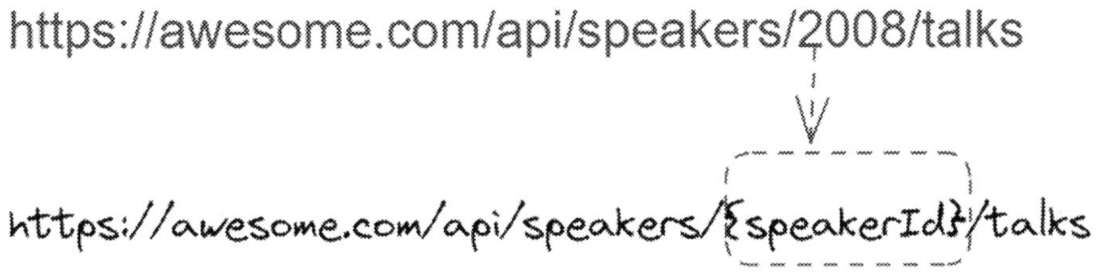

https://awesome.com/api/speakers/2008/talks

https://awesome.com/api/speakers/{speakerId}/talks

Figure 8-5. *Parameter binding*

Now if we look at the Swagger starting page, shown in Figure 8-6, it has picked up our new action and displays it under the documentation list.

TalksForSpeakers

`GET`   `/api/speakers/{speakerId}/talks`

Figure 8-6. *Talks for speakers*

Now, let's try to make a request to the endpoint using Postman. Open Postman and in the URL section write or copy the URL path: `https://localhost:7068/api/speakers/2008/talks`.

If we pass 2008 as the value of the `speakerId` we will obtain the list of talks for our speaker, as shown in Figure 8-7.

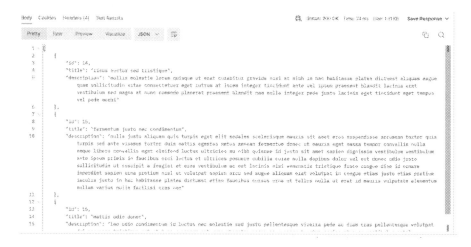

Figure 8-7. *Response to our request*

Similarly, since we now have the "root" URL already defined for our controller, we can add the next action, which returns a specific talk for a specific speaker.

When we implement this action, we will add another parameter corresponding to the ID of the talk, as shown in Listing 8-17.

Listing 8-17. Adding the Action-level Parameter

```
[HttpGet("{talkId}", Name = "GetTalkForSpeaker")]
public ActionResult<TalkModel> GetTalkForSpeaker(int speakerId,
int talkId)
{
}
```

This second parameter will also be bound from the URL only if the first part of the URL matches the route template. The first part is "inherited" from the controller Route("api/speakers/{speakerId}/talks")], and then the second part is appended, [HttpGet("{talkId}].

In our case, if the route matches, both parameters of the GetTalkForSpeaker will have a value. In Listing 8-18, you can see the full implementation of the method.

Listing 8-18. Full Implementation of GetTalksForSpeaker

```
[HttpGet("{talkId}", Name = "GetTalkForSpeaker")]
public ActionResult<TalkModel> GetTalksForSpeaker(int
speakerId, int talkId)
{
    if (!speakersService.CheckIfExists(speakerId))
    {
        return NotFound();
    }

    var talkForSpeaker = talksRepository.GetTalk(speakerId,
    talkId);

    if (talkForSpeaker == null)
    {
        return NotFound();
    }
    var talk = talksRepository.GetTalksForSpeaker(speakerId);
    var talkModel = mapper.Map<IEnumerable<TalkModel>>(talk);
    return Ok(talkModel);
}
```

In our method, I chose to check the existence of both the speaker and the talk and return a 404 Not found status code for each, or the talk itself if we find it. This way, we prevent asking for data in the URL that we don't use at all.

Issuing a request to `https://localhost:7068/api/speakers/2008/talks/15` will result in a `200 OK` status code, with a response body, since we know this talk belongs to this specific speaker.

In any other cases, we will have to return an appropriate status code.

Summary

In this chapter, we learned what all the route components are and how these fit into the larger URL and model-binding ecosystem. We learned how to create a custom route constraint and use it, and then we learned that the controller name we have doesn't necessarily have to be visible to the URL. We then created our first hierarchical route.

In the next chapter, we will take a deeper look at what a middleware component is and how we can insert functionality into the request pipeline.

CHAPTER 9

Middleware

In web development, the term *middleware* often refers to software that acts as an intermediary between an operating system and the applications running on it. In the context of a Web API, middleware is a layer that sits between the incoming HTTP requests and the application's final response (Figure 9-1).

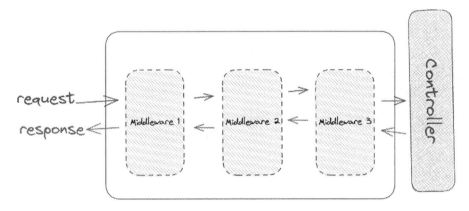

Figure 9-1. *Middleware ecosystem*

Middleware is a C# class that handles requests and responses, adds additional functionality (e.g., authentication, logging, input validation), and controls the response execution flow.

© Irina Dominte 2023
I. Dominte, *Web API Development for the Absolute Beginner*,
https://doi.org/10.1007/978-1-4842-9348-5_9

Middleware can do several things, such as the following:

- Handle requests and generate HTTP responses

- Handle the request, modify the request, and pass it on to other middleware

- Process an outgoing HTTP response, modify it, and pass it to other middleware

A pipeline can be thought of as a series of steps or stages that a request goes through before a response is generated. Think of it as a factory assembly line, where each worker (piece of middleware) has a specific job to do in order to create a finished product. In the same way, a request to a Web API goes through a series of steps, or middleware components, before a response is generated.

The pipeline helps to ensure that each request is handled consistently and that the necessary functions are performed in the correct order.

Middleware components are pluggable request/response pipeline blocks that are executed in a specific order, as shown in Figure 9-2. In this figure, Middleware 3 gets inserted between the last two middleware components, and their order of execution changes. Number three becomes number four in the execution chain.

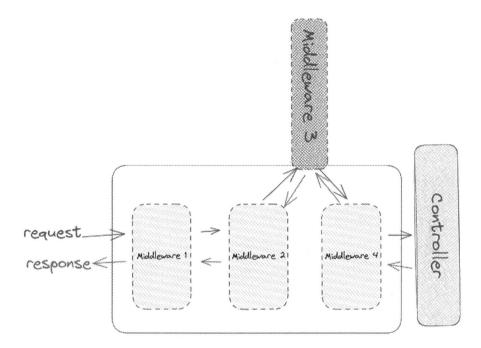

Figure 9-2. *Adding another middleware in the pipeline*

These middleware components allow developers to build reusable components that can be easily added or removed from the pipeline as needed.

There are many middleware components available out of the box for Web API, but we will name just a few. You can see an extensive list <u>here</u>, in the official documentation. They include the following:

- **Authentication middleware** – Implements authentication mechanisms such as cookies, JWT tokens, or OAuth.

- **Authorization middleware** – Controls access to resources based on user roles and permissions.

- **Routing middleware** – Routes incoming requests to the correct endpoint based on the URL.

- **Exception-handling middleware** – Captures and logs any unhandled exceptions that occur during the processing of a request.

- **CORS middleware** – Implements Cross-Origin Resource Sharing (CORS) to allow communication between different domains.

- **Static file middleware** – Serves static files, such as HTML, CSS, and JavaScript files.

- **Request-logging middleware** – Logs incoming requests for debugging and auditing purposes.

- **Request body parsing middleware** – Parses the body of an incoming request and maps it to an object.

These are just a few examples of the many middleware components that can be used in a Web API. The specific middleware used will depend on the requirements of the application.

We already covered the `Map` and `MapWhen` scenarios in Chapter 3, and in the next sections we will focus on understanding how full-fledged middleware can be used. These are more likely to be encountered in real life.

Middleware Usage Scenarios

Before .NET Core we had different mechanisms. In most cases, custom middleware was used to log information about the current request.

Usage scenarios could be as follows:

- Log information about the current request.

- Associate the request with a relevant user by decoding some tokens.

- Set the language or culture for the current request.

- Extract a custom value from a header.

- Add or remove headers.

Introducing Custom Middleware

As I mentioned, middleware are just C# classes that have access to the current HttpContext and can be plugged into the request pipeline. To have such a class we need to respect a few requirements.

HttpContext is a fundamental object that encapsulates all HTTP-specific information about an individual HTTP request and response. It provides access to information such as the request headers, query string parameters, form data, and response headers, as well as other contextual information related to the request and response. This object is created by the runtime for each incoming HTTP request to a Web API, and it is then used by the pipeline to handle the request and generate a response. The object is passed through the pipeline to each stage of processing, where it can be accessed and modified as needed.

No matter the intended purpose, any class that wants to play the middleware role must include the following:

- A public constructor with a parameter of type RequestDelegate.

- A public method named Invoke or InvokeAsync.

This method must do the following:

- Return a Task.

- Accept a first parameter of type HttpContext.

You can see in Listing 9-1 a skeleton for such a class. The actual logic will be written in the InvokeAsync method.

Listing 9-1. A Skeleton of a Middleware

```
public class ExampleMiddleware
{
    private readonly RequestDelegate _next;

    public ExampleMiddleware(RequestDelegate next)
    {
        _next = next;
    }

    public async Task InvokeAsync(HttpContext context)
    {
        //do something
        // Call the next delegate/middleware in the pipeline.
        await _next(context);
    }
}
```

There might be cases when we need to access other parameters along with the required parameters—ones that get their values from the Dependency Injection Container. Middleware components can resolve their dependencies through constructor parameters, as long as those are explicit.

In terms of lifetimes, middleware components are constructed when the application starts. Therefore they live as long as the application is up and running, and we need to pay a little extra attention to what types we are using here.

Create Your Own Middleware to Add Headers

Having to work with custom middleware components is not unusual. Some libraries give access to their functionality by exposing an extension method that wraps their internal logic, or a middleware component. This is very useful because we can toggle features and functionality as needed.

Now, let's get started and create a new class called SecurityHeadersMiddleware and follow the skeleton we talked about, as shown in Listing 9-2. For the moment, before passing the control to the next middleware, add the highlighted line. This line will add a header property named We with the value AreAwesome.

Listing 9-2. Our Security Middleware

```
public class SecurityHeadersMiddleware
{
    private readonly RequestDelegate next;

    public SecurityHeadersMiddleware(RequestDelegate next)
    {
        this.next = next;
    }

    public async Task Invoke(HttpContext httpContext)
    {
        httpContext.Response.Headers.Add("We", "AreAwesome");
        await this.next.Invoke(httpContext);
    }
}
```

Now we have the code, but it has not been added to the pipeline yet. To add it, we will create an extension method.

Making an Extension Method for Our Middleware

Creating extension methods to wrap middleware components is a good practice because it keeps the code tidy and doesn't pollute the class that bootstraps your application.

Add a new file named MiddlewareExtensions to hold the middleware-related extensions (Listing 9-3). Make this class static, since we need only one instance per application, and we will have only extension methods inside.

Listing 9-3. MiddlewareExtension Class

```
public static class MiddlewareExtensions
{
}
```

Inside the empty class, we need to add our actual code for the extension method. For this, we need to extend the IApplicationBuilder class, which allows us to insert code into the pipeline ourselves, as shown in Listing 9-4. Here, we named the extension method UseSecurityHeaders because it follows the same naming conventions as built-in middleware, and inside it returns a call to the generic method UseMiddleware<T>, where T is our class containing all the logic.

Listing 9-4. Extension Methods for Our Middleware

```
public static IApplicationBuilder UseSecurityHeaders(this
IApplicationBuilder application)
{
 return application.UseMiddleware<SecurityHeadersMiddleware>();
}
```

Next, to see it in action, we will add our UseSecurityHeaders call right after the UseAuthorization(), as shown in Figure 9-3. Doing this will allow the insertion of our functionality into the pipeline, as Middleware 3 was in Figure 9-2.

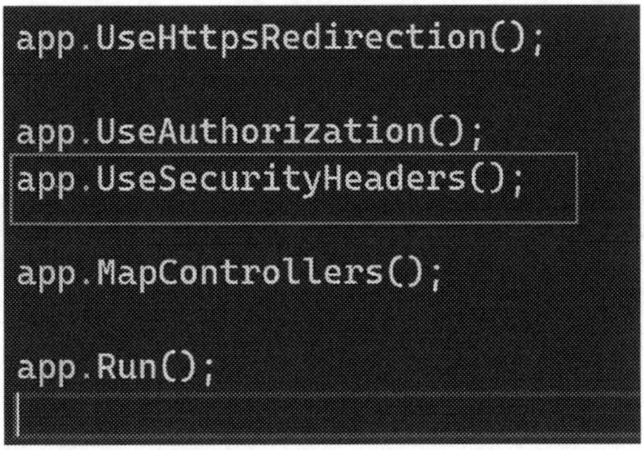

```
app.UseHttpsRedirection();

app.UseAuthorization();
app.UseSecurityHeaders();

app.MapControllers();

app.Run();
```

Figure 9-3. *Using the extension method*

Now let's make a test call to one of our endpoints, let's say /api/ speakers (Figure 9-4).

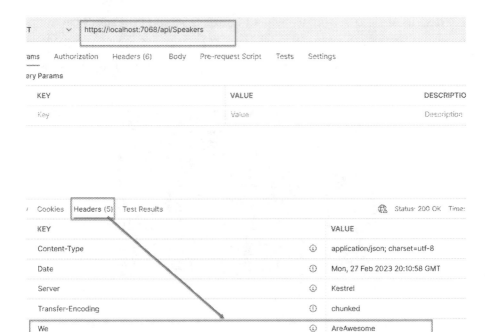

Figure 9-4. *We = AreAwesome header added by the middleware*

We see this working as expected, and now we can add some header fields, which can be used with real-world applications, as shown in Listing 9-5. These headers play an important role when it comes to security audits, and each of them will be explained briefly in the next section, "Understanding the Security Headers We Added."

Listing 9-5. Adding Security-related Headers

```
httpContext.Response.Headers.Add("X-Xss-Protection", "1;
mode=block");
httpContext.Response.Headers.Add("X-Content-Type-Options ",
"nosniff");
httpContext.Response.Headers.Add("X-Frame-Options", "DENY");
httpContext.Response.Headers.Add("X-Permitted-Cross-Domain-
Policies", "none");
```

Understanding the Security Headers We Added

Security headers are directives that browsers or API consumers must follow and travel with the response. Some of these play an a major role in security attack prevention, and is important at least to mention the most common.

X-Content-Type-Options

The X-Content-Type-Options header is an HTTP response header that is used to control how the browser should handle content–type mismatches between the declared MIME type and the actual content of a resource. This header can help protect web applications from MIME-type sniffing attacks, which occur when an attacker tricks a browser into interpreting a file as a different MIME type than what it actually is, potentially leading to security vulnerabilities.

The X-Content-Type-Options header has only one possible value, as follows:

- **Nosniff** – This value instructs the browser to prevent MIME-type sniffing and to always respect the declared MIME type of a resource, rather than trying to infer it based on the content of the file.

X-Frame-Options

X-frame-options is used to control whether a web page can be displayed inside an iframe on another website. In an API context, the X-Frame-Options header can be used to prevent clickjacking attacks, where an attacker attempts to trick a user into clicking a button or link on a web page that is hidden inside an iframe.

The X-Frame-Options header can have one of the following values:

- DENY – This value instructs the browser to prevent the web page's being displayed inside an iframe on any website. This is the most secure option but can also break some legitimate uses of iframes.

271

- SAMEORIGIN – This value instructs the browser to allow the web page to be displayed inside an iframe on the same domain as the parent web page. This can be useful for legitimate uses of iframes, such as displaying content from the same domain in a separate frame.

- ALLOW-FROM URI – This value instructs the browser to allow the web page to be displayed inside an iframe on the specified domain or URL. This can be useful for legitimate uses of iframes, such as embedding a video from a trusted third-party site.

X-Permitted-Cross-Domain-Policies

The X-Permitted-Cross-Domain-Policies header field is a security-related HTTP response header that is used to control whether and how content from different domains can be loaded and accessed within a web application. This header is used as a defense against cross-site scripting (XSS) attacks and clickjacking attacks.

When a web browser receives a response from a web server that includes the X-Permitted-Cross-Domain-Policies header field, the browser will use the information in this header to determine whether it is allowed to load content from other domains within the web application. The header field can include one of the following values:

- none – Indicates that no cross-domain policies are permitted and content from other domains will not be loaded.

- master-only – Allows content to be loaded from the same domain as the web application, but not from any other domains.

- `by-content-type` – Allows content to be loaded from other domains that have been declared safe by the web application based on the content type of the resource being loaded (e.g., images, scripts, or stylesheets).

- `by-ftp-filename` – Allows content to be loaded from other domains that have been declared safe based on the filename of the resource being loaded.

- `all` – Allows content to be loaded from any domain.

By setting the `X-Permitted-Cross-Domain-Policies` header field to an appropriate value, web developers can help protect their web applications from attacks that attempt to load malicious content from other domains. It is recommended that web developers set this header field to an appropriate value based on the security requirements of their web application.

X-XSS-Protection

The `X-XSS-Protection` header can have one of the following values:

- `0` – Disables the browser's built-in XSS protection mechanism. This is not recommended as it leaves the web application vulnerable to XSS attacks.

- `1` – Enables the browser's built-in XSS protection mechanism, which will attempt to block potentially dangerous content.

- `1; mode=block` – Enables the browser's built-in XSS protection mechanism and instructs the browser to block the entire page if it detects any potentially dangerous content.

By setting the X-XSS-Protection header to an appropriate value, web developers can help protect their Web APIs from XSS attacks. However, it is important to note that this header should not be relied upon as the only defense against XSS attacks. Developers should also implement other security measures, such as input validation and output encoding, to further reduce the risk of XSS vulnerabilities.

Summary

In this chapter, we learned that middleware is a core component of Web API. It has access to both incoming requests and outgoing responses. By using these small classes we can inject functionality into the pipeline that may perform some processing logic and then pass that request to the next middleware for further processing, or may terminate (short-circuit) the request pipeline whenever required. These small components are executed in the order in which they are added to the pipeline, and it is very important to control this order because changes might have unwanted effects.

PART III

Beyond Basics

CHAPTER 10

Model Binding

In this chapter, we will learn about different ways we can customize default behavior to obtain values for the parameters bound to our actions. We will learn how to create our own model binder, modify the place from which a parameter value is bound, and exclude parameters from the binding process.

What Is Model Binding?

Model binding in Web API is the process of mapping data received in an HTTP request to a model or a parameter in a controller action. It allows the framework to automatically populate objects with data from the request based on the HTTP method and the data format.

When a Web API controller action is executed, the framework inspects the incoming HTTP request to determine how to bind the request data to the parameters of the action method. This process is called parameter binding. If the parameters of the action method match the names of values in the HTTP request, and the routing constraints are satisfied, the framework automatically maps the data to the corresponding parameters.

This is easy to observe if the parameters are bound from the URL, but not so obvious if the parameters come from a request's body or headers.

If we look at Figure 10-1, the binding is quite straightforward. This is populated from the route because we defined the route template as such and the route matches.

© Irina Dominte 2023
I. Dominte, *Web API Development for the Absolute Beginner*,
https://doi.org/10.1007/978-1-4842-9348-5_10

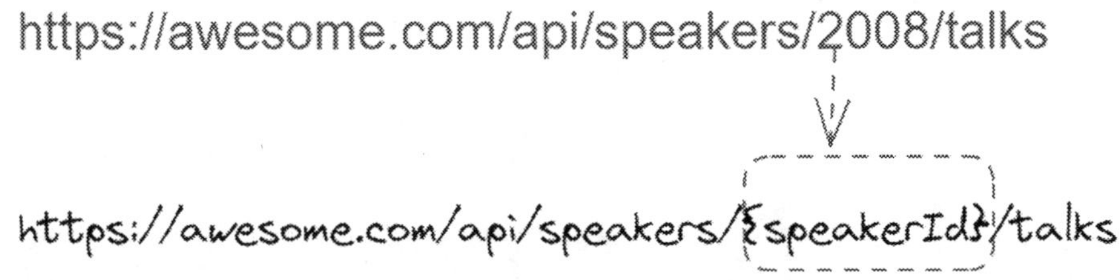

https://awesome.com/api/speakers/2008/talks

https://awesome.com/api/speakers/{speakerId}/talks

Figure 10-1. *Binding a parameter from a route*

Model binding is a smart and simple "translator" between an HTTP request and a C# action method. It lets us declare actions with parameters (complex or simple ones), and, like magic, the parameters will get values, without intervention. We won't have to inspect, parse, or process the incoming data unless we want to make a special model binder.

When it comes to model binding and action parameters we can perform a few operations, such as the following:

- Bind from simple types – such as int, strings, decimals

- Bind from complex types – Allows data from the request to be mapped to a model object, rather than just individual parameters. Model binding can be useful when working with complex data structures or when you want to validate the incoming data. You can see an example in Figure 10-2.

- Exclude properties from binding

- Specify the source of binding – We can decorate our model class with attributes that specify how the data in the request should be mapped to the model properties. For example, we can use the [FromBody] attribute to specify that the data should be read from the request body.

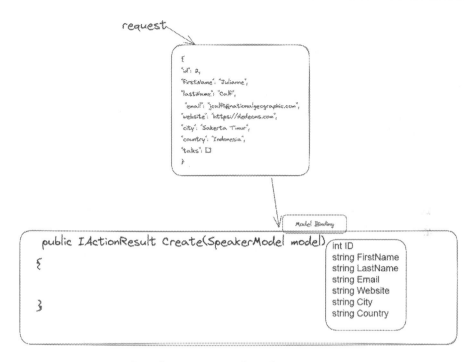

Figure 10-2. *Binding from a complex object*

Model binders can populate almost any data type out of the box as long as the type is common, such as the following:

- Simple types, like `int`, `string`, `DateTime`, and `bool`.

- Complex types, defined by class, record, or struct.

- Collection types, like arrays and lists.

Model-binding Sources

The process of setting values to parameters in actions is relatively straightforward if we point the platform to the place from which we want the values to be set.

For that, we can use one of the available attributes and decorate the parameters and models with them. There are cases when we may need a certain parameter to be bound from a custom header property, and others from the request body or query string. The platform is flexible enough to allow this. In the next section, we will talk individually about each of the source-indicating attributes.

FromRoute

The [FromRoute] attribute is used to bind a parameter in a controller action method to a value from the route data explicitly.

Route data is information that is extracted from the URL of an incoming request and used to determine which controller action method should handle the request. By default, Web API uses the route data to match the names of the parameters in the action method to the corresponding segments in the URL.

Using the [FromRoute] attribute can be helpful when we need to specify the source of a parameter's value explicitly. It can also be useful when we want to customize the binding behavior for a particular parameter, such as by applying custom validation or coercion rules.

FromQuery

FromQuery allows us to bind one or more parameters from the query string of the request, in action's parameters, as follows:

```
public ActionResult<IEnumerable<SpeakerModel>>
GetAll([FromQuery] List<string>? country)
```

FromBody

FromBody will automatically try to search and bind values from the request body. Based on the names and value types it will populate parameters in the action method. This means that, as in Listing 10-1, the values sent in the body will populate the filter object.

Listing 10-1. FromBody Example

```
[HttpGet]
public IActionResult GetAll([FromBody] FilterModel filter)
{
    var speakers = speakersService.GetAll();
    return Ok(speakers);
}
```

FromHeader

FromHeader will allow us to search and bind values from the request's header properties, use them as independent values, and act on them (Listing 10-2).

Listing 10-2. FromHeader and Specifying Header Name

```
[HttpGet]
public IActionResult GetAll([FromHeader(Name = "Accept")]
string accept)
{
    var speakers = speakersService.GetAll();
    return Ok(speakers);
}
```

This means that if we make a request with Accept: custom/media-type, it will be bound to the Accept parameter exactly as it is, as shown in Figure 10-3. From there, we can use the value extracted in our parameters in our code, just as we would with any other parameter.

```
[HttpGet]
0 references | 0 changes | 0 authors, 0 changes
public IActionResult GetAll([FromHeader(Name = "Accept")] string accept)
    < 6.900m elapsed                                    accept   Q View ▾ "custom/media-type"
        var speakers = speakersService.GetAll();
        return Ok(speakers);
}
```

Figure 10-3. *Bind values from headers*

Attribute Scope

When it comes to the scope of where the attributes have applicability, we are talking about the following places:

- **Applied to an action method parameter** – This will have effects only on this instance of that class that is bound for that action method.

  ```
  IActionResult GetAll([FromQuery]
  QueryValues values)
  ```

  In this case, the binding will always be made from the query string, and the QueryValues type can be reused.

- **At the model level** – This has a wider effect on all the actions on which this class will ever be used. In Listing 10-3, the GetAll action method has no binding-related attribute applied, but in the HeaderValues object parameter, each property has a strict indication in regards to where to get its value from.

Listing 10-3. Different Sources for Each Parameter

```
Public IActionResult GetAll(HeaderValues values)
{
...
}
```

```
public class HeaderValues
{
    [FromHeader]
    public string Accept { get; set; }

    [FromHeader(Name = "Culture")]
    public string Culture { get; set; }

    [FromHeader(Name = "Language")]
    public string Language { get; set; }
}
```

This case covers scenarios where we need a more than decent number of parameters in an action and we wrap them in a class, and it also gives us enough flexibility to specify more sources.

Binding-related Attributes

So far, we've seen attributes that can indicate the source of values for a parameter, and now we need to talk about how we can aid, or ignore, the binding process.

Selectively Bind Properties

There are a few attributes already available that let us specify what to bind from the request, or not. These attributes are as follows:

- BindProperties

- BindProperty

- BindNever

In Web API, you can selectively bind properties from an HTTP request to a controller-level property by using the [BindProperties] attribute.

First, we need to annotate the controller with the `BindProperties` attribute. The `SupportsGet` parameter is, by default, set to false, which makes the binding mandatory only for POST requests, but if we set it to True, it will work for GET requests. Once we do this, values will be bound to the class-level property and not to the parameters in the action. You can see in Figure 10-4 how this works.

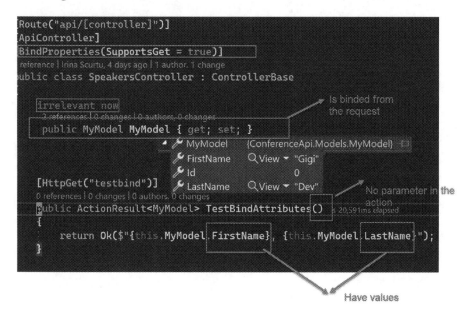

Figure 10-4. *Binding to controller properties*

This is particularly useful when we have parameters that are needed in all actions. This way, we can set them at the controller level and use them from there.

Another attribute that can be used is [BindProperty], which is similar to [ModelBinder] (Listing 10-4). We will talk about it later in this chapter.

Listing 10-4. Bind a Single Property and Specify the Source Name

```
[BindProperty(Name = "user", SupportsGet = true)]
public string username { get; set; }
```

Excluding Properties from Being Bound

In the context where there is a property to hold some state or value at the controller level, there is an attribute that can be applied to prevent the binding from happening. This attribute is [BindNever], and it can be applied to those properties.

In our previous example, you saw the Id property of the MyModel class' being 0, because a [BindNever] was applied on top of it, as shown in Listing 10-5.

Listing 10-5. BindNever Example

```
public class MyModel
{
    [BindNever]
    public int Id { get; set; }

    public string FirstName { get; set; }
    public string LastName { get; set; }
}
```

Create a Custom Model Binder

In this section, we will implement a custom model binder that receives a simple parameter (an ID) and populates an entire object action parameter.

For this, we will rewrite our GetById action in the Speakers controller to have a different signature than before, as shown in Listing 10-6.

Listing 10-6. Specify a ModelBinder

```
[HttpGet("{id}")]
public IActionResult GetbyId([ModelBinder(Name = "id")]
SpeakerModel speaker)
{
}
```

Our action will have a `SpeakerModel` object as a parameter instead of a simple ID, as we had before—`public IActionResult GetbyId(int id).`

This will require the following steps:

- Receive a simple parameter.

- Uses Entity Framework Core to fetch the entity with the ID sent in the request.

- Populate the associated entity as an argument to the action method.

We will start by adding a new class named `SpeakerEntityBinder` that implements `IModelBinder`.

This interface asks us to implement a single member, named `BindModelAsync`, which will give us access to a `ModelBindingContext` object. From this context we can extract useful information related to binding, allowing us to intervene in the process (Listing 10-7).

Listing 10-7. ModelBinder Example

```
public class ExampleBinder : IModelBinder
{
  public Task BindModelAsync(ModelBindingContext
  bindingContext)
  {
    throw new NotImplementedException();
  }
}
```

Getting back to implementing our class, we can inject dependencies in the constructor. In our case, we will inject the ConferenceContext and the Imapper.

In Listing 10-8, you can see the constructor and dependencies for our class.

Listing 10-8. SpeakerEntityBinder Dependencies

```
public class SpeakerEntityBinder : IModelBinder
{
        private readonly ConferenceContext _context;
        private readonly IMapper mapper;

        public SpeakerEntityBinder(ConferenceContext context,
        IMapper mapper)
        {
            _context = context;
            this.mapper = mapper;
        }}
}
```

We need the database to search for a speaker by the ID received as a parameter, and we need the IMapper for transforming the Speaker entity we retrieve to a SpeakerModel since this is the object we are using in the controller.

In this phase, we need to access the context, take the model name, extract its value, and, based on that, do all the other operations.

Next, we will start adding small pieces of code; I will explain them step by step.

1. Check if the binding context is not null and throw an exception if it is. This part can also be skipped, but I add it to emphasize that it is very important to validate parameters, especially in such important constructs:

```
public Task BindModelAsync(ModelBindingContext
bindingContext)
{
 if (bindingContext == null)
 {
    throw new ArgumentNullException(nameof(binding
    Context));
 }
}
```

2. Get the name of the model from the
    `ModelBindingContext`:

    ```
    var modelName = bindingContext.ModelName;
    ```

3. Use the extracted name and check if there is
    a value associated. If there is no value, return
    a `CompletedTask` and stop everything else by
    returning the following:

    ```
    // Try to fetch the value of the argument by name
     var valueProviderResult = bindingContext.
     ValueProvider.GetValue(modelName);

    if (valueProviderResult == ValueProviderResult.None)
    {
        return Task.CompletedTask;
    }
    ```

4. Set the newly extracted value on the `ModelState`:

    ```
    bindingContext.ModelState.SetModelValue(modelName,
    valueProviderResult);
    ```

5. Check if the argument is null or empty and terminate the execution:

```
if (string.IsNullOrEmpty(value))
{
    return Task.CompletedTask;
}
```

6. Try to parse the extracted value to ensure we don't allow string values. We could also enforce this on the routing, but it is good practice to prevent it here too. If the passed value is a non-integer we will cause an error and stop the execution:

```
if (!int.TryParse(value, out var id))
{
    // Non-integer arguments result in model
    state errors
    bindingContext.ModelState.TryAddModelError(
        modelName, "Speaker Id must be an integer.");

    return Task.CompletedTask;
}
```

7. Search for the Speaker in the database using the ID we obtained:

```
var model = _context.Speakers.Find(id);
```

8. Convert the Speaker entity to a SpeakerModel object:

```
var finalModel = mapper.Map<SpeakerModel>(model);
```

9. Set the SpeakerModel as a successful binding and
    return a CompletedTask to finish and return from
    the binder:

    ```
    bindingContext.Result = ModelBindingResult.
    Success(finalModel);
    return Task.CompletedTask;
    ```

With all the pieces assembled, we should have the implementation
shown in Listing 10-9.

Listing 10-9. Complete Implementation of SpeakerEntityBinder

```
public Task BindModelAsync(ModelBindingContext bindingContext)
{
    if (bindingContext == null)
    {
        throw new ArgumentNullException(nameof(binding
        Context));
    }

    var modelName = bindingContext.ModelName;

    // Try to fetch the value of the argument by name
    var valueProviderResult = bindingContext.ValueProvider.
    GetValue(modelName);

    if (valueProviderResult == ValueProviderResult.None)
    {
        return Task.CompletedTask;
    }

    bindingContext.ModelState.SetModelValue(modelName,
    valueProviderResult);
```

```
    var value = valueProviderResult.FirstValue;

    // Check if the argument value is null or empty
    if (string.IsNullOrEmpty(value))
    {
        return Task.CompletedTask;
    }

    if (!int.TryParse(value, out var id))
    {
        // Non-integer arguments result in model state errors
        bindingContext.ModelState.TryAddModelError(
            modelName, "Speaker Id must be an integer.");

        return Task.CompletedTask;
    }

    // Model will be null if not found, including for
    //out-of-range id values (0, -3, etc.)
    var model = _context.Speakers.Find(id);

    var finalModel = mapper.Map<SpeakerModel>(model);
    bindingContext.Result = ModelBindingResult.
    Success(finalModel);
    return Task.CompletedTask;
}
```

Using the Custom ModelBinder

With the SpeakerEntityBinder now implemented, we need to use the binder in our code. For that, we will go into our controller and change the signature of the action, as shown in Listing 10-10.

Listing 10-10. Change the Signature of GetById

```
[HttpGet("{id}")]
 public IActionResult GetbyId([ModelBinder(Name = "id")]
 SpeakerModel speaker)
```

We annotate the parameter with the [ModelBinder(Name="id")] attribute, telling the platform that we will need to search for a parameter named "id" in the incoming request.

Next, we go into our SpeakerModel class and annotate it with the [ModelBinder] attribute. This time, we pass it the type of binder we want to use, as shown in Listing 10-11.

Listing 10-11. Specifying a ModelBinder on a Class

```
[ModelBinder(BinderType = typeof(SpeakerEntityBinder))]
public class SpeakerModel
{
}
```

The two annotations we added work in conjunction with each other. The first one takes the string passed as a parameter and passes it on to the binder specified for the SpeakerModel class. This makes it possible to access the bindingContext.ModelName and extract its value.

You can see a schematic of the entire flow in Figure 10-5.

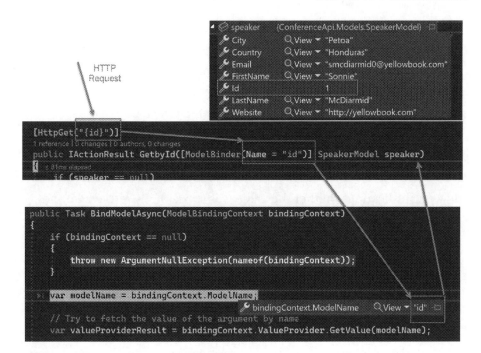

Figure 10-5. *ModelBinding flow*

Value Providers

In the context of C# Web API, a value provider is a component that provides the values for the parameters of a controller action method during the model-binding process. When a Web API controller action is invoked, the framework uses a value provider to retrieve the values for the parameters of the action method.

Value providers can obtain parameter values from various sources, such as query strings, HTTP headers, form data, route parameters, and more. The Web API framework includes several built-in value providers for common sources of parameter values, such as the QueryStringValueProvider and the RouteDataValueProvider.

In addition to the built-in value providers, we can also create our own custom value providers to retrieve parameter values from other sources. To create a custom value provider, we need to implement the IValueProvider interface, which defines a single method, GetValue.

The GetValue method takes two parameters: the name of the parameter to retrieve the value for, and a flag indicating whether to perform a case-insensitive search for the parameter name. The method returns a ValueProviderResult object, which contains the retrieved value and a flag indicating whether the value was successfully retrieved or not.

Listing 10-12 shows an example of a custom value provider that retrieves parameter values from a configuration file.

Listing 10-12. Value Provider Example

```
public class ConfigValueProvider : IValueProvider
{
    private readonly IConfiguration config;

    public ConfigValueProvider(IConfiguration config)
    {
        this.config = config;
    }

    public Task<ValueProviderResult> GetValueAsync(string key)
    {
        string value = this.config[key];

        if (value != null)
        {
            return Task.FromResult(new
            ValueProviderResult(value));
        }
        else
        {
```

```
        return Task.FromResult(ValueProviderResult.None);
      }
   }
}
```

In this example, the `ConfigValueProvider` class retrieves parameter values from an `IConfiguration` object, which is typically populated from a configuration file or other configuration source. The `GetValueAsync` method searches for the parameter value with the specified key in the configuration object and returns a `ValueProviderResult` object containing the retrieved value, if any.

Overall, value providers are an important part of the model-binding process in C# Web API, allowing us to retrieve parameter values from a wide variety of sources and customize the behavior of the framework to suit our needs.

When to Use a Value Provider

In general, we should use a value provider whenever we need to retrieve parameter values from a source that is not directly supported by the built-in model-binding system or when we need to transform the values that come from these sources.

Here are some common scenarios where you might want to use a custom value provider in C# Web API:

- **Retrieving parameter values from a custom data source** – If you have parameter values stored in a custom data source, such as a database or a third-party API, you can create a custom value provider that retrieves the values from that source and returns them to the model-binding system.

- **Converting parameter values to a different data type** – If the parameter values in your API request are in a different format or data type than what is expected by the controller action method, you can create a custom value provider that performs the necessary conversions before returning the values to the model-binding system.

- **Securing parameter values** – If you need to perform custom validation or authorization on the parameter values before they are bound to the controller action method, you can create a custom value provider that performs the necessary security checks and only returns the values if they pass the checks.

Implement a Custom Value Provider

To give a little context, we will need to add one parameter to our GetAll action to allow us to filter the speakers by the country they live in (Listing 10-13). We will change our signature by adding a nullable List<string> named country.

Listing 10-13. Future Method Signature for GetAll

```
[HttpGet]
public ActionResult<IEnumerable<SpeakerModel>>
GetAll([FromQuery] List<string>? country)
{
    ...
}
```

In this section, we will implement our own value provider that will extract a list of countries received as a single query string parameter.

By default, whenever we have lists as parameters for the actions, if we have more than one value passed in the URL, the name of the model needs to be duplicated like this: /api/speakers?country=Romania&country=Germany&Country=France.

In our example, to make the default ModelBinder work, we would need to repeat the name parameter for every new country we would want to include in our filter.

Though such a URL works just fine, it is rather unpleasant and not clean, especially if the string country keeps repeating and exhausts URL characters, or we would have several such filters.

We will fix this repetition issue by writing a value provider that allows us to write a list of countries separated by a comma, like this: /api/speakers?country=Romania,Germany,France.

Without a custom value provider, if we made a request to this URL we would see that only the first item in the list of strings had values, as shown in Figure 10-6. We are working with strings, after all, and it would make sense that the parameter would be bound as a single value.

Figure 10-6. *Binding without the value provider*

Now, we could get this list and split it at the action level, and then use the newly obtained values. From an architectural point of view, that's not the place to do that.

We need a different method that will allow us to reuse the same logic whenever we need lists like these in our code. Let's go ahead and right-click the Infrastructure folder and add there a new folder named ValueProviders. In there, add a new class named CommaQueryStringValueProvider.

This class should extend QueryStringValueProvider since we are using the existing query string (Listing 10-14).

Listing 10-14. CommaQueryString Constructor

```
public class CommaQueryStringValueProvider :
QueryStringValueProvider
{
    private readonly string separator = ",";

    public CommaQueryStringValueProvider(IQueryCollection
    values)
        : base(BindingSource.Query, values, CultureInfo.
        InvariantCulture)
    {
    }
}
```

We add our comma as the separator for this, and we pass parameters to the base constructor, reusing the logic inside the base.

Next on our list is to override the GET method in the base class (Listing 10-15). This will be the place where we actually access the parameter, and if we find them separated by a comma, we will return an actual list.

Listing 10-15. The Implementation of the GetValue Method

```
public override ValueProviderResult GetValue(string key)
{
 var result = base.GetValue(key);
 if (result != ValueProviderResult.None && result.
 Values.Any(x => x.IndexOf(separator, StringComparison.
 OrdinalIgnoreCase) > -1))
 {
```

```
var splitValues = new StringValues(result.Values.
SelectMany(x => x.Trim().Split(new[] { separator },
StringSplitOptions.None)).ToArray());
return new ValueProviderResult(splitValues, result.
Culture);
}

return result;
}
```

Now that we have this implementation, we need to create a ValueProviderFactory that will insert our ValueProvider in the list of already available ones.

Value Provider Factory

In C# Web API, a value provider factory is a component that creates instances of value providers for the model-binding process. Value provider factories are used by the Web API framework to determine which value providers to use for each parameter of a controller action method.

When a Web API request is received, the framework uses the value provider factories to create instances of value providers for each parameter of the controller action method. The value providers are then used to retrieve the parameter values from various sources, such as the query string, form data, route data, HTTP headers, and more.

Value provider factories are typically classes that implement the IValueProviderFactory interface, which defines one method:

- CreateValueProviderAsync – This method creates an instance of a value provider for a specific parameter.

Let's add a new class in our folder and name it
CommaQueryStringValueProviderFactory (Listing 10-16).

Listing 10-16. Implementing CommaQueryStringValue
ProviderFactory

```
public class CommaQueryStringValueProviderFactory :
IValueProviderFactory
{
    public Task CreateValueProviderAsync(ValueProviderFactory
    Context context)
    {
        context.ValueProviders.Insert(0, new
        CommaQueryStringValueProvider(
          context.ActionContext.HttpContext.Request.Query));
        return Task.CompletedTask;
    }
}
```

Our class has the sole purpose of inserting a new instance of our
value provider in the list of all existing providers and passing the required
parameters.

In Web API you will often encounter classes that have a name ending
with the suffix Factory. All of them have the role of creating other
specialized objects and are implementations of the factory design pattern.

To use our CommaQueryStringValueProvider, we have the following
options:

- Register it globally.

- Create an attribute so we can use it selectively
  whenever we apply it.

Apply the Value Provider Globally

To use a value provider globally, we would need to go to `Program.cs` and register it with the `AddControllers`. See Listing 10-17.

Listing 10-17. Registering a Value Provider

```
builder.Services.AddControllers(options =>
{
    options.ValueProviderFactories.Add(
                    new CommaQueryStringValueProvider
                    Factory());
    options.ReturnHttpNotAcceptable = true;
    options.RespectBrowserAcceptHeader = true;
});
```

This way, the `CommaQueryStringProvider` will be executed every single time, even for situations where we don't need a parameter to be checked if it contains a comma and is split into a list.

Apply the Value Provider Selectively Using an Attribute

In Listing 10-18, you can see the best option for using value providers for our case. We create an attribute that we can selectively apply to only the actions that need such a binding (Listing 10-19), provided by our `CommaQueryString`.

Listing 10-18. Creating an Attribute

```
[AttributeUsage(AttributeTargets.Method | AttributeTargets.
Class, Inherited = true, AllowMultiple = false)]
public class CommaQueryStringAttribute : Attribute,
IResourceFilter
{
    private readonly CommaQueryStringValueProviderFactory
    factory;

    public CommaQueryStringAttribute()
    {
        factory = new CommaQueryStringValueProviderFactory();
    }

    public void OnResourceExecuted(ResourceExecutedContext
    context)
    {
        // will be implemented
    }

    public void OnResourceExecuting(ResourceExecutingContext
    context)
    {
        context.ValueProviderFactories.Insert(0, factory);
    }
}
```

Listing 10-19. Using the Attribute on Method

```
[HttpGet]
[CommaQueryString]
```

```
public ActionResult<IEnumerable<SpeakerModel>>
GetAll([FromQuery] List<string>? country)
{
    ...
}
```

Applying our attribute on top of our action will allow us to make sure we have the list specified as a parameter populated correctly, and only when we need to have it. Using the attribute will prevent the value provider from being executed for every single action and prevent small performance penalties.

With our attribute applied, you can see in Figure 10-7 how making a request to the action will populate the parameter correctly, as expected.

Figure 10-7. *CommaQueryString attribute in action*

Summary

This chapter covered the topic of model binding in Web API, which refers to the process of extracting data from an HTTP request to populate an action method's parameters. The various sources of data that can be bound to an action method's parameters were discussed, including FromRoute, FromQuery, FromBody, and FromHeader.

Additionally, we learned that attributes can have different scopes by applying them at the action level or class level. The chapter also delved into binding-related attributes, such as BindRequired, BindNever, and BindProperties, and explained how to selectively bind or exclude properties from the binding process, although these are often avoided in Web API.

The creation of a custom model binder was explained as a way to bind complex types or handle special cases. Furthermore, the chapter discussed value providers, which provide values to model binders, and when it's appropriate to use them. The chapter explained how to implement a custom value provider and how to use a value provider factory to dynamically create value providers.

In conclusion, the chapter emphasized the significance of model binding for creating robust and efficient ASP.NET Core applications. Knowing how to properly bind data to an action method's parameters is crucial for developing dependable and maintainable code. Custom model binders and value providers can be utilized to personalize the model-binding process to meet specific requirements, resulting in improved application performance and flexibility.

CHAPTER 11

Versioning the API

Versioning an API refers to the practice of assigning a unique identifier or version number to each iteration of an API. This is done to enable developers to make changes to the API without disrupting the functionality of applications that depend on it.

The versioning approach depends on the specific needs and requirements of the API and its consumers. However, it is generally recommended to use a consistent and easy-to-understand versioning scheme that is well documented and understood by the API consumers. It is also important to ensure that older versions of the API are supported for a reasonable period of time to allow consumers to migrate to newer versions at their own pace.

When it comes to versioning, the sky is the limit. You can see some examples here, all of which are valid and have a meaning to a specific business:

- /api/foo?api-version=1.0
- /api/foo?api-version=2.0-Alpha
- /api/foo?api-version=2015-05-01.3.0
- /api/v1/foo
- /api/v2.0-Alpha/foo
- /api/v2015-05-01.3.0/foo

© Irina Dominte 2023
I. Dominte, *Web API Development for the Absolute Beginner*,
https://doi.org/10.1007/978-1-4842-9348-5_11

You will often hear the term *semantic versioning*, where the version number has a specific format and each of the numbers has a specific meaning.

The version number sometimes has the format shown here:

```
<major version>.<minor version>.<patch version>
```

- The major version is incremented when there are significant changes that are not always backward compatible with previous versions.

- The minor version is incremented when new functionality is added in a backward-compatible manner.

- The patch version is incremented when minor changes and bug fixes are made.

For example, if the current version of a software product is 2.1.3, this means that it is the second major version, the first minor version, and the third patch version.

If a backward-incompatible change is made, such as removing a feature or changing the API, the major version number should be incremented to indicate that the new version is not backward compatible with the previous version.

If a new feature is added in a backward-compatible manner, the minor version number should be incremented. Finally, if a bug is fixed or a minor improvement is made, the patch version number should be incremented.

Whether the number used for versioning is semantic or not, the place where we add this number is more important.

There are several approaches to versioning an API, including the following:

- **URI versioning or URL path versioning** – In this approach, the version number is included in the URI (Uniform Resource Identifier) of the API, often as a path.

  For example: `https://api.example.com/v1/speakers`.

- **Query parameter versioning** – In this approach, the version number is included as a query parameter in the URI of the API.

  For example: `https://api.example.com/speaker?v=1`

- **Header versioning** – In this approach, the version number is included as a header in the request made to the API.

  For example, the `Accept-Version` header can be used to indicate the version of the API to be used, or `X-Version`, or anything custom and documented can be used.

- **Media type versioning** – In this approach, the version number is included as part of the media type of the response returned by the API.

  For example: The `Content-Type` header can be used to indicate the version of the API response.

Versioning-related Libraries

There are several libraries available that include everything that we need to version an API, but I advise you to use the `Asp.Versioning.Http` NuGet package. It is an open-source library, is well maintained, and is a continuation of one of the official libraries.

In the source code /ch11/start folder, you will find the project with some updates to Program.cs. We will talk about them in Chapter 12, where we discuss documenting our API. I chose to make the updates here to make it easier for you to observe changes.

Getting Started

Open the project, and you will see that the Asp.Versioning package is already installed (Figure 11-1).

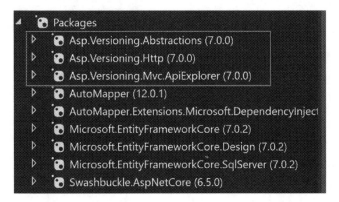

Figure 11-1. *Asp.Versioning* packages*

These packages will give us access to a lot of features related to versioning that we will see in the next sections.

To work with the library, we need to add middleware to our services:

```
builder.Services.AddApiVersioning();
```

Preparing the Project

Our end goal is to see how we can use different types of versioning and how the code might look when we have versioning involved.

We will prepare our SpeakerController to support two different versions. First, we will add a new model named SpeakerModelV2 with the content shown in Listing 11-1.

Listing 11-1. SpeakerModelV2 Class

```
public class SpeakerModelV2
{
 public int Id { get; set; }
 public string FirstName { get; set; }
 public string LastName { get; set; }
 public string Bio { get; set; }
 public string Position { get; set; }
 public string Company { get; set; }
}
```

Then, go to the AutoMapper profiles and register the Speaker to SpeakerModelV2 mapping, as shown in Listing 11-2. We add this now because we already know what the next steps are.

Listing 11-2. Creating Speaker to SpeakerModelV2 Mapping

```
CreateMap<Speaker, SpeakerModelV2>();
```

APIs can evolve or change development directions, and we want to be able to have two different versions (representations) of the same resource.

In this case, version 2 for our SpeakerModel is different, having had a few properties removed and three extra ones added.

Now that we have added the model, let's go ahead and add another controller, named SpeakersControllerV2. This controller will be similar to our previous SpeakersController, and will have the same dependencies, but it will return a new version for one of our actions. You can see in Listing 11-3 what the constructor should look like. For the moment, we will leave everything as it is because we will need to group the two versions under the same umbrella using the [Route] attribute.

Listing 11-3. SpeakersControllerV2 Controller and Dependencies

```
[Route("api/[controller]")]
[ApiController]
public class SpeakersControllerV2 : ControllerBase
{
  private readonly ISpeakersService speakersService;
  private readonly IMapper mapper;

  public SpeakersControllerV2(ISpeakersService speakersService,
  IMapper mapper)
   {
     this.speakersService = speakersService;
     this.mapper = mapper;
   }
}
```

Next, we will focus on one method only, GetbyId. This will be the only action that will have two versions.

In SpeakersControllerV2, copy and paste the GetById action from SpeakersController.

If you run the project now, you will see that the Swagger page has noticed that we have added another endpoint, and it will show it here (Figure 11-2).

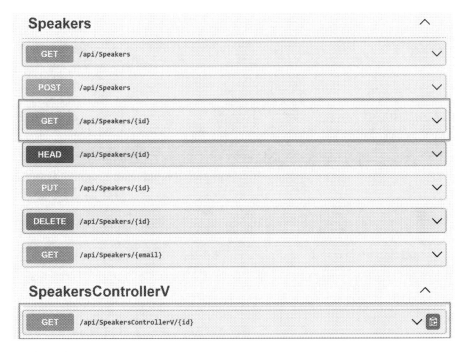

Figure 11-2. *Swagger page displaying the new controller action*

Next, let's annotate our controllers with an attribute so we can tell them apart in the next step, when we add the same route for them.

This attribute is [ApiVersion]. We need to annotate our two versions of SpeakersController with the right version numbers. SpeakersController will have [ApiVersion("1.0")], and SpeakersControllerV2 will have [ApiVersion("2.0")], as shown in Listing 11-4.

Listing 11-4. Adding ApiVersion Attribute

```
[Route("api/[controller]")]
[ApiVersion("1.0")]
[ApiController]
 public class SpeakersController : ControllerBase
```

311

```
{
...
}

[Route("api/[controller]")]
[ApiController]
[ApiVersion("2.0")]
public class SpeakersControllerV2 : ControllerBase
{
...
}
```

Running the program again, we will notice that the last endpoint is moved from the v1 version and resides under the v2 API definition, and now we have both versions displayed in the Definition dropdown, as shown in Figure 11-3.

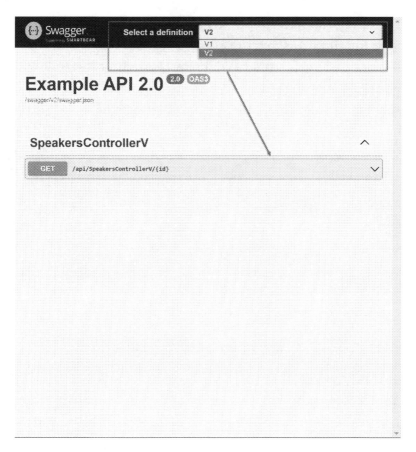

Figure 11-3. *V2 endpoint*

The updates you noticed in the project were made so that dropdown would be displayed correctly.

We have a few more things to put in place. The purpose of versioning is to allow us to obtain different representations of a Speaker entity by using the version differentiator.

Looking at Figure 11-4, we see the two endpoints side by side and notice that they have different routes, which means two separate URIs. Now, it doesn't matter how many controllers we have scattered in our solution; what matters is what we expose to the outside world. The API's consumers should see only one endpoint, not two, or more, for the same resource.

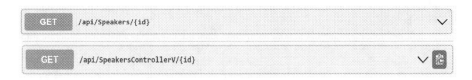

Figure 11-4.   *The two endpoints side by side*

We will fix this by using the route attribute to put the two endpoints under the same umbrella, as shown in Listing 11-5.

Listing 11-5.   Same Route for the Two Controllers

```
[Route("api/speakers")]
[ApiVersion("1.0")]
[ApiController]
public class SpeakersController : ControllerBase

[Route("api/speakers")]
[ApiController]
[ApiVersion("2.0")]
public class SpeakersControllerV2 : ControllerBase
```

Testing to see the updates in action, and looking at Figure 11-5, we notice that in versions 1 and 2 the endpoints are the same.

Figure 11-5. *Fixed the two endpoints*

However, there is still a small issue remaining. Even though the two controllers are under the same routing, the Swagger page sees them as having two different names. We can fix that by using the [ControllerName] attribute on top of the controller with the out-of-the-ordinary name SpeakersControllerV2, as shown in Listing 11-6. This way we ensure that we don't leak any name-related information for our controllers.

Listing 11-6. Adding the Same Name for Controllers

```
[Route("api/speakers")]
[ApiController]
[ControllerName("Speakers")]
[ApiVersion("2.0")]
public class SpeakersControllerV2 : ControllerBase
```

Now that we have one endpoint, one name, and two versions, we need to change the v2 code to return our SpeakerModelV2. The only thing we will change is shown in Listing 11-7, mapping from Speaker (returned from the repository) to SpeakerModelV2.

Listing 11-7. Returning a SpeakerModelV2

```
[HttpGet("{id}")]
public IActionResult GetbyId(int id)
{
    var speakerToReturn = speakersService.Get(id);
```

315

```
if (speakerToReturn == null)
{
    return NotFound();
}
return Ok(mapper.Map<SpeakerModelV2>(speakerToReturn));
}
```

If we open one of our endpoints in Swagger, we will notice that each of them now has a required parameter, named by default api-version.

This is automatically added by the AddApiVersion middleware, and once we start versioning, it assumes that all controllers with a version annotation will require this parameter, as shown in Figure 11-6.

Figure 11-6. *Required parameter api-version*

In the next section, we will see how we can tweak some options in the middleware.

API Version Options

There are several options available, which can be turned on or off to provide a more pleasant experience for the consumer of our APIs. One of them is related to providing a default version for the API and making the api-version parameter not required.

Default API Version

In Listing 11-8, you can see AssumeDefaultVersionWhenUnspecified flag is set to true. This will remove the need to require the version-related parameter with every endpoint.

The second parameter, DefaultApiVersion, allows us to provide an instance of the ApiVersion object that will be treated as the default version.

Listing 11-8. Adding Implicit API Version

```
builder.Services.AddApiVersioning(options =>
{

    options.AssumeDefaultVersionWhenUnspecified = true;
    options.DefaultApiVersion = new ApiVersion(1.0);
})
```

The two parameters work hand in hand and will make the parameter optional for all the actions that are not versioned, as shown in Figure 11-7.

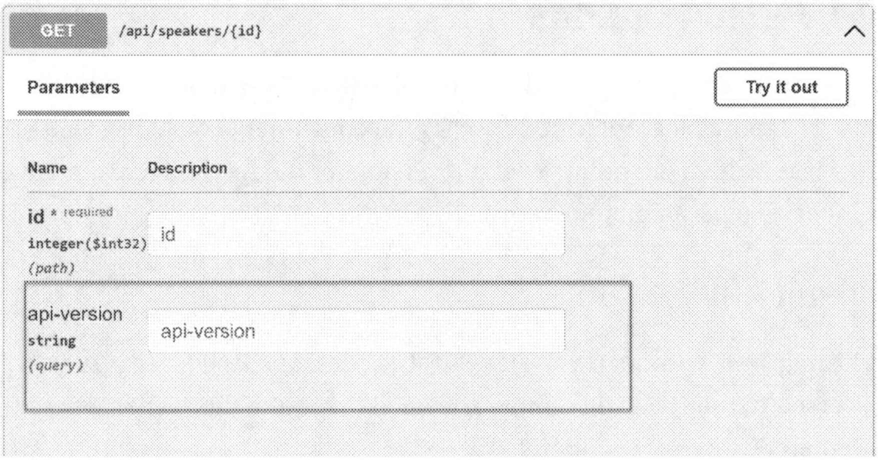

Figure 11-7. *Not requiring an api-version parameter*

This means that all actions that are not versioned, and our GetById action from the Speakers controller, won't require this parameter, and it will be required only by the GetById in version SpeakersControllerV2.

Being aware of and using these features will make the experience more pleasant and time-saving for our API consumers, even if we are among the consumers.

Reporting the API Versions

When this property is set to true, the HTTP headers api-supported-versions and api-deprecated-versions will be added to all valid service routes. This information is useful for advertising which versions are supported or scheduled for deprecation to clients. This information is also useful when supporting the OPTIONS method.

```
options.ReportApiVersions = true;
```

In Figure 11-8 you can see a header that will always be included in the responses because we set ReportApiVersions to true.

api-supported-versions   ⓘ   1.0

Figure 11-8. *Supported API versions header field in response*

Ways of Versioning

By default, whenever we add the versioning middleware it is enabled to use the query string as the versioning strategy.

Our `Asp.Versioning` library supports all four versioning types by allowing us to use the right implementation for the `IApiVersionReader` interface they provide.

To specify a versioning strategy, we assign an implementation that corresponds to what we need for the `ApiVersionReader` property (Listing 11-9).

Listing 11-9. Assigning a Versioning Strategy

```
options.ApiVersionReader = new
QueryStringApiVersionReader("api-version");
```

In Listing 11-10, you can see the four available implementations. Each of the constructors allows us to specify the parameter name (if we want/need something other than the default one).

Listing 11-10. Available IApiVersionReader Implementations

```
new QueryStringApiVersionReader("api-version");
new HeaderApiVersionReader("api-version");
new MediaTypeApiVersionReader("application/json");
new UrlSegmentApiVersionReader();
```

Versioning in QueryString

This option is the default one when we use the middleware, and we saw an example of this in practice. You can manually specify the versioning strategy by creating an instance of QueryStringApiVersionReader and passing the parameter name, as shown in Listing 11-11. See Figure 11-9.

Listing 11-11. QueryStringApiVersion Reader

```
options.ApiVersionReader = new
QueryStringApiVersionReader("api-version");
```

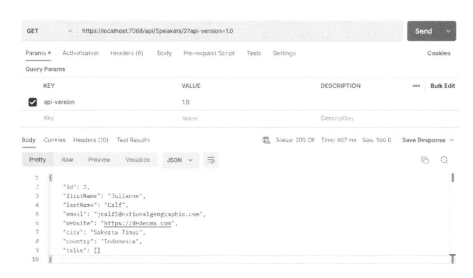

Figure 11-9. *Api-Version parameter in a request*

We can also change the name of the default parameter, as shown in Listing 11-12.

Listing 11-12. Changing the Version Parameter Name

```
options.ApiVersionReader = new QueryStringApiVersionRe
ader("v");
});
```

Now we will use "v" as the name of the parameter in charge of versioning, and this change is global. All the versioning parameters will now have this new name, as shown in Figure 11-10.

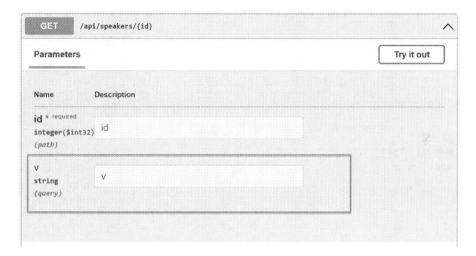

Figure 11-10. *Changing the parameter name*

Here are some key things to keep in mind when versioning an API using query strings:

- It's important to keep the version number separate from other parameters in the query string to avoid any confusion or conflicts.

- Use a consistent naming convention for the version parameter to make it clear that it indicates the API version. Using v is a common convention, but other names like version, api-version, or x-version can also be used.

- Make sure to document the versioning scheme clearly and thoroughly so that developers using the API can easily understand how to specify the version number in the query string.

- Support multiple versions of the API to allow developers to continue using older versions if needed. This can involve maintaining separate code paths for each version or using version-specific controllers.

- Make sure to handle versioning gracefully by providing helpful error messages and appropriate responses when a request is made with an invalid or unsupported version number.

Versioning in Headers

Versioning our API by using headers requires just a simple change. We assign HeaderApiVersionReader to the ApiVersionReader, and we are set (Listing 11-13).

Listing 11-13. Using HeaderApiVersionReader

```
options.ApiVersionReader = new HeaderApiVersionReader(
"api-version");
```

If we look at the documentation pages, shown in Figure 11-11, you can see that the api-version parameter is now a header field.

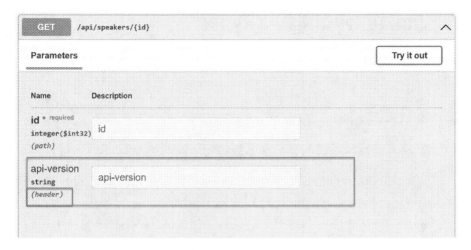

Figure 11-11. *Header versioning*

If we make a request to our API, asking for version 2, we need to specify this header field, or else it will be implied as being version 1 (since this is how we configured it to behave). See Figure 11-12.

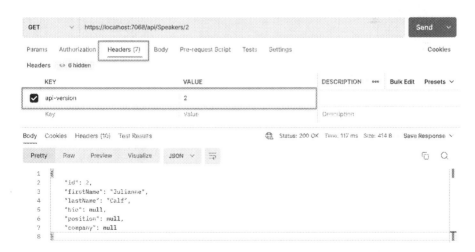

Figure 11-12. *ApiVersion in the header*

Versioning with Media Types

As before, to change the versioning strategy, we just need to assign the right instance to the `ApiVersionReader` parameter (Listing 11-14).

Listing 11-14. MediaTypeApiVersionReader

```
options.ApiVersionReader = new MediaTypeApiVersionReader();
```

The `MediaTypeApiVersionReader` uses, as the default parameter name, the string `v` and the `Content-Type` header field.

We can see in Figure 11-13 how we would make such a request to our version 2 endpoint. We pass the `Content-Type` field value as we would normally do and append the `v=2.0` string. We also need to separate the two values by using the `";"` character.

Figure 11-13. *Versioning by using a media type*

If we look at the Swagger pages, we won't see anything there indicating that there is a way to send versioning-related information through media types.

This is the default behavior, but we could customize it by restricting our actions to accept a different media type than application/json and changing the parameter name.

For more advanced scenarios, like using custom media types, we can build our template, as shown in Listing 11-15.

Listing 11-15. Custom Media Type with Version

```
var builder = new MediaTypeApiVersionReaderBuilder();

options.ApiVersionReader = builder.Template("application/vnd.
my.company.{version}+json")
                                      .Build();
```

Even though this is possible, you will need to provide the extra information related to documenting your API with the custom media types and providing InputFormatters and OutputFormatters to be able to read and write these. The versioning library doesn't provide other support beyond matching the API version from the media type in the incoming request.

Versioning in the URL Path

URI versioning or URL versioning is the practice of including a version number in the Uniform Resource Identifier (URI) of an API endpoint to indicate which version of the API is being used.

In Listing 11-16 you can see an example of how a URI would look in a route template.

Listing 11-16. An Example with URL Versioning

```
[Route("api/v1/users")]
public class UsersController : ControllerBase
{
}
```

In this example, the [Route] attribute is used to specify the URI of the API endpoint. The URI includes the version number (v1) as a prefix to indicate that this is the first version of the API.

If a new version of the API is released, a new controller with a different URI can be created to handle requests for the new version. See Listing 11-17.

Listing 11-17. Second Controller

```
[Route("api/v2/users")]
public class UsersControllerV2 : ControllerBase
{

}
```

In this example, the URI of the new endpoint includes the version number v2 to indicate that this is the second version of the API.

To enable the use of this versioning strategy, as before we assign the right implementation in the middleware, as in Listing 11-18.

Listing 11-18. Adding UrlSegmentApiVersionReader

```
options.ApiVersionReader = new UrlSegmentApiVersionReader();
```

After that, our simple route /api/speakers, in both our controllers, would need to receive a parameter related to the version. We add that as shown in Listing 11-19 by also prefixing it with the letter "v". This way, we will get v1 and v2 in route names automatically.

Listing 11-19. Adding the Version Parameter in the Route

```
[Route("api/v{version:apiVersion}/speakers")]
```

If we open the Swagger page now, we would see some funky-looking endpoints, as in Figure 11-14. Now all our endpoints make use of the version parameter we added on top of our controllers, but since we have a dropdown taking care of the version, we will fix this by adding a configuration option in the middleware that displays this page.

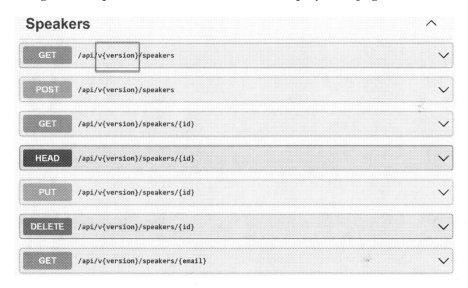

Figure 11-14. *Version parameter displaying in endpoints*

Go to Program.cs and add the option highlighted in Listing 11-20. This is related more to documentation than versioning, but these two often go hand in hand.

Listing 11-20. Substitute the Version in the URL

```
.AddApiExplorer(o =>
{

    o.GroupNameFormat = "'v'VVV";
    o.SubstituteApiVersionInUrl = true;

});
```

Once we have added the parameter number, we will see that, for the first version of our API, we have the v1 parameter in the URL now, substituted correctly, and it has disappeared from the parameters list, as shown in Figure 11-15.

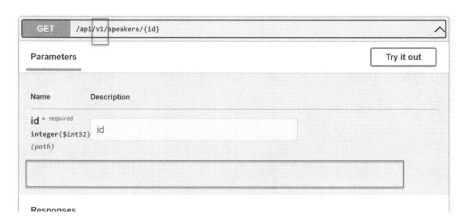

Figure 11-15. *Version parameter substituted in URL, removed from the parameters list*

Combining Versioning Strategies

This library provides a way to combine versioning strategies. Combining them is not a regular practice, but if ever in need, you can use something like in Listing 11-21.

Listing 11-21. Combining Versioning Strategies

```
options.ApiVersionReader = ApiVersionReader.Combine(
        new HeaderApiVersionReader("api-version"),
        new UrlSegmentApiVersionReader());
```

General Rules about Versioning

When it comes to versioning an API, several general rules should be followed to ensure that changes to the API are communicated clearly and effectively to developers who use the API. Here are some of the common practices:

- **Use semantic versioning** – This means using a three-part version number (e.g., 1.2.3) that indicates the major, minor, and patch versions. Major version changes indicate significant changes that are not backward compatible, minor version changes indicate new features or improvements that are backward compatible, and patch version changes indicate bug fixes or other small changes that are backward compatible.

- **Use version numbers in such a way that they don't affect consumers** – One of the best versioning strategies is using the header or the media type. Changing the URI to reflect a new version is a bad practice because we sometimes don't know who our API consumers are. We wouldn't want to break them by suddenly changing the URL they know. Roy Fielding— who coined the term *REST*—said that "cool URIs don't change," and we should strive to keep it that way.

- **Provide backward compatibility** – Whenever possible, try to maintain backward compatibility with previous versions of the API. This means that existing code that uses the API will continue to work, even if the API is updated with new features or changes.

- **Use deprecation warnings** – If a feature or endpoint is going to be removed in a future version of the API, provide a warning in the current version so developers have time to update their code.

- **Plan for future changes** – When designing an API, think about how it may evolve over time and plan for future changes. This can include designing the API with flexibility in mind and providing ways to extend or customize it.

By following these general rules, we can help ensure our APIs are robust and evolvable and our API consumers are happy.

Deprecating Versions

After a while, when APIs evolve, we need them to be able to announce that some versions are deprecated so as to prepare our API consumers for transitioning to newer versions. To do that, we have to mark the controller or the endpoint with an attribute (Listing 11-22; Figure 11-16).

Listing 11-22. Deprecating a Version

```
[Route("api/speakers")]
[ApiVersion("1.0", Deprecated = true)]
[ApiController]
public class SpeakersController : ControllerBase
```

Figure 11-16. *Advertising the deprecated version*

Summary

In this chapter, we discussed the importance of versioning an API properly and learned about different versioning strategies. As software developers, we need to understand that versioning is an important aspect of API development.

We explored various ways of versioning an API, including URL-based, query string–based, header-based, and media-type-based versioning. Each approach has its advantages and disadvantages, so it's essential to choose the right versioning strategy for your project.

We also discussed the process of deprecating an API and the importance of having a clear deprecation strategy in place. Deprecating an API can be a challenging process, especially if you have clients using older versions of the API. Therefore, it's crucial to communicate any changes to your clients effectively and provide a clear timeline for deprecation.

Whether you opt for route-based, query string–based, or header-based versioning, it's crucial to ensure that your API remains backward compatible and easy to use for your clients. By choosing the right versioning strategy, you can ensure that your API remains scalable, maintainable, and consumer friendly.

CHAPTER 12

Documenting the API

The process of documenting an API should be given a well-deserved place in the API development process. Ultimately, we develop APIs to be consumed by different systems, whether inside our organization or not. Part of this process is related to interacting with an API in a simple manner.

In this chapter, we will learn what tools we can use and how we can use them to make API documenting an enjoyable step in our development process. We will learn about OpenAPI and then dive into using the Swashbuckle library. We will customize our documentation process so that anyone can understand what operations are supported in our APIs.

Introducing OpenAPI

OpenAPI, is a specification, with tools formerly known as Swagger. Is an open-source specification for building and documenting RESTful APIs (Application Programming Interfaces). It is designed to make it easier for developers to interact with APIs by defining the format of the API requests and responses, as well as the available endpoints and operations.

The Swagger project was donated to the OpenAPI Initiative in 2015 and has since been referred to as OpenAPI. Both names are used interchangeably. However, *OpenAPI* refers to the specification. *Swagger* refers to the family of open-source and commercial products from SmartBear that work with the OpenAPI specification. Subsequent open-source products, such as OpenAPIGenerator, also fall under the Swagger family name, despite not being released by SmartBear.

OpenAPI provides a standardized way to describe an API's functionality, including the parameters that can be passed to each endpoint, the responses that can be returned, any error messages that might be generated, and the status codes that might be returned. This allows developers and testers to easily understand how to use an API without having to consult extensive documentation or rely on trial and error.

The OpenAPI specification is written in a YAML or JSON format and can be used to generate client libraries, server stubs, and interactive API documentation. It is widely used in the industry, with many popular APIs such as Google, Stripe, and GitHub providing OpenAPI specifications for their services.

When we say that OpenAPI is a specification, we mean that it is a document that defines a set of rules and guidelines that must be followed when designing and implementing RESTful APIs. The OpenAPI specification outlines a common language for describing the structure and functionality of an API, including the available endpoints, operations, input and output data formats, authentication requirements, and more.

The specification itself does not provide any implementation details or code but rather serves as a blueprint for building an API. By following the rules and guidelines laid out in the OpenAPI specification, developers can ensure that their API is consistent, well documented, and interoperable with other systems that adhere to the same standard.

One of the key benefits of having a standardized specification like OpenAPI is that it enables automated tooling, such as code generators and testing frameworks, to be built on top of it. This makes it easier and faster for developers to create and consume APIs, reducing development time and increasing productivity.

Introducing Swashbuckle

Swashbuckle is an open-source library for ASP.NET Core that automatically generates an OpenAPI specification for RESTful APIs. It provides a set of middleware components that integrate with Web API, scanning the application's controllers and actions to generate a complete and accurate OpenAPI specification.

With Swashbuckle, developers can easily document their APIs and make them discoverable to developers or tools. Through the interactive API documentation, developers can explore and test the API's endpoints and operations directly from the browser. The generated documentation includes examples of API requests and responses, as well as details about any authentication requirements.

Swashbuckle can be customized to fit the specific needs of an API or team, and it provides many customizations.

For example, developers can use Swashbuckle to add custom descriptions and annotations to their API's endpoints and operations or to exclude certain endpoints or actions from the generated specification. It also supports customization of the generated documentation page, allowing the addition of branding and styling.

Working with Swashbuckle

Swashbuckle comes with a set of core libraries and several extension libraries made by the community. In Table 12-1 and Table 12-2, you can see a list of the most common packages.

Table 12-1. *Core Swashbuckle Components*

Package	Description
Swashbuckle.AspNetCore.Swagger	The main package
Swashbuckle.AspNetCore.SwaggerGen	This particular implementation generates OpenApiDocument(s) from your routes, controllers, and models
Swashbuckle.AspNetCore.SwaggerUI	Exposes an embedded version of the Swagger user interface (UI). You specify the API endpoints where it can obtain Swagger JSON, and it uses them to power interactive docs for your API.

Table 12-2. *Additional Swashbuckle Components*

Package	Description
Swashbuckle.AspNetCore. Annotations	Includes a set of custom attributes that can be applied to controllers, actions, and models to enrich the generated Swagger
Swashbuckle.AspNetCore.Cli	Provides a command line interface (CLI) for retrieving Swagger directly from a startup assembly and writing to file
Swashbuckle.AspNetCore.ReDoc	Exposes an embedded version of the ReDoc UI (an alternative to Swagger UI)

Documentation Steps

In this section, we will look at the available attributes and features related to documentation so you have a complete overview by the end. We won't go into advanced topics, but will cover the bare minimum you will most likely encounter in most projects.

Define Supported Request Content Types

By default, an action supports all available request content types, and it is up to us if we need anything other than application/json or application/xml. This becomes particularly useful when we want to leverage media types to their fullest to have different actions that respond to different content types sent for the requests.

The [Consumes] attribute forces an action to respond only to a specific content type, as shown in Listing 12-1. This is very useful when working with custom media types.

Listing 12-1. Consumes Attribute

```
[HttpPost]
[Consumes("application/xml")]
public IActionResult CreateSpeaker(Speaker speaker)

[HttpPost]
[Consumes("application/json")]
public IActionResult CreateSpeakerFromJson(Speaker speaker)

[HttpPost]
[Consumes("text/vcard")]
public IActionResult CreateSpeakerFromVCard(Speaker speaker)
```

337

The [Consumes] attribute allows us to have actions that have different names, similar parameters, and the same route, being distinguished only by the content type they respond to. This wasn't possible in previous .NET versions; the platform forced us to have only one action/verb/parameter.

In this case, if the request doesn't specify a Content-Type header of application/xml, a 415 Unsupported Media Type response will result.

Define the Possible Status Codes

If we need to specify a different status code and/or additional response formats, or our actions return IActionResult instead of an ActionResult<T> model, we can explicitly describe responses with the ProducesResponseTypeAttribute. See Figure 12-1.

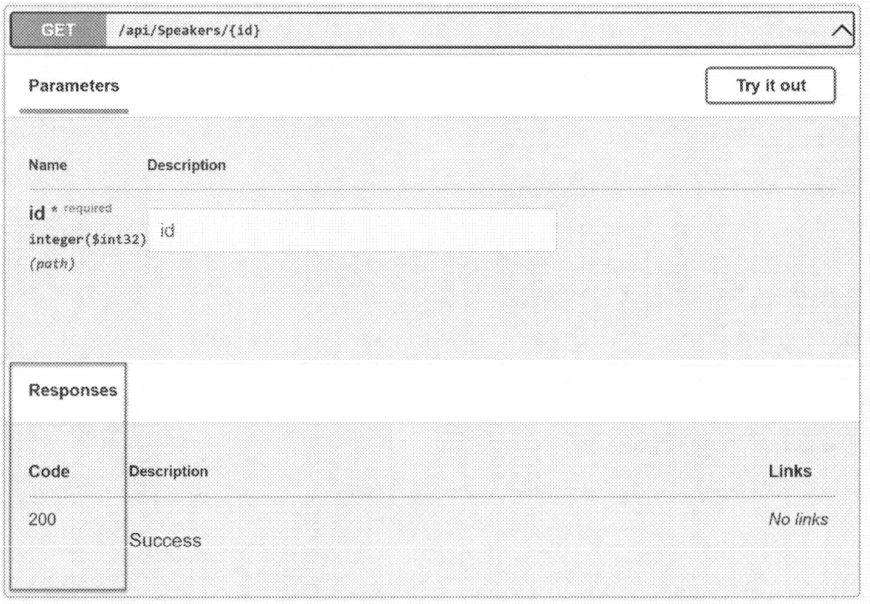

Figure 12-1. *Standard status code in Swagger*

If we look at our implementation, we will notice that we have two different status codes that are available for this action, but only one of them shows up on the Swagger page (Listing 12-2).

Listing 12-2. Status Codes Returned by GetByID

```
[HttpGet("{id}")]
public IActionResult GetbyId(int id)
{
    var speakerToReturn = speakersService.Get(id);
    if (speakerToReturn == null)
    {
        return NotFound();
    }
    return Ok(speakerToReturn);
}
```

By default, the `ApiController` attribute assumes that every single action responds with a 200 OK status code. All other status codes that might be returned from the action are up to you to specify and document (Listing 12-3).

Listing 12-3. Documenting the Returning Status Codes

```
[HttpGet("{id}")]
[ProducesResponseType(StatusCodes.Status200OK)]
[ProducesResponseType(StatusCodes.Status404NotFound)]
 public IActionResult GetbyId(int id)
```

The [ProducesReponseType] attribute supports another parameter that allows us to add the type that is returned with each status code as shown in Listing 12-4.

```
[ProducesResponseType(StatusCodes.Status200OK, Type =
typeof(SpeakerModel))]
```

Using the second parameter will add another section to the Swagger page, as shown in Figure 12-2. This displays the model, in the media type specified, with all the properties. Using this, you know what model to expect in case of a success status code.

Figure 12-2. *Swagger page adding the SpeakerModel type blueprint*

Define the Content Type of the Response

Listing 12-4. Produces Attribute in Action

```
[HttpGet("{id}")]
[ProducesResponseType(StatusCodes.Status200OK)]
[ProducesResponseType(StatusCodes.Status404NotFound)]
[Produces("application/json")]
public IActionResult GetbyId(int id)

[Produces(MediaTypeNames.Application.Json)]
public IActionResult GetbyId(int id)
```

We have two ways of using the attribute: specifying the media type as a string or using a strongly typed one. We are allowed to use only one attribute at once on top of our actions.

At the same time, if we know that all actions in a controller produce the same content type, we can annotate the controller, and all the actions inside will be documented as producing the same response type, as shown in Listing 12-5.

Listing 12-5. Using MediaTypeNames

```
[Produces(MediaTypeNames.Application.Json)]
[Route("api/[controller]")]
[ApiController]
[BindProperties(SupportsGet = true)]
 public class SpeakersController : ControllerBase
 {
 }
```

As an effect of using this attribute, the Swagger page will preselect and limit all the available options in the dropdowns related to the Accept header. This way it prevents you from doing requests with an unsuitable value.

The Swagger page limits all the options in Figure 12-3 to only the one specified in the attribute, shown in Figure 12-4. Removing the extra options limits the cases where an API consumer could issue requests with a type that is not supported.

Figure 12-3. *All available media types for Accept header*

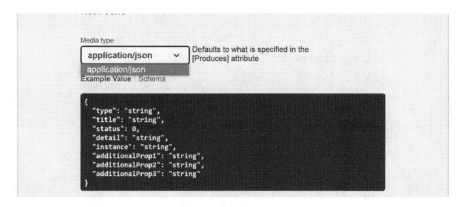

Figure 12-4. *Media type list limited to the value specified in the Produces attribute*

Describing Endpoints

To include comments that describe our endpoints, we will need to allow the Software Development Kit (SDK) to generate a documentation file. This documentation file is an XML file containing text added between special characters. These special characters are three backslashes, as shown in Listing 12-6.

Listing 12-6. Describing an Action

```
/// <summary>
/// Returns all speakers filtered by country
/// </summary>
/// <param name="country"></param>
/// <returns></returns>
```

After these characters, we can have special nodes that help describe the methods. You can see in Table 12-3 a short list of the supported notes and their usage.

Table 12-3. *Comments Nodes*

Node	Description	Example

`<summary></summary>`	Describes the action	`/// <summary>`
		`/// Returns all`
		`speakers filtered`
		`by country`
		`/// </summary>`

`<param name="">`
`</param>`
	Describes the parameters, one by one	`<param name="Country">`
		`This is the country`
		`parameter</param>`

`<returns></returns>`	Describes what is returned	

`<response code="">`
`</response>`
	Allows us to specify the returned status codes	`<response code="201">`
		`Returns the newly`
		`created item</response>`

`<remarks>` `</remarks>`	Allows us to add information related to other areas, like examples	

In Figure 12-5, you can see an example where the <response> node is used to add extra details about it, like "If the id is not found."

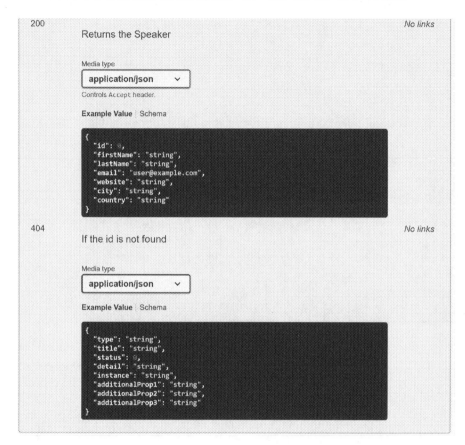

Figure 12-5. *Displaying info about the returned status code*

Using the <remarks> node, you can help with testing by providing an example request, as shown in Figure 12-6.

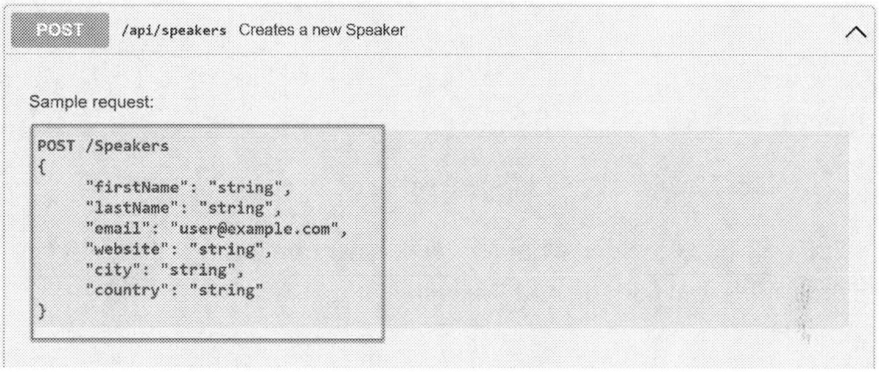

Figure 12-6. *Documented request example*

Corresponding to this result, you can see the full code in Listing 12-7.

Listing 12-7. Adding a Full Description for an Action

```
/// <summary>
/// Creates a new Speaker
/// </summary>
/// <param name="model"></param>
/// <returns></returns>
/// <remarks>
/// Sample request:
///
///     POST /Speakers
///     {
///         "firstName": "string",
///         "lastName": "string",
///         "email": "user@example.com",
///         "website": "string",
```

345

```
///             "city": "string",
///             "country": "string"
///     }
///
/// </remarks>
[HttpPost]

public IActionResult Post(SpeakerModel model)
```

Once we have decided what we need to document, we will right-click the project file and add the node seen in Listing 12-8.

Listing 12-8. Enable Documentation File Generation

```
<PropertyGroup>
  <GenerateDocumentationFile>true</GenerateDocumentationFile>
</PropertyGroup>
```

Enabling documentation file generation is a feature of the .NET SDK, and it allows the platform to output this file as part of the build process.

Once we have this file, we need to configure Swagger and point it to the file location, as shown in Listing 12-9. Our example uses reflection to identify the file, but if you have other paths, or you want to use other discovery methods, you can also do that. You just need to make sure the file exists and is discoverable.

Listing 12-9. Enable Comments in Swagger

```
builder.Services.AddSwaggerGen(options =>
{
var xmlFilename = $"{Assembly.GetExecutingAssembly().GetName().
Name}.xml";
    options.IncludeXmlComments(Path.Combine(AppContext.
    BaseDirectory, xmlFilename));
});
```

To test if this works, run the API. We should be able to observe some extra details about our endpoints, as shown in Figure 12-7.

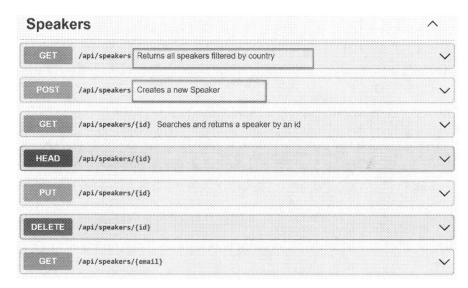

Figure 12-7. *Add comments from XML describing the actions*

API Conventions

In the context of ASP.NET Core Web API, an *API convention* is a set of default behaviors and rules that are applied to controller actions, routes, and other aspects of the API.

This helps standardize the way that controllers and actions are defined and documented, making it easier for developers to understand and use the API.

Using a convention removes a lot of the tedious work related to documenting the API. We can apply the attribute [ApiConventionType] to the controller shown in Listing 12-10.

Listing 12-10. DefaultApi Conventions Applied to the Entire Controller

```
[ApiConventionType(typeof(DefaultApiConventions))]
[ApiVersion("1.0")]
[Route("api/speakers")]
[ApiController]
public class SpeakersController : ControllerBase
```

We can also apply the convention as shown in Listing 12-11, where we use the [ApiConventionMethod] attribute. This requires the type of convention and also the method in the convention that we want to be applied.

Listing 12-11. DefaultApiConventions Applied to an Action

```
[HttpGet]
[CommaQueryString]
[ApiConventionMethod(typeof(DefaultApiConventions),
            nameof(DefaultApiConventions.Get))]
public ActionResult<IEnumerable<SpeakerModel>>
GetAll([FromQuery] List<string>? country)
```

Looking at the implementation of this convention, shown in Listing 12-12, we see that it contains a list of status codes that supposedly should be returned from every action that responds to an HTTP GET.

Listing 12-12. Default GET-related Convention

```
public static class DefaultApiConventions
{
    #region GET
    /// <summary>
    /// Get convention.
    /// </summary>
```

```
/// <param name="id"></param>
[ProducesResponseType(StatusCodes.Status200OK)]
[ProducesResponseType(StatusCodes.Status404NotFound)]
[ProducesDefaultResponseType]
[ApiConventionNameMatch(ApiConventionNameMatchBehavior.
Prefix)]
public static void Get(
    [ApiConventionNameMatch(ApiConventionNameMatchBehavior.
    Suffix)]
        [ApiConventionTypeMatch(ApiConventionTypeMatch
        Behavior.Any)]
        object id)
{ }

/// <summary>
/// Find convention.
/// </summary>
/// <param name="id"></param>
[ProducesResponseType(StatusCodes.Status200OK)]
[ProducesResponseType(StatusCodes.Status404NotFound)]
[ProducesDefaultResponseType]
[ApiConventionNameMatch(ApiConventionNameMatchBehavior.
Prefix)]
public static void Find(
    [ApiConventionNameMatch(ApiConventionNameMatchBehavior.
    Suffix)]
        [ApiConventionTypeMatch(ApiConventionTypeMatch
        Behavior.Any)]
        object id)
{ }
#endregion
```

In this default implementation, we notice that API conventions are implemented using the [ApiConventionType] attribute, which is a new feature in .NET 6 and later versions. The ApiConventionAttribute allows you to define a set of conventions for controller actions and apply them to all actions in a controller, or specific actions using a combination of HTTP method and action name.

Here are some examples of API conventions that can be defined using the ApiConventionAttribute:

- **Response type conventions** – Specify the default response types for successful and error responses returned by actions in a controller.

- HTTP method conventions – Define the default HTTP method for action methods with specific names.

In Listing 12-13, there is an example of how to use the ApiConvention attribute to define a convention for the response type of a Web API action method.

Listing 12-13. Using a Default Convention on an Action

```
[HttpGet("{id}")]
[ApiConventionMethod(typeof(DefaultApiConventions),
    nameof(DefaultApiConventions.Get))]
public ActionResult<User> GetUser(int id)
{
    var user = _userRepository.GetUserById(id);

    if (user == null)
    {
        return NotFound();
    }

    return user;
}
```

In this example, the ApiConventionMethod attribute is used to specify that the GetUser method should use the default response type convention defined in the DefaultApiConventions class for the HTTP GET method. The DefaultApiConventions.Get method specifies that the default response type for a successful GET request should be an ActionResult<T> where T is the type of the return value.

By using API conventions, you can simplify the implementation of your Web API and improve its consistency and usability for developers. API conventions can help to reduce the amount of boilerplate code that you need to write and make it easier for other developers to understand and use your API.

The [ApiController] attribute can be applied to a controller class to enable the following opinionated, API-specific behaviors:

- Attribute routing requirement

- Automatic HTTP 400 responses

- Binding source parameter inference

- Multipart/form-data request inference

- Problem details for error status codes

Creating an API Convention

If our controllers follow some common patterns, or if we want them to follow a pattern—e.g., they are all primarily CRUD endpoints—and we aren't already using ProducesResponseType or Produces to document them, we should consider using API conventions. These let us define the most "common" return types and status codes that we use and globally apply them. In a way, these conventions are a substitute for decorating individual actions with ProducesResponseType attributes and are also great ways to identify areas of our application that are lacking Swagger documentation and correct them.

The easiest way to create our convention is to start from the existing one by copying and pasting the code and then adapting it. I propose doing this because this feature is not very extensive.

Let's add a new class, named MyApiConventions, and paste the existing code.

We will focus only on one specific action, and I will let you, the reader, implement the rest.

Find the method with the name Find (pun intended)–public static void Find–and modify it as shown in Listing 12-14. Add another ProducesResponseType attribute with Status418ImATeapot and remove any other attribute near the method name, leaving it plain and simple.

Listing 12-14. Adding an Extra Status Code on a Convention

```
[ProducesResponseType(StatusCodes.Status200OK)]
[ProducesResponseType(StatusCodes.Status404NotFound)]
[ProducesResponseType(StatusCodes.Status418ImATeapot,
StatusCode = 418)]
[ProducesDefaultResponseType]
 public static void Find(
 object id)
 { }
```

Now go into SpeakersController and modify the previously used convention with our own (Listing 12-15).

Listing 12-15. Apply Our Custom Convention

```
[ApiConventionType(typeof(MyApiConventions))]
[ApiVersion("1.0")]
[Route("api/speakers")]
[ApiController]
public class SpeakersController : ControllerBase
```

Then, change the GetById action name to Find to make it match our convention, exactly as shown in Listing 12-16.

Listing 12-16. Rename to "Find"

```
[HttpGet("{id}")]
public IActionResult Find(int id)
```

Now, if we run our API, we should see the 418 I'm a teapot status code displayed on our Swagger page, as shown in Figure 12-8.

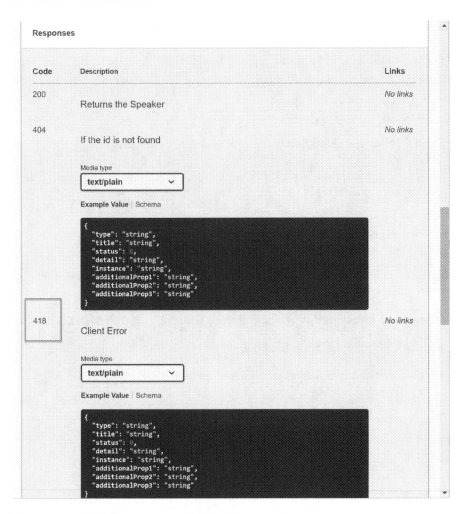

Figure 12-8. *Using custom MyApiConventions to generate status codes*

Summary

In this chapter, we talked about OpenAPI, a specification for building APIs that allows developers to define, document, and interact with web services in a standardized way. We have also discussed the usage of Swashbuckle, a popular tool for generating OpenAPI documentation for .NET Core Web APIs.

We have covered the importance of defining the supported request content types and possible status codes for each API endpoint. This information provides valuable guidance to API clients on how to interact with the service and handle different scenarios.

Finally, we discussed the use of comments to describe API endpoints within the codebase, and we created our API convention.

OpenAPI and Swashbuckle are powerful tools for building and documenting RESTful web services. By using them and following a few practices, developers can create APIs that are easy to use, understand, and maintain, ultimately leading to a better experience for both developers and API consumers.

CHAPTER 13

Testing the API

Testing an API means verifying that it functions as expected by testing its inputs, outputs, and behaviors. This involves making requests to the API using a variety of input values and verifying that the API responds with the expected output.

The testing process can involve a combination of automated and manual tests. Automated tests can be used to verify the basic functionality and integration of the API, while manual tests can be used to verify the accuracy of the results, the user experience, and other factors that cannot be tested automatically.

API testing can also involve testing for security vulnerabilities, such as unauthorized access or data leaks. Security testing can be performed using automated tools or manual penetration testing to identify potential vulnerabilities.

Overall, API testing is an important part of the software development process and helps ensure that the API meets the functional, security, and performance requirements of the system it is integrated with.

Why Is Testing an API Important?

Testing an API is important for the following reasons:

- **Functionality** – Ensures that it performs the functions it was designed for and that it works as expected. This ensures that the API provides the correct results and returns the right data in response to various inputs.

© Irina Dominte 2023
I. Dominte, *Web API Development for the Absolute Beginner*,
https://doi.org/10.1007/978-1-4842-9348-5_13

- **Reliability** – Helps to identify any issues or bugs that may arise during usage. By discovering these problems early, developers can work on fixing them, improving the reliability of the API.

- **Security** – APIs can be a potential attack vector for hackers to gain access to an application or system. Testing an API can help identify potential security vulnerabilities and enable developers to patch them before they become a security threat.

- **Performance** – This can help identify how it performs under various loads and conditions. This can help developers optimize the performance of the API and ensure that it can handle large volumes of traffic and requests.

- **Compatibility** – APIs are often used by multiple applications and systems. Testing an API helps ensure that it is compatible with different systems and platforms and that it can be integrated smoothly into other applications.

Testing an API is crucial to ensure that it is reliable and secure, and performs as expected, which is essential for providing a good user experience and achieving the desired business outcomes.

Terminology

Even if we already know how to code or write tests, it is equally important to know the right terms that describe what we do. With testing, this becomes paramount because it can lead us to understand why one of our tests fails even thought it should be passing. Here we will have a look over some terms, and progress towards putting these into practice.

Test Doubles

Test double is a term used to describe fake dependencies in tests that are used instead of real dependencies to facilitate testing. The term comes from the concept of a stunt double in movies. Test doubles are useful for testing because they are non-production-ready and can be passed to the system under test instead of real dependencies, which may be difficult to set up or maintain.

SUT

SUT stands for *system under test,* which refers to the software component or module that is being tested in unit testing. In C#, the SUT is typically a class or a method that is being tested for its behavior and correctness. The purpose of unit testing is to isolate the SUT and verify that it behaves as expected when given certain inputs or conditions. By testing the SUT in isolation, we can catch bugs and errors early in the development cycle and ensure that the code functions as intended.

Mock

A *mock* is a simulated object or component that is used to replace a real object or component in order to test the behavior of the code. Mocks are used to isolate the code under test and remove dependencies on other components or systems that may not be available or suitable for testing.

Mocks are created with the same interface as the real object, and we can interact with it the same way we would interact with a real object, but we specify what to return instead. That return type can be used further to test if the behavior is correct.

In Listing 13-1 you can see an example of what such a substitution looks like.

Listing 13-1. Substituting a Class

```
var calculator = Substitute.For<Calculator>();
```

In Listing 13-2, we define a mocked `ISpeakerService` that can be passed down as a dependency to another class, which is our system under test. This will allow us to call methods from that class and test them.

Listing 13-2. Substituting a Dependency

```
private readonly ISpeakersService speakersService = Substitute.
For<ISpeakersService>();
```

Stub

A *stub* is a type of test double that provides canned responses to method calls made during a test. Stubs are typically used to simulate a specific behavior of a component that is being called by the system under test, but that is not the focus of the test. For example, suppose a test needs to verify the behavior of a system under test that makes a network call to retrieve some data. If the network call is slow or unreliable, it could cause the test to fail or take a long time to run. In this case, a stub could be used to simulate the network call and return a simulated response that the system under test is expecting, without actually making a real network call. This makes the test faster and more predictable and allows the focus to remain on the behavior being tested rather than the reliability of the network.

Test Types

There are other types of tests that can be performed on an API to ensure its functionality, performance, and security are as expected. Some of the common types of tests that can be performed on an API include the following:

- **Functional testing** – Testing the API's functionality and behavior in response to different input values and requests to ensure that it meets the functional requirements.

- **Performance testing** – Testing the API's performance under different load and stress conditions to ensure that it can handle large volumes of requests and responses.

- **Security testing** – Testing the API for vulnerabilities such as authentication and authorization issues, injection attacks, and data leaks.

- **Usability testing** – Testing the user experience of the API, including ease of use, accessibility, and overall user satisfaction.

- **Acceptance testing** – Testing the API against predefined acceptance criteria to ensure that it meets the desired quality standards and requirements.

- **Smoke testing** – This is a quick and simple test that verifies the basic functionality of the API. The purpose of a smoke test is to check whether the API is up and running, responding to requests, and returning expected results. Typically, a smoke test involves sending a few simple requests to the API and checking that the responses are valid. For example, a smoke test might involve sending a GET request to retrieve a resource and verifying that the response contains the expected data, status code, and headers. If the API fails the smoke test, it indicates that there may be fundamental issues with the API that need to be addressed before further testing can be done.

Overall, a combination of these tests can be used to ensure that the API is functional, reliable, and secure and that it meets the desired business and user requirements.

I can't emphasize enough the importance of testing applications. The testing pyramid in Figure 13-1 illustrates the importance of having a solid foundation of unit tests and building up from there to integration tests and end-to-end tests. The idea is to catch issues as early as possible in the development cycle, when they are cheaper and easier to fix. By focusing on a solid testing strategy that includes all three types of tests, teams can ensure that their software is reliable, functional, and meets the needs of their user.

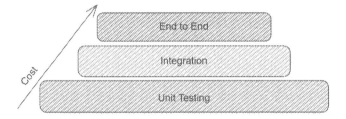

Figure 13-1. *Testing pyramid*

1. **Unit tests** – At the base of the pyramid are unit tests, which focus on testing individual units of code in isolation. These tests are typically written by developers and are intended to catch bugs early in the development process. Unit tests are fast, cheap to write, and run frequently, making them an essential part of any testing strategy.

2. **Integration tests** – In the middle of the pyramid are integration tests, which focus on testing how different units of code work together. Integration tests are written by developers or dedicated testers and are intended to catch bugs that arise when

different components interact. These tests are more expensive to write and run than unit tests, but they are still critical for ensuring that the system as a whole functions correctly.

3. **End-to-end tests** – At the top of the pyramid are end-to-end tests, which test the entire system from end to end, often using a User Interface. These tests are typically written by dedicated testers or automation engineers and are intended to catch bugs that arise when the entire system is integrated. End-to-end tests are the most expensive and time-consuming tests to write and run, but they are still necessary for ensuring that the system works as intended in production.

In the next section, we will focus on unit testing and learn how we can unit test an API and what the general guidelines are that we can use. Then, we will move to a more advanced concept—integration testing.

Unit Tests

Unit tests are small methods that test independent, isolated chunks of code with the sole purpose of obtaining feedback related to the correctness of a specific method, in a fast and repeatable manner.

Anatomy of a Unit Test

Writing a good unit test should follow a clear pattern, named the AAA pattern. This, similar to cooking, involves three steps. Preparing the ingredients (*arrange*), mixing them (*act*), and enjoying the final product (*assert*).

Let's take the example of a simple method, shown in Listing 13-3, that computes the sum of two numbers.

Listing 13-3. Sum Two Numbers

```
public class Calculator
{
    public int Sum(int a, int b)
    {
        return a + b;
    }
}
```

If we wanted to test it, we would do something similar to Figure 13-2, where we can see the full code.

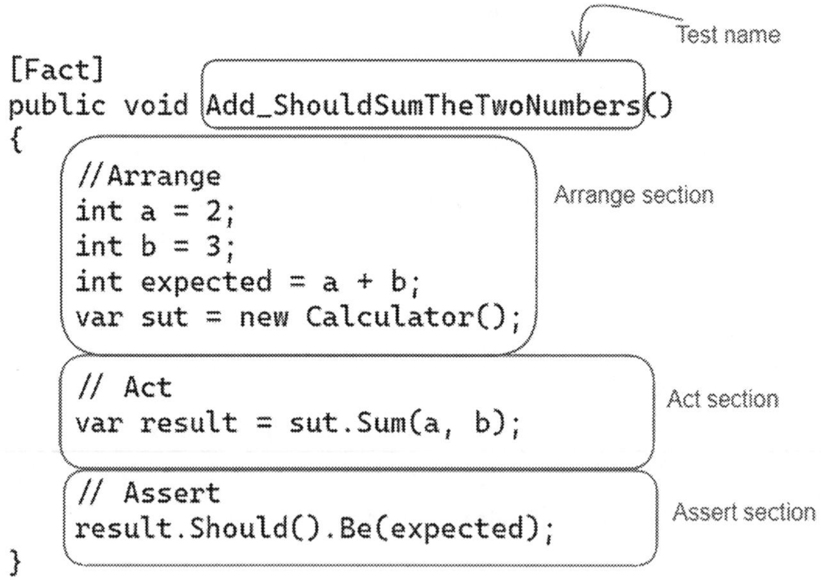

Figure 13-2. *Structure of a test*

Arrange

The arrange part is where we set the ground rules for our tests, instantiate classes using mocking libraries like NSubstitute or Moq, assign values to variables, decide what to return from methods, and so on. This is usually the most extensive part of a test because we have to mock every statement that happens in our original code.

For example, if we check the uniqueness of an email by calling a method, we will have to establish what that method returns.

In Listing 13-4, there is a check we do in our code. In our test in Listing 13-5, we show that this method call needs to return true by using the Returns() method.

Listing 13-4. Original code

```
if (!speakersService.IsEmailUnique(model.Email))
{
...
}
```

Listing 13-5. Same Code in a Test

```
speakersService.IsEmailUnique(model.Email).Returns(true);
```

This Returns() method is part of the NSubstitute library, and it helps us to set the return types or values for our tests.

Act

In the act part, we call methods that we expect to return values (Listing 13-6). Usually, this part is just a line of code or a method call, and it is the core of the unit we want to test.

Listing 13-6. Examples of act

```
// Act
var result = sut.Sum(2, 3);

var result = (CreatedAtActionResult)sut.Post(model);
```

Assert

In this last part, we verify the outcome of our test. We determine if the test passes or fails given the conditions we created in the arrange part and check the expected result. These assertions can be related to expecting a specific status code, a specific value, or a certain characteristic of the result. In Listing 13-7 you can see two examples of asserting the result of a SUT. In the first one, the expected status code of a result is a 201 Created, and in the second one, the result should be true.

Listing 13-7. Examples of Assert using FluentAssertions

```
result.StatusCode.Should().Be(201);

// Assert
result.Should().BeTrue();
```

The AAA pattern provides a uniform structure to all tests. Once you get used to it, tests will be easier to read, manage, and maintain. The look and feel of a test might be different due to the different libraries used, but the principles of writing unit tests are the same.

A regression is a bug introduced in your code. Sometimes it is interchangeably used with a software bug.

Library Types You Might Encounter

For unit testing APIs in .NET 7, there are several libraries that can be used, depending on the specific needs and requirements of the project. Detailed next are some of the most popular and widely used libraries for unit testing APIs in .NET 7, and we can split them into three categories.

Testing Libraries

These libraries come with a series of attributes and methods that facilitate testing. For example, XUnit uses the [Fact] attribute to make a test method runnable by the test runner, and NUnit uses the [Test] attribute and so on. The libraries are different in more than one aspect, but in the end the general rules apply to all of them. What it matters is to write tests for our code.

The following are libraries you are most likely to encounter in the real world:

- **NUnit** – NUnit is a widely used unit testing framework for .NET that supports testing APIs and other software components. It provides a rich set of assertions and test runners, as well as support for test fixtures and suites.

- **xUnit** – xUnit is another popular unit testing framework for .NET. It is similar to NUnit but has some differences in syntax and features. It also supports testing APIs and other software components and provides a range of assertions and test runners.

- **Microsoft.VisualStudio.TestTools.UnitTesting** – This is the built-in testing framework for Visual Studio and provides a range of testing features, including support for testing APIs. It provides a variety of test runners, assertions, and test fixtures.

Mocking Libraries

Mocking libraries help us by simulating an interface or an abstract-type implementation. We instantiate a 'mock' object of the interface or type and we instruct this mock what it should return if a method or property is called against the mock, by essentially simulating the behavior of the component in a controller way

- **Moq** – Moq is a popular mocking library for .NET that provides a way to create mock objects for testing APIs and other software components. It allows developers to isolate components and test them in isolation, without the need for a full system environment.

- **NSubstitute** – This is an open-source .NET library used for creating test doubles in unit testing. It provides a simple and friendly API for creating stubs and mocks, which are then used to isolate the system under test from its dependencies. With NSubstitute, developers can easily create test doubles without needing to write boilerplate code or set up complex arrangements. NSubstitute provides a fluent syntax for setting up the expectations and behaviors of the test double, allowing developers to focus on writing tests rather than on managing dependencies. NSubstitute also provides features such as auto-mocking and call info for advanced scenarios.

- **FakeItEasy** – This is an open-source .NET library used for creating test doubles in unit testing. It provides a simple and fluent API for creating mocks, stubs, and spies, which are used to isolate the system under test from its dependencies. `FakeItEasy` allows developers to create test doubles with minimal setup and configuration. It provides a fluent syntax for setting up the expectations and behaviors of the test double, which makes it easier to write readable and maintainable tests.

A test spy is a testing technique that verifies the behavior of a SUT by capturing and recording the interactions between the object and its collaborators. It allows us to observe and make assertions about the calls made to the collaborator objects.

Asserting Libraries

Assertions libraries are used in software testing to make assertions or check whether specific conditions hold true during the execution of the test.

- **Fluent Assertions** – Fluent Assertions is a popular assertion library for .NET that provides a fluent interface for writing assertions in unit tests. It supports testing APIs and other software components and provides a range of built-in assertions for common scenarios.

A fluent interface is a design pattern in object-oriented programming that aims to create code that is easy to read and understand by providing a more expressive and fluid syntax. It allows method chaining, where multiple methods can be called on an object in a single line of code, giving a feeling of a natural flow. Example:

```
int result = new Calculator()
    .Add(5).Subtract(3).Add(10).GetResult();
```

This way of writing code is preferred by some developers due to the way it can be read and chained.

- **Shouldly** – This is an open-source .NET library that provides a fluent syntax for unit testing in C#. It aims to make tests more readable and maintainable by providing a more expressive way to write assertions.

These are just some of the most popular libraries for unit testing APIs in the .NET ecosystem, but there are many others available. The choice of libraries used will depend on the specific requirements and preferences of the project, as well as on the expertise and experience of the development team.

Creating Our First Unit Tests

In the following examples, we will use XUnit, NSubstitute, and FluentAssertions.

Open the project folder /ch13/start. In there you will see an empty folder named tests. That will be our starting point.

Go ahead and create a new project in the empty folder named ConferenceApi.Tests.Unit (Figure 13-3).

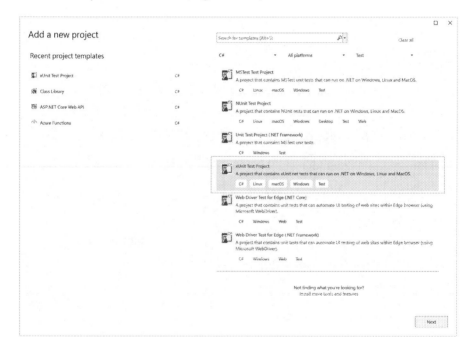

Figure 13-3. *Available test projects*

I like to use this convention when naming test projects. This is made of {ProjectThatWeTest}.Tests.{TypeOfTests}. This way, for me at least, it is easier to distinguish between unit, integration, or any other kind of test that I might have. With ConferenceApi.Test.Unit or ConferenceApi. Tests.Integration, you can see right away what the tests are addressing, and the names are self-explanatory.

Testing the Controller

We will add a new file, naming it SpeakersControllerTests. Here, too, we follow a convention. If we test, for example, SpeakersController, we will add a .cs file named SpeakersControllerTests, similar to how we named our controllers when we first added them. Inside this file, we will create tests for a few of the actions, just enough for you to get the hang of it.

Let's go ahead and add a constructor for our file. Usually, for tests, we use the constructor to instantiate our SUT (SpeakersController) and mock the dependencies necessary for it to be instantiated.

Looking at the constructor, shown in Listing 13-8, we notice that we have two dependencies to inject. In our code, those are provided by the Dependency Injection container, but we would have to obtain them from it somehow.

Listing 13-8. SpeakersController Signature

```
public SpeakersController(ISpeakersService speakersService,
IMapper mapper)
```

In our SpeakersControllerTest, we need to prepare the dependencies individually. In Listing 13-9, you can see that we add the dependencies, using their interfaces, as private fields.

Listing 13-9. SpeakersController State

```
private readonly ISpeakersService speakersService;
private IMapper mapper;

private readonly SpeakersController sut;
public SpeakersControllerTests()
{
...
}
```

In the next step, shown in Listing 13-10, we take these private fields and substitute them with mocks, using NSubstitute, and then we pass them to our SUT.

Listing 13-10. Controller Substitutions

```
public SpeakersControllerTests()
{
  this.mapper = Substitute.For<IMapper>();
  speakersService = Substitute.For<ISpeakersService>();
  //pass the dependencies to our SUT
  sut = new SpeakersController(speakersService, mapper);
}
```

Our mapper needs a few updates in order to pass along the correct mapping profile. This helps it map from one object to another. We will get to this when we actually need it in the next section.

As shown in Figure 13-4, you now add a new method, GetById_ReturnsNotFound_WhenSpeakerDoesntExists, and annotate it with the attribute [Fact]. This attribute, applied to a method, indicates the fact that it should be run by the test runner. You can see a full implementation in Figure 13-5.

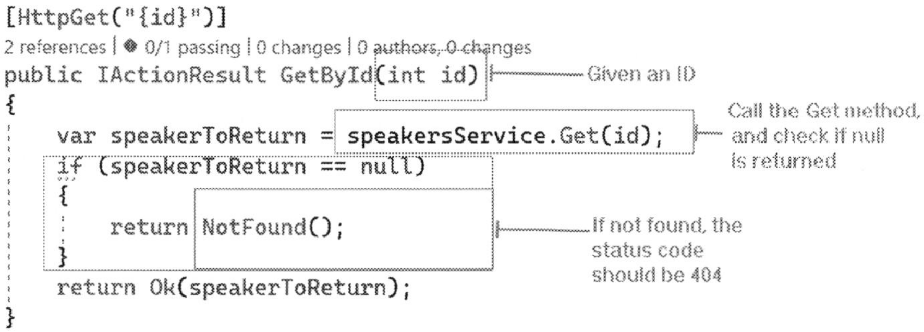

```csharp
[HttpGet("{id}")]
2 references | ● 0/1 passing | 0 changes | 0 authors, 0 changes
public IActionResult GetById(int id)  |————— Given an ID
{
    var speakerToReturn = speakersService.Get(id);   |— Call the Get method,
    if (speakerToReturn == null)                         and check if null
    {                                                    is returned
        return NotFound();          |————— If not found, the
    }                                            status code
    return Ok(speakerToReturn);                   should be 404
}
```

Figure 13-4. *The GetById action logic*

```csharp
[Fact]
● | 0 references | 0 changes | 0 authors, 0 changes
public void GetById_ReturnsNotFound_WhenSpeakerDoesntExists()
{
    // Arrange
    speakersService.Get(Arg.Any<int>()).ReturnsNull();

    // Act
    var result = (NotFoundResult)sut.GetById(1);

    // Assert
    result.StatusCode.Should().Be(404);
}
```

Figure 13-5. *Full implementation with AAA pattern*

In Figure 13-6, by following the step numbers you can see what the test method looks like compared to the method being tested.

We are focusing only on the scenario where a given ID is not found, and the result should be a 404 Not Found status code. The happy path should and will be tested with a different test method. The whole purpose of unit testing controller actions is to make sure that, given the right conditions (in the arrange section), you get the expected result (in the assert section), when acting on a given action.

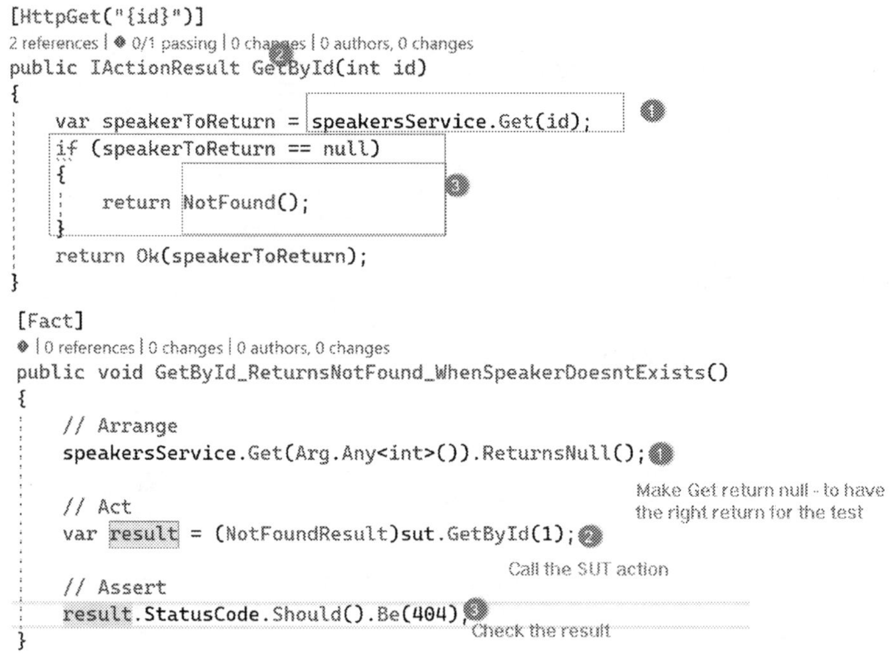

```
[HttpGet("{id}")]
2 references | ◆ 0/1 passing | 0 changes | 0 authors, 0 changes
public IActionResult GetById(int id)
{
    var speakerToReturn = speakersService.Get(id);      ❶
    if (speakerToReturn == null)
    {
        return NotFound();                               ❸
    }
    return Ok(speakerToReturn);
}

[Fact]
◆ | 0 references | 0 changes | 0 authors, 0 changes
public void GetById_ReturnsNotFound_WhenSpeakerDoesntExists()
{
    // Arrange
    speakersService.Get(Arg.Any<int>()).ReturnsNull();   ❶
                                                          Make Get return null - to have
    // Act                                                the right return for the test
    var result = (NotFoundResult)sut.GetById(1); ❷
                                                          Call the SUT action
    // Assert
    result.StatusCode.Should().Be(404)❸
                                          Check the result
}
```

Figure 13-6. *Comparing SUT and test*

Now that the code is written, it is time to put the test runner to work.

Go to Visual Studio ➤ View Menu, and select Test Explorer, as shown in Figure 13-7. This will open the Test Explorer window.

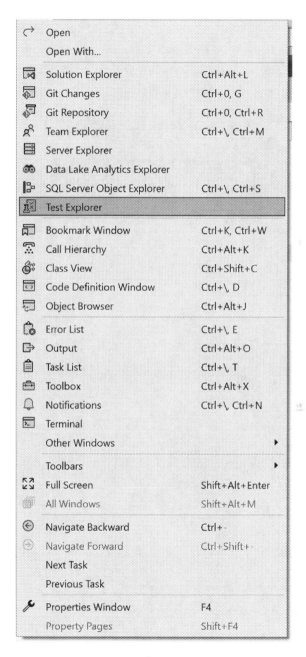

Figure 13-7. *View menu, test explorer*

Inside the Test Explorer window, as in Figure 13-8, you will see all the tests in the project, grouped by files (highlighted by step numbers here), and you can run, explore, or debug them individually. One of them has failed, so you can see what it looks like when this happens.

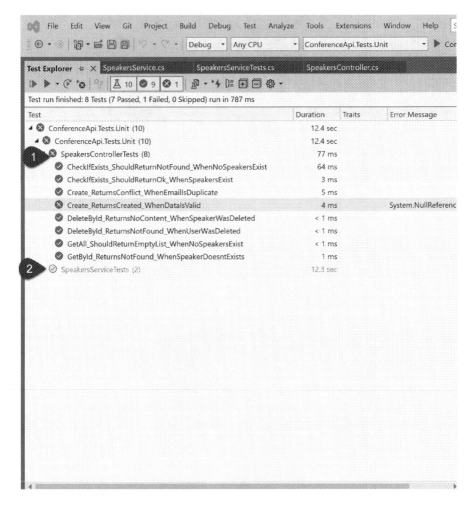

Figure 13-8. *Test Explorer window*

You can right-click on an individual item and use one of the options, as shown in Figure 13-9. This will affect only the selected item. You can also create playlists so that you can run at once just a selection of the tests and so on.

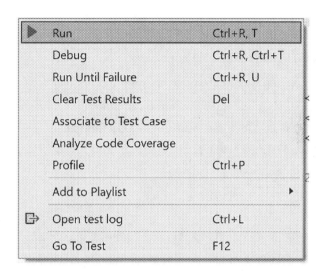

▶	Run	Ctrl+R, T
	Debug	Ctrl+R, Ctrl+T
	Run Until Failure	Ctrl+R, U
	Clear Test Results	Del
	Associate to Test Case	
	Analyze Code Coverage	
	Profile	Ctrl+P
	Add to Playlist	▶
⤵	Open test log	Ctrl+L
	Go To Test	F12

Figure 13-9. *Individual test options*

Select the test, right-click, and select Run. After a moment, you will see the result of the test, similar to what is shown in Figure 13-10. The test either passes or fails, and the result is shown in the window, along with an exception detail in the case of failure.

❌ SpeakersControllerTests (8)	93 ms	
❌ CheckIfExists_ShouldReturnNotFound_WhenNoSpeakersExist	80 ms	
✓ CheckIfExists_ShouldReturnOk_WhenSpeakersExist	3 ms	
✓ Create_ReturnsConflict_WhenEmailIsDuplicate	5 ms	
❌ Create_ReturnsCreated_WhenDataIsValid	4 ms	System.NullReference

Figure 13-10. *A passing test*

Now that we have written our first unit test, let's move a bit further and cover the case where the Delete action returns a 204 No Content status code as a result of a successful item deletion.

Add a new method named DeleteById_ReturnsNoContent_ WhenSpeakerWasDeleted and annotate it with the [Fact] attribute.

To see what we have to do, we will first analyze the SUT, shown in Listing 13-11, and look at the highlighted sections.

Listing 13-11. The Delete Action

```
[HttpDelete("{id}")]
public IActionResult Delete(int id)
{
    var speakerFromDb = speakersService.Get(id);
    if (speakerFromDb == null)
    {
        return NotFound();
    }
    speakersService.Delete(speakerFromDb);
    return NoContent();
}
```

To prepare for writing our first test, we need to clarify a few things:

1. Arrange section

   a. By sending any ID to the Get method of the SpeakerService, we should receive a Speaker object (this means we found it in our database and can delete it). If we need to receive such an object, it also means that we need to return it from our mock.

   b. Call the Delete method of the speakerService and expect it to be executed successfully.

2. Act section – Call the Delete action of the SUT.

3. Assert section – Expect the result of the Delete call to be a NoContentResult.

You can see the full implementation of the test in Figure 13-11.

In the Arrange section, we set the stage, send any integer, and ensure that we receive a new `Speaker` object from the mock. Then we pass any `Speaker` object, and we make sure the `Delete` method call executes successfully (returning `true` in this case).

For the Act section, we call the SUT's `Delete` action and pass an integer, and we convert it to a `NoContentResult` type so that we can assert it in the last step.

```
[Fact]
◈ | 0 references | 0 changes | 0 authors, 0 changes
public void DeleteById_ReturnsNoContent_WhenSpeakerWasDeleted()
{
    // Arrange
    speakersService.Get(Arg.Any<int>()).Returns(new Speaker());

    speakersService.Delete(Arg.Any<Speaker>()).Returns(true);

    // Act
    var result = (NoContentResult)sut.Delete(new int());

    // Assert
    result.StatusCode.Should().Be(204);
}
```

Figure 13-11. *Implementation for ReturnsNoContent_ WhenSpeakerWasDeleted*

Testing a Service

Since we now know how to write test methods for our controller actions, we can test services or repositories using the same approach.

First, let's add a new class to our test project named `SpeakersServiceTests.` Here, too, we will follow the same convention, relative to naming our files. We are testing the `SpeakersService`, and the test file will be named starting with our test subject.

Inside we will prepare our dependencies so that we can have a full-fledged SUT—SpeakerService, in our case.

In Listing 13-12, you can see the SpeakerService constructor dependencies, and based on what we have here, we will prepare our mock objects.

Listing 13-12. SpeakerService Constructor Signature

```
public SpeakersService(ISpeakersRepository speakersRepository)
```

This is fairly straightforward as we have only one dependency to mock, using NSubstitute, to instantiate our SUT.

Listing 13-13 shows how our test controller will look.

First, we declare two private readonly fields to hold our dependency (ISpeakerRepository mock) and SUT. Inside the constructor, we use Substitute.For<T> to mock the ISpeakerRepository and then instantiate a new SpeakerService, passing the mock as a dependency.

Listing 13-13. SpeakerServiceTests Constructor and Private Fields

```
private readonly ISpeakersRepository speakersRepository;
private readonly ISpeakersService sut;

public SpeakersServiceTests()
{
 this.speakersRepository = Substitute.
 For<ISpeakersRepository>(); ;
 this.sut = new SpeakersService(speakersRepository);
}
```

With the setup ready, we can create our first test method. We aim to test the same methods we tested in the controller, so we can make sure we covered everything with tests.

Let's create a public method named Get_ShouldReturnSpeaker_
WhenSpeakerExists and implement the three sections to follow the AAA
pattern. We will dissect them here, but you can see the full implementation
in Figure 13-12.

- **Arrange** – In this section, we need to create a new
  Speaker entity and populate it with an ID. This is the
  minimum required field for this scenario, but you
  might want to create an actual object, giving values to
  all properties. Here, I chose to fill in only the FirstName
  and the LastName. We will use this object to pretend
  that it is returned from the repository.

  We take this object and pass the Id to the
  speakersRepository.Get method, and then make
  sure it returns the entire object. You will notice that,
  with unit testing, everything is like a game of make-
  believe that has the purpose of helping us create
  more robust code.

- **Act** – In this section, we just use the method in the
  SUT, passing the same parameter as before (the
  existingSpeaker.Id).

- **Assert** – In here, we expect that, given the setup we
  made, the result we get should be equivalent to the
  object we created in the arrange section.

It is a common practice to have objects that need values to be
"saved" at the class level or the project level and then be reused. The
reuse of these objects removes a lot of the setup we have to do for
each of the test methods, but beware of scenarios where values get
changed. It can lead to flaky tests.

```
[Fact]
⊘ | 0 references | 0 changes | 0 authors, 0 changes
public void Get_ShouldReturnSpeaker_WhenSpeakerExists()
{
    // Arrange
    var existingSpeaker = new Speaker
    {
        Id = 2,
        FirstName = "Irina",
        LastName = "Dominte"
    };

    speakersRepository.Get(existingSpeaker.Id).Returns(existingSpeaker);

    // Act
    var result = sut.Get(existingSpeaker.Id);

    // Assert
    result.Should().BeEquivalentTo(existingSpeaker);
}
```

Figure 13-12. *ReturnSpeaker when the speaker exists*

Now, let's run it in the Test Explorer window. Opening the window, we should be able to see our new test. Right-click and select Run.

In Figure 13-13, you can see that (in my case) the execution took 68 ms, and it was successful.

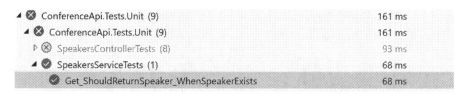

◢ ⊗ ConferenceApi.Tests.Unit (9)	161 ms
◢ ⊗ ConferenceApi.Tests.Unit (9)	161 ms
▷ ⊗ SpeakersControllerTests (8)	93 ms
◢ ✔ SpeakersServiceTests (1)	68 ms
✔ Get_ShouldReturnSpeaker_WhenSpeakerExists	68 ms

Figure 13-13. *Get_ShouldReturnSpeaker_WhenSpeakerExists successful run*

Other Useful Attributes

So far, we have talked about the [Fact] attribute, but others can be applied to a test too.

Such an example is the [Theory] attribute. Data theories are tests that are given various bits of data from a data source that then correspond to parameters in the test method. If the data source contains multiple rows, then the test method is executed multiple times (once with each data row). Data is provided by attributes that derive from Xunit.Sdk.DataAttribute (notably, Xunit.InlineDataAttribute and Xunit.MemberDataAttribute).

The [InlineData] attribute provides a data source for a data theory, with the data coming from inline values.

We'll look at a test that uses both the [Theory] and the [InlineData] attributes. You will notice that the [InlineData] attribute supports an array of objects as parameters, usually real values.

The values provided with the [InlineData] attribute become actual values for the parameters of the test method when the test runs.

The parameters that we add in the test method (int a, int b, int expected) in Figure 13-14 can be used in the act and assert sections and allow us to have more dynamic tests.

By adding parameters to our test method and using actual values, we can test several cases or more than one value per test. This is particularly useful when we have scenarios where we could have tricky edge cases and we want to cover them all. Sometimes, providing more test values might uncover bugs or unwanted behavior in our code.

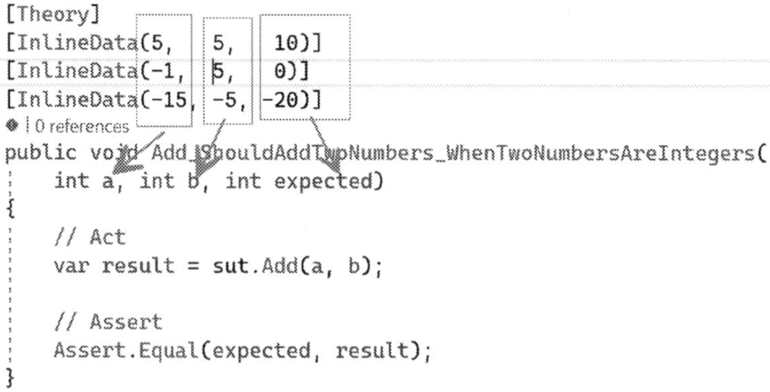

```
[Theory]
[InlineData(5,    5,   10)]
[InlineData(-1,   5,    0)]
[InlineData(-15, -5,  -20)]
◆ | 0 references
public void Add_ShouldAddTwoNumbers_WhenTwoNumbersAreIntegers(
    int a, int b, int expected)
{
    // Act
    var result = sut.Add(a, b);

    // Assert
    Assert.Equal(expected, result);
}
```

Figure 13-14. *A test that uses Theory attribute*

Integration Tests

Integration testing from an API perspective is a type of testing that focuses on the interactions and integrations between different components of the API. It involves testing the API's ability to communicate and exchange data with other systems and components, such as databases, web services, or other APIs.

Integration testing helps ensure that the API functions correctly in real-world scenarios, where it is integrated with other systems and components. It can help identify issues with the API's input/output handling, data transfer, error handling, and other integration-related issues that may not be apparent during unit testing.

Some examples of integration testing for APIs include the following:

- Testing the integration between the API and the database to ensure that data is correctly retrieved and stored.

- Testing the integration between the API and other web services to ensure that data is correctly exchanged between systems.

- Testing the integration between the API and other components of the system, such as user interfaces, to ensure that the system works as expected.

Integration tests are more extensive and involve calling the API's endpoints, instead of calling methods. An integration test will touch a database; it will go further than mocking the services, repositories, and objects we interact with. A particular database, depending on preferences and project specificity and what the team wants to achieve, might use an in-memory database (SQL or SQL in-memory) or an actual database. In the latter case, these integration tests, with some customizations, can be used to do some performance testing on the app.

When we do integration tests, we act like as we would act by using external tool like Postman to test the endpoints. We prepare the data, set headers, parameters, and request body, execute the request, and then analyze what we get as a response.

In terms of AAA, these too should respect the same pattern, but it likely involves more arranging and asserting for each. For example, we would want to make sure we receive a 400 Bad Request error, and a ValidationProblemDetails for the response body, and from it we might want to assert that we receive a specific error.

For the integration tests, we will create a new project. This time we will need a bit more setup since we will want to work on a new database.

In our tests folder, add a new xUnit project named ConferenceApi. Tests.Integration.

In this project, we will use the same libraries we used for unit testing, xUnit and FluentAssertions, so go ahead and add the NuGet packages.

Then add a new class named SpeakersControllerTests.cs. In here, we will write our tests, but not before we introduce some concepts.

Long story short, when running integration tests, we need to provide an instance of our Program.cs, which contains services and configuration-related bits, and allow the platform to run an instance of our API. This API instance will be called from inside our tests.

To do this, we will use the `Microsoft.AspNetCore.Mvc.Testing` package, which contains a special kind of factory named `WebApplica tionFactory<TEntryPoint>`. This allows us to create an instance of our application for testing purposes. It is used to simulate the hosting environment of our application in memory and provides a way to make requests against our application's endpoints without the need to deploy it to a real web server.

Usually, this entry point is the `Program.cs`, or in older .NET Core versions, the `Startup.cs`. Irrespective of the class name, it simulates the hosting environment.

For example, our `SpeakersControllerTests` will implement an `IClassFixture<T>`, where T is a `WebApplicationFactory<Program>`.

Traditionally, we could have a class that looks like Listing 13-14, but we will create a custom `WebApplicationFactory` because we want to alter a few things, like removing the existing `DatabaseContext` and creating a new database.

Listing 13-14. SpeakersControllerTest Class

```
public class SpeakersControllerTests : IClassFixture
<WebApplicationFactory<Program>>
```

Let's look at Listing 13-15 to see what an example integration test would look like. First, the class `MyIntegrationTest` implements an `IClassFixture<T>`, where T is a `WebApplicationFactory<TEntryPoint>`, and `TEntryPoint` is exactly our `Program.cs`. This provides disposal capabilities and simulates an in-memory hosting environment. The factory field maintained as a state at the class level will allow us to create `HttpClients` or access things from the hosting environment that we have configured in `Program.cs`.

You can further see that there is a test method named `TestEndpoint`, annotated with the `[Fact]` attribute. In this test method, we obtain an `HttpClient` from the factory and then make an HTTP GET request to the api/test endpoint (the act section). Then, in the assert section, we expect the endpoint call to be successful, and, if it is, we assert that the content read from the response body equals the "Expected response" string. Although very simplistic, this is the main philosophy behind integration tests—calling endpoints to make sure the whole system works as expected.

Listing 13-15. An Example Class

```
public class MyIntegrationTest : IClassFixture<WebApplicationFa
ctory<Program>>
{
    private readonly WebApplicationFactory<Program> factory;

    public MyIntegrationTest(WebApplicationFactory<Program>
    factory)
    {
        this.factory = factory;
    }

    [Fact]
    public async Task TestEndpoint()
    {
        // Arrange
        var client = this.factory.CreateClient();

        // Act
        var response = await client.GetAsync("/api/test");

        // Assert
        response.EnsureSuccessStatusCode();
        var content = await response.Content.ReadAsStringAsync();
        Assert.Equal("Expected Response", content);
    }
}
```

An `HTTPClient` is a class that provides a way to send HTTP requests and receive HTTP responses from a web server. It is a powerful and flexible class that can be used to perform a wide variety of HTTP operations, and it gives access to everything we would have access to in an HTTP request/HTTP response.

What Is a Fixture?

`IClassFixture<T>` is an interface that allows us to define a fixture class that is shared among all the tests in a test class. A *fixture* is a set of data and objects that are used in multiple tests, and by using a fixture we can ensure that the same data is used across all tests, making them more reliable. The `IClassFixture<T>` interface has a single generic parameter, T, which is the type of the fixture class. When we implement this interface, xUnit will create a new instance of the fixture class for each test class that uses it, and then dispose of it when all the tests in the class have been completed. To use `IClassFixture<T>`, we need to define a class that implements the interface and provides any required setup and teardown logic for the fixture. Then, we can use the fixture in our test classes by adding it as a constructor parameter or by injecting it using an DI container.

Creating a Custom WebApplicationFactory

Creating a custom `WebApplicationFactory` is a useful approach for integration testing in ASP.NET Core because it allows us to create a test server with a specific configuration that mimics our production environment, or that has a configuration that is specific only to the test project.

To create a custom WebApplicationFactory, we extend the generic WebApplicationFactory and override its methods to configure the test server.

We can have access to all the methods we usually use with our API, like ConfigureLogging, ConfigureServices, and so on. In Listing 13-16 we can see just a few that are specific to the test server.

Listing 13-16. A Custom WebApplication Factory

```
public class CustomWebApplicationFactory<TStartup> :
WebApplicationFactory<TProgram>
    where TProgram : class
{
    protected override void ConfigureWebHost(IWebHostBuilder
    builder)
    {
        builder.UseEnvironment("Test");

        builder.ConfigureTestServices(services =>
        {
            // Add custom services for testing
        });

        builder.UseTestServer();
    }
}
```

We will add a new class, and call it ConferenceApiFactory. In this class, we will add more capabilities, as shown in Listing 13-17, by creating a constant that will hold the connection string for our test database, named ConferenceDemoTest.

Listing 13-17. ConferenceApiFactory Constructor and State

```
public class ConferenceApiFactory<TProgram> :
WebApplicationFactory<TProgram> where
    TProgram : class
{
    private const string ConnectionString = @"Data Source=
    (localdb)\MSSQLLocalDB;Initial Catalog=Conference
    DemoTest";
    public ConferenceApiFactory()
    {
    }
}
```

The next thing that we will do is to override one of the exposed methods to ensure we use only the settings required for testing. One of these settings is related to the database we use. In Listing 13-18, we override the ConfigureWebHost method, and inside it we set the environment as being Test. This is useful when in our Program.cs we have checks or configurations specific to the development or production environment. For example, in development we want to seed the database with some data, and in our test environment we do so with different data, or not at all.

Listing 13-18. Overriding the ConfigureWebHost Method

```
protected override void ConfigureWebHost(IWebHostBuilder
builder)
{
  builder.UseEnvironment("Test");
}
```

The next thing we want to do is to configure the services specific to our test environment in relation to the database. In Listing 13-19, in the highlighted section, we remove any references that might contain a connection string pointing to any other environments (since our class will have access to the entry point of our API—Program.cs). In the following lines, we just call AddDbContext<ConferenceContext> and pass the local connection string that points to our test database, named ConferenceDemoTest.

Listing 13-19. ConfigureTestServices

```
builder.ConfigureTestServices(services =>
{
    var dbContextDescriptor = services.SingleOrDefault(
    d => d.ServiceType ==
        typeof(DbContextOptions<ConferenceContext>));

    services.Remove(dbContextDescriptor);

    services.AddDbContext<ConferenceContext>(options =>
    {
        options.UseSqlServer(ConnectionString);
        options.EnableSensitiveDataLogging();
    });
});
```

In this context, we can add configuration items as we would in our main application. These things are related to ensuring the database is created and deleted for every test run, or populated with some pre-made test data, as shown in Listing 13-20.

Listing 13-20. Ensuring the Test Database Is Created

```
var sp = services.BuildServiceProvider();

using (var scope = sp.CreateScope())
{
  var scopedServices = scope.ServiceProvider;
  var db = scopedServices.GetRequiredService<ConferenceC
  ontext>();

  db.Database.EnsureDeleted();
  db.Database.EnsureCreated();
}
```

Also, here we can globally configure the HTTPClient that we will obtain from the factory with custom header fields, cookies, and base address, as shown in Listing 13-21.

Listing 13-21. Configuring Base Client

```
services.AddHttpClient("local", httpClient =>
{
 httpClient.BaseAddress = new Uri("https://localhost:7068/api/");
});
```

Now that we have our custom WebApplicationFactory implemented, we can use it with our integration test classes. In Listing 13-22, you can see what the class looks like. In the constructor, we set the base address for the HttpClient as being our root API address, we create the controller, and we keep it at the class level to be used in our test methods.

Listing 13-22. SpeakersControllerTest

```
public class SpeakersControllerTests : IClassFixture<Conference
ApiFactory<Program>>
{

 private readonly HttpClient httpClient;
 public SpeakersControllerTests(ConferenceApiFactory<Program>
 appFactory)
 {
     appFactory.ClientOptions.BaseAddress = new Uri
     ("https://localhost:7068/api/");
     this.httpClient = appFactory.CreateClient();
 }
 }
```

Writing an Integration Test

The first method we want to implement is an easy one. We want to test that
a NotFound status code is returned when the speaker is not found in our
database.

To do that, we will add a method named Get_ReturnsNotFound_
WhenSpeakerDoesNotExist and try to follow the AAA pattern. Listing 13-23
shows the skeleton of our method.

Listing 13-23. Get_ReturnsNotFound

```
[Fact]
public async Task Get_ReturnsNotFound_WhenSpeakerDoesNotExist()
{ //Arrange
  //Act
  //Assert

}
```

First, we want to obtain a random ID to pass as a parameter to our endpoint. We do that by using Random and picking an interval.

```
//Arrange
Random rnd = new Random();
int ID = rnd.Next(1, 30);
```

Then, we need to call the endpoint that handles our case—/api/speakers/{id} and pass the random integer as the parameter.

```
// Act
var response = await httpClient.GetAsync($"speakers/{ID}");
```

The last part—the assert—is a bit more extensive, and it should be to make sure we don't get a false positive. In Listing 13-24, we check that the status code should be HttpStatusCode.NotFound. If that is true, we dig into the response body to see that it has the format it should have.

We try to read the body into a ValidationProblemDetails object and then check each of the properties we need. If the read is successful, we check that the Title property equals Not Found and the Status field is 404.

Listing 13-24. Asserting a NotFound

```
// Assert
response.StatusCode.Should().Be(HttpStatusCode.NotFound);
var problem = await response.Content.ReadFromJsonAsync<Validation
ProblemDetails>();
problem!.Title.Should().Be("Not Found");
problem.Status.Should().Be(404);
```

If we run the test, it should pass since we have no records in our database that should be retrieved by searching with the randomly generated ID.

The next test we want to do implies creating a speaker, which requires a bit more preparation in the arrange section.

Let's create a new method, `Post_CreatesSpeaker_WhenDataIsValid`, and fill in the AAA gaps.

In the arrange section, shown in Listing 13-25, we will need to create a valid `SpeakerModel` to send as part of the request that, if valid, would be inserted in the test database. We don't use the ID field since that will be assigned by the database.

Listing 13-25. Create a Valid Object

```
// Arrange
var speaker = new SpeakerModel
{
    City = "Iasi",
    Country = "Romania",
    Email = "masssil@mail.com",
    FirstName = "Irina",
    LastName = "Dominte",
    Website = "https://irina.codes",
};
```

Next, we need to call our `/api/speakers` endpoint and pass the valid model to issue an HTTP `POST` request, as shown in Listing 13-26. The methods like `PostAsJsonAsync` are part of the `HttpClient` we keep at the class level.

Listing 13-26. Act on Post

```
// Act
var response = await httpClient.PostAsJsonAsync("speakers",
speaker);
```

The last section, the assert, shown in Listing 13-27, involves checking that the returned status code is a 201 Created, represented by the HttpStatusCode.Created.

If this assertion is true, then we need to look at what we received in the body of the response and try to convert it to a strongly typed object— SpeakerModel or Speaker entity. The last part, highlighted, expects the Location header field to be present and to have a value equivalent to the expectedHeaderValue.

When you write tests, it starts to matter what you return from your actions because you can use the types to make assertions. If we return an IActionResult, everything is very generic, but if we return an ActionResult<T>, where T is a Speaker, or a SpeakerModel in our case, it becomes easier. You will often notice that some methods would be better renamed or refactored to be more clear. I encourage you to do so every time you get the feeling that something is not right, either in code or in tests.

Listing 13-27. Assert Created Speaker

```
// Assert
response.StatusCode.Should().Be(HttpStatusCode.Created);

var speakerReponse = await response.Content.ReadFromJsonAsync<S
peakerModel>();

var expectedHeaderValue = $"{httpClient.BaseAddress}speakers/
{speakerReponse.Id}";

var actualLocationHeader = response.Headers.Location!.ToString()
actualLocationHeader.Should().BeEquivalentTo(expectedHeaderValue);
```

The last integration test that we will implement together involves testing if a *model validation* works as expected. We will check that, when sending a bad value for an email, we get back a `400 Bad request` status code.

We will create a new method named `Post_ReturnsValidationError_WhenEmailIsInvalid`.

In the assert section, we will prepare an object that has a bad email value. Listing 13-28 shows that.

Listing 13-28. Assert in ValidationError Test

```
// Arrange
 const string invalidEmail = "blllllaaaah.com";
var currentSpeaker = new SpeakerModel
{
    City = "Iasi",
    Country = "Romania",
    Email = "masssil@mail.com",
    FirstName = "Irina",
    LastName = "Dominte",
    Website = "https://irina.codes",
};

 currentSpeaker.Email = invalidEmail;
```

Since we now have two methods that use a `SpeakerModel` instance, I think we should talk a little about these objects. To reuse the same object, we could extract one instance at the class level and use it from there when we need it, but there is a caveat with this approach. What if two or more tests are running in parallel and change the object at the same time? We would end up having bad data or flaky tests, and that's why we should try copies that are local to our methods.

We should either create them manually in each test method (which is not recommended) or try to reuse them as much as we can. Or, we could use libraries that can help us generate such objects with valid or invalid properties. Our examples have a simple object, but you might have cases when you have 40 or more properties to give values to. I wouldn't want to do this manual work more than once.

A library that does things very well is Bogus, created by Brian Chavez and maintained by the community.

Bogus is a popular open-source library for .NET that allows us to generate realistic fake data for testing and prototyping purposes. It provides a simple and flexible API that can create randomized data for a variety of data types, including names, addresses, phone numbers, emails, dates, times, and more.

In Listing 13-29 you can see an example of a fake object generated using the Bogus library.

Listing 13-29. An Object Generated with Bogus Library

```
var speakerFaker = new Faker<Speaker>()
.RuleFor(s => s.Name, f => f.Name.FullName())
.RuleFor(s => s.Email, f => f.Internet.Email())
.RuleFor(s => s.Topic, f => f.Company.BS())
.RuleFor(s => s.Bio, f => f.Lorem.Sentences(3));
```

The act section is similar to the previous test, as we pass the object we created to the speakers' endpoint and wait for the response, shown in Listing 13-30.

Listing 13-30. Act Section of Our Test

```
// Act
var response = await httpClient.PostAsJsonAsync("speakers",
currentSpeaker);
```

In the assert section, Listing 13-31, we expect to receive a 400 Bad Request status code and a specific body format. If we get the bad request, we try to look at the response body and extract the ValidationProblemDetails from there, just as we did in the previous integration test.

Then we check the Status field of the error object to make sure it is a 400 Bad Request. The next step is to check the Title property and ensure it indicates an error by inspecting the string "One or more validation errors occurred."

If the Title property is as expected, then we need to make sure that the error displayed is related to our Email field. We do this by making sure the Errors array has the string "The Email field is not a valid e-mail address" for the Email key since that is the default error message for the [Email] validation attribute.

Listing 13-31. Asserting the Invalid Email

```
//Assert
response.StatusCode.Should().Be(HttpStatusCode.BadRequest);

var error = await response.Content.ReadFromJsonAsync<Validation
ProblemDetails>();

error!.Status.Should().Be(400);

 error.Title.Should().Be("One or more validation errors
 occurred.");
error.Errors["Email"][0].Should().Be("The Email field is not a
valid e-mail address.");
```

Unit versus Integration Tests

Although both are types of automated tests and are written by developers to ensure quality and increase trust in their code, they target different levels of the software stack.

Unit tests aim to cover the smallest testable parts of an application, such as individual functions or methods. They are typically written by developers and run in isolation from the rest of the system, using mock or stub objects to simulate dependencies. Unit tests aim to verify that each unit of code is working as expected, and they help catch bugs early in the development cycle before they can become more complex and difficult to fix.

Integration tests, on the other hand, test the interaction between different components or modules of an application. They verify that the different parts of the system work together correctly, and they can help catch problems that might not be apparent in unit tests. Integration tests are typically written by developers or QA engineers, and they can be run either manually or automatically. They can be more time-consuming and complex than unit tests, as they involve testing a larger part of the system.

Although with different scopes, both types can be integrated into the CI/CD pipelines and executed before deployments to upper environments, preventing major production bugs or regressions.

Summary

Throughout this chapter, we learned about the importance of testing APIs and the different types of libraries that we may encounter while testing. We discussed different categories of libraries, like mocking libraries and asserting libraries, and how they can be used to improve the quality of our code.

Then we gained an understanding of the anatomy of a unit test, including the Arrange, Act, and Assert phases. We also learned the terminology associated with testing, like SUT and mock, and we created our first unit test by covering a controller and a service.

Additionally, we discussed integration tests and their importance in ensuring that all components of an API work together as expected. We learned about what a `Fixture` is and how to create a custom `WebApplicationFactory` for integration tests.

Finally, we compared unit and integration tests, highlighting their differences and when to use each type of test.

Index

A, B

W, X, Y, Z

Printed in the United States
by Baker & Taylor Publisher Services